MW00441242

The Supplied Life

*Selected portions
for daily reading*

Bill Freeman

Ministry Publications
Scottsdale, Arizona

ISBN 0-914271-70-9

Library of Congress
Catalog Number: 95-79841

Available from the Publishers:

Ministry Publications
P.O. Box 12222
Scottsdale, Arizona 85267
(602) 948-4050

Printed in the United States of America

Contents

Preface

The very nature of the Christian life requires that we live a life of being daily supplied. We begin this life by receiving, and we go on by receiving.[*] The Christian life is a supplied life. It is a life that has already been lived out and preserved for us in the Holy Spirit.[‡] Now, that "lived out life" is received and supplied to us. The Christian life is not dependent on our own resources or any potential in ourselves. It has everything to do with the rich resources of Another life. Indeed, *The Supplied Life* is Christ Himself.[§] He has been prepared by God for us and is now being supplied and furnished to us. The way God does this is by organically joining us as branches to Christ, the true Vine (John 15:1, 4-5). Thus, the supplied life comes by abiding as a branch in the Vine. Our daily need is to spend time with the Lord cultivating our life of abiding in Him so as to receive all the riches of His Person and work.

Our understanding of the Christian life needs to be renewed to see that our one unique need is to learn how to *receive* from the Lord. Paul's statement to the Corinthians sums up this spiritual principle: "What do you have that you did not receive?"[†] This shows us that everything in the Christian life is supplied to us. It is for this reason that we need to spend time cultivating such a life. For Christ to be everything to us in our daily life, we need daily supply.

In our time with the Lord, a number of things may take place. To begin, we may need to cast all our preoccupations and anxieties

---

[*] John 1:12, 16; Col. 2:6
[‡] John 16:13-16
[§] Phil. 1:19, 21
[†] 1 Cor. 4:7

v

upon Him (1 Pet. 5:7). Then we may spend time just feeding upon the Word by praying over a verse or part of a verse. We can take the very words of Scripture themselves and make them our prayer, as the apostle Paul tells us: *"Take . . . the sword of the Spirit, which is the word of God, by means of all prayer* and petition, praying at every time in spirit."[§] Following this we may sense the need to wait upon the Lord quietly, allowing the love-life of the Father and the Son to be cultivated within our hearts (Gal. 4:6; Rom. 5:5). We may find ourselves making melody in our heart to the Lord by singing a hymn or chorus. Paul and Silas blended their praying with singing: "Now, about midnight Paul and Silas while they were praying were also singing praises to God, mingling petition with songs of praise . . ."[‡] Our time with the Lord may include a blend of several ways of contacting Him. However we spend our time with the Lord and whatever we do during that time should usher us into God Himself. It is a time to have direct contact with Him in spirit,[*] where nothing is mere routine. It is this contact that nourishes, supplies, and furnishes Christ to us as *The Supplied Life.*

The selections here have been taken from spoken messages that are now published in various books. May these daily selections be an added stimulus to feed upon the Lord Himself, in order that His eternal purpose would be fulfilled through a daily supply of His life.

—Bill Freeman
November 1995

[§] Eph. 6:17-18, Alfred Marshall, *The Interlinear Greek-English N. T.*
[‡] Acts 16:25, Wuest
[*] John 4:24

The Scripture quotations are primarily taken from the *New King James Version.* Additional translations we have used are as follows:

1. ASV
2. NASV
3. KJV
4. Amplified
5. J. N. Darby
6. K. S. Wuest
7. R. F. Weymouth

When quoting from these various translations, we have included minor changes from time to time to give a more accurate rendering of the Hebrew or Greek texts. Due to the nature of this book, we have not called attention to these changes in order not to encumber the reading with the more detailed matters of translation.

January

"But as many as received Him, to them He gave authority to become children of God, even to those who believe in His name." JOHN 1:12

A great deal of importance is placed upon the word "receive" in the New Testament. You might ask, What does it mean to receive Christ? When do I receive Him? At what point can I say I have received Him? In the above verse, the answer to these questions does not mention joining a church or merely subscribing to doctrinal statements; neither does it require us to go through a religious ritual. It simply says — "as many as *received* Him." Then it says, "to them He gave authority to become children of God." The word "become" implies that we were not children of God, but by the act of receiving, an authority is imparted to us by Christ Himself to become children of God. It is by *receiving* Him that I *become* a child of God.

At this point may I ask, Have you received Him? Do you have the assurance that Christ is in you? If not, you can receive Him *now*. You can receive Him at any time and in any place. You can receive Him by yourself or with others. While you are reading this daily selection, you can take the step to receive Him. It is as simple as receiving a gift. For example, someone may offer a pen to you. They can say, "This pen is for you. It is a gift." They can offer the pen to you all day long, but for the pen to become yours, you need to receive it. Then it actually becomes yours. In a similar way the Lord Jesus offers Himself to us through the gospel. But He is like a gentleman. He waits for our act of receiving. Whenever anyone receives Him, He instantly comes into them.

It is a momentous thing to receive the Lord Jesus. You receive by confessing with your mouth, "Lord Jesus, I receive You." At that moment He gives you the authority to become His child. There is more authority in simply saying, "Jesus, right now I open to You, come into me," than in all the form prayers you have ever prayed and all the rituals you have ever practiced. The authority to become a child of God is yours by the act of receiving Him. You can do it now, if you have not already.

The need to be supplied   January 2nd

"For I know that this shall turn out to my salvation, through your supplication and the bountiful supply of the Spirit of Jesus Christ."
PHILIPPIANS 1:19 (ASV)

The very nature of the Christian life requires that we spend time with the Lord, because the Christian life is a supplied life. It is a life that is supplied to us. It has nothing to do with our own resources or any potential in ourselves. It has everything to do with our opening up to Another life to be supplied by that life from beginning to end. The Christian life is a life that has been prepared for us and is then furnished to us by God. He intends to continually supply Himself to us. It is for this reason that we need to spend time with the Lord — to receive the supply.

When we hear the truth from the Scriptures or from others, we may take it as a personal demand upon us and feel threatened. We may think, "I'm not like that. I could never do that. I can't imagine that I could ever feel that way. I just can't live up to that." With these kinds of thoughts and feelings, if we do not realize that the Christian life is a supplied life, we may conclude that this life is not for us and give up.

But listen to this. Every word that God has spoken in the Bible, whatever it is, whatever apparent demand it brings, God wants to supply that very thing into our being. It is not that we are expected to "measure up," or come up with the ability to perform in ourselves. No, God intends to continually supply Himself to us. We must understand the Christian life in this way — it is a supplied life. From beginning to end, it is supplied to us. And this supply comes to us and is dispensed into us in a very special and enjoyable way — *by spending time with the Lord.*

God is in your desire   January 3rd

"Work out your own salvation with fear and trembling; for it is God who works in you both to will and to do for His good pleasure."
PHILIPPIANS 2:12-13

We may live for years having desires to spend time with the Lord in a regular way. We may experience these desires to a greater or lesser degree, depending upon our spiritual situation. Nevertheless, we may not be aware of the fact that the very existence of these desires stirring within us *is* God operating in us. God works in your will to incline you to spend time with Him. He operates to that extent. But He does not take us over, obliterating our faculties and human responsibility and forcing us to spend time with Him. He works in us to a point. Then it is up to us to take the initiative to follow through by cooperating with His worked-in inclinations and desires. In other words, God's part is to supply the desire and the inclination to be with Him. Our part is to find a private place, set the alarm clock, rise up from our bed, wash our face, get our Bible, hymnal, and other spiritual books, and begin to wait upon the Lord by reading, praying, singing, or just quietly being in His presence to enjoy Him and behold Him.

We need to realize that our desires to be with the Lord *are* God Himself. It is not just you. It is not just your desire. It is not merely your own thought that you should spend time with the Lord. It is God! God is in *your* desire! God is in *your* inclination! God is in *your* thought! Now you must work out what God has worked in. Just go along with that still small voice, that slight sensation that you should withdraw yourself to pray and spend time with Him. If you obey those small nudges, you are obeying God operating within you.

Unconditional love   January 4th

"The LORD did not set His love on you nor choose you because you were more in number than any other people, for you were the least of all peoples; but because the LORD loves you."
DEUTERONOMY 7:7-8

To speak of God's unconditional love is to utter a wonderful fact about God's nature. He loves because He *chooses* to love and for no other reason. His love is not dependent upon finding something in us that merits His love. His love is without conditions — it is *un*conditional. It is this kind of love that is expressed to Israel in the above verses. In other words, God loves because He chooses to love, not because of a reason found outside of Himself.

God's unconditional love is revealed throughout the Old and New Testaments, but the most detailed description of His love is found in the book of Hosea. When we touch this book that unveils the nature of God's love, we are treading ground that we have never trod before. We see God's unconditional love coming to the least likely object of love.

Gomer, the name of the woman Hosea was to take as a wife, reveals the depths of the nature of God's unconditional love. Gomer is derived from a Hebrew word *(gamar)* that means "cease, come to an end, and fail." In other words, God was telling Hosea, "Go take *failure* to be your wife," or "Go take *that which has come to an end* to be your wife." This illustrates the nature of God's love to us. He loves us when we have no potential, no victory, when we have come to an end — when we are nothing but failure. Gomer not only means

4

failure, but it also has the meaning of "completion" or "perfection." So this woman was complete or perfected in her failure. She was a harlot. She filled up the measure of harlotry to the uttermost. She committed not merely one transgression but a thousand transgressions. She reached a state of completion and is ironically spoken of as being perfected in harlotry. She was that low, that base. She was perfected in her harlotry because she was fully experienced in sinning and in rebellion. She was fully developed, perfected, and completed in the realm of failure. She was not partially a failure, but she was a total failure. Yet God tells Hosea to *take* this "wife of harlotry" to be his wife (Hosea 1:2). Later, God tells him to *love* her. This demonstrates the Lord's love toward us. He takes us and then lavishes His love on us, despite our failed condition.

Unlock the floodgate of the Spirit   January 5th

"That the righteous requirement of the law might be fulfilled in us who do not walk according to the flesh but according to the Spirit." ROMANS 8:4

The subject of the Spirit's writing on our hearts in the new covenant is *the law of God* as it is described by the Lord Himself in Matthew 5—7. In these chapters, what the Lord spoke is the righteous requirement of the law. It is the inner reality of the outward law. Now this uplifted law is being written upon our hearts by the Spirit. It is this Spirit-writing that constitutes the Lord's voice within us.

The evidence of our hearing the Lord's voice is both the consciousness we have within our hearts as well as the inclination of our hearts. For example, the very consciousness and prompting within us forbidding us to take a certain course of action or hold a certain attitude is His speaking within. The consciousness itself is the Lord's voice. This kind of consciousness may also be understood as a consciousness of life, because the nature of the consciousness is an inner awareness that is being supplied to us by the life of God. If we cooperate with this consciousness, or in other words, if we listen to the Lord's voice within, and by faith obey His forbidding feeling, we will unlock the floodgate of the Spirit of life into our whole being. It is important to know that His voice always comes with this supply of His presence and grace.

The prompting within   January 6th

"My sheep hear My voice, and I know them, and they follow Me." JOHN 10:27

The uniqueness of our new covenant relationship with the Lord is this: it is not a matter of our keeping outward commands, but of discovering His voice as an inner consciousness. Thus, it is not being outwardly *told* what to do; it is being *prompted* from within concerning what to do. So expect the Lord's voice to come from within you. And the way you will discover His voice is by His inner operation that manifests itself by inward promptings. What is important then is how we respond to these promptings.

Let me give an illustration. The most basic function of a PC computer is a little blinking "C" at the bottom of the screen, known as the "C prompt." Its appearance on the screen tells you that the computer is operating and is prompting you to enter a command. The prompt is the computer's way of speaking to you; it is the computer's voice. Of course, when you respond to the prompt by entering a command, you open up a wealth of information on the screen. Everything is instantly available to you by simply responding to the "prompt."

In the same way, as believers indwelt by the life of God, we have promptings within us. These promptings are the Lord's way of speaking to us. The promptings *are* the Lord's voice. They are telling us that God is operating in us to open up all the riches of His life to our inward parts. However, to get the benefit of God's life within, we need to respond properly to the prompting. In our daily life, when we say "Amen" to the prompting within and go along with it, we are obeying the voice of the Lord.

Vision governs us   January 7th

"Therefore, King Agrippa, I was not disobedient to the heavenly vision." ACTS 26:19

These words are Paul's own testimony about his calling and constitute a summary of what governed his life. It was vision! He was governed by a heavenly vision that controlled and directed him. The Lord appeared to him, spoke to him, and gave him a revelation of his mission — to open people's eyes to see the light of God's plan and to usher them into God's heart's desire.

When we have vision, we have something to govern and direct our lives day by day. Vision gives us something to which we can render our obedience. If we do not have a heavenly vision, what do we obey? What is the vision that directs our life? What do we see? What controls us? Is there vision in our life? Or are we just spending our days passively waiting to go to heaven? We need to see what God's purpose is right now in time.

When vision governs us, our lives are properly controlled and directed. When there is no vision, then our lives are spent in vanity. We sit at home and watch television, read the newspaper, go to work, acquire an abundance of material possessions, and exist with a sense of futility and emptiness about life. We go through the cycle of life without any governing vision. There is nothing that shapes and directs our lives. So we must see how crucial vision is to us.

The vision that Paul speaks of as the heavenly vision was the factor that governed his plans and practical life. Immediately after

7

receiving this vision, he "declared first to those in Damascus and in Jerusalem, and throughout all the region of Judea, and then to the Gentiles..." (v. 20). In other words, first comes vision; then comes a controlled and directed life in practical service. It was vision that gave Paul direction and caused him to spread the gospel and build up local churches in an ever-increasing sphere. The apostle Paul was under a mandate because he was under vision.

Vision restrains us   January 8th

"Where there is no vision, the people cast off restraint."
PROVERBS 29:18

To "cast off restraint" can also be translated to "run wild." Thus, vision in our lives is not only a controlling and directing factor, but a restraining factor. If we have no vision, we cast off restraint. We run wild. We have nothing directing us. We have nothing controlling us. There is no governing principle for our lives. To live in this age without heavenly vision is to become vulnerable to the breakdown of the moral fabric of society. Man's thoughts, concepts, values, and degraded morals are gradually taking over. Today there is increasing moral looseness. There are more things taking place that are without restraint, and more things happening that at one time would not have been allowed by the general social conscience.

Surely in the unsaved world there is no vision and no God, so the people cast off restraint. The same can be true with believers. The fact that Paul had to admonish the Ephesians to "no longer walk as the rest of the Gentiles walk, in the vanity of their mind" (Eph. 4:17) indicates that it *can* happen even to believers. As children of God we must have a directing heavenly vision in our lives. Otherwise, we could fall into the condition spoken of in Matthew 24:12: "And because lawlessness will abound, the love of many will grow cold."

8

This verse indicates that an increasing lack of restraint is being released on the earth. The mystery of lawlessness is at work. It is infecting mankind more and more as the hour approaches for the Lord's coming. Thus, we need a clear heavenly vision to control us, direct us, and restrain us.

Stand in your justification   January 9th

"Blessed is the man to whom the Lord will not reckon sin."
ROMANS 4:8 (ASV)

To be a justified man means that my sin is no longer accounted to me. Before God my history of sins and even the present sin nature in my flesh are not counted against me. I am accounted righteous by faith. I am a justified man. Not only have I been forgiven, but I have been clothed with Christ, who is now my righteousness. To be justified means that before God I have fulfilled the law. I have kept it — every jot and tittle. God could not be happier with me. When Christ is my righteousness, it means I am not only forgiven, negatively, but I also have a positive standing. I am positively admired in Christ, my robe of righteousness. Not only is nothing counted against me, but also I am in all that He is as righteousness. He obeyed the law. He fulfilled it. And now He has become my righteousness. So I really feel wonderful about myself, because Christ is my righteousness.

Are you related to yourself as a justified person? Do you know what it means in your experience to stand in your justification? Or do you take condemnation? Maybe you are feeling horrible about yourself, but you cannot pinpoint anything definite that you have done to bring on those feelings of condemnation. Yet you feel wrong. If there was something you could point to, some sin that you had committed, then you would simply say, "Lord, thank You for the forgiveness in Your blood." But these feelings are vague, like something intangible hanging over you. In that moment do you carry the load of those feelings? Or do you know how to exercise your spirit and say, "Thank You, Jesus. Thank You for justifying me. Nothing is reckoned against me!" This is how to stand in your justification.

Into the bosom   January 10th

"No one has seen God at any time. The only begotten Son, who is into the bosom of the Father, He has declared Him." JOHN 1:18

The concentration of the divine love is presently existing in the Son of God. When the apostle John describes the only begotten Son as being into the bosom of the Father, he is unveiling the intimacy of the divine love existing between the Father and the Son. The Greek preposition in this verse is not *in* but *into*. Thus, it is more accurately translated *"into* the bosom of the Father" rather than *"in* the bosom."

In his *Commentary on the Gospel of John,* Frederick Godet talks about the love relationship existing between the Father and the Son in John 1:18. He says, "This present participle, *Who is*, refers to the permanent relation of the Son to the Father through all the stages of His divine, human, and divine-human existence. He ever presses anew, with an equal intimacy into the bosom of the Father, who reveals Himself to Him in a manner suitable to His position and His work at every moment. The Greek form '*into* the bosom,' instead of 'in the bosom' (the preposition of motion, instead of that of rest), expresses precisely this active and living relation. The bosom of the Father is not a place, but a life; one is *there* only in virtue of a continual moral act." The indication here is that there is a continuous, intimate love relationship going on between the Father and the Son. He is ever *into* the bosom of the Father.

May God grant that *this* love-life would become our portion and our experience in the middle of our weakness, so that instead of being *into* our depression, we would constantly be *into* the bosom. We would not be into our bad and unworthy feelings that cause morbid introspection, but *into* a love-life that nourishes and cherishes us in our weaknesses.

His relationship — our relationship   January 11th

"In this the love of God was manifested toward us, that God has sent His only begotten Son into the world, that we might live through Him." 1 JOHN 4:9

To understand the Christian life properly, it is important to see that *Christ is our relationship with everything.* In Galatians 2:20, when the apostle Paul said, "It is no longer I who live, but Christ lives in me," he opened up a profound revelation concerning our life — Christ is now our relationship with all things. If Christ now lives in me, with the "I" crucified and no longer in the picture, then I do not have a separate, independent relationship with God. My relationship with God is Christ! In fact, one of the most refreshing things to my spirit is to declare that I do not have a relationship with God. I have declared it many times, and said out loud — "My relationship with God is *Jesus Christ!*"

God has established one unique relationship, and that relationship is with His *only* begotten Son (John 1:14, 18; 3:16, 18). First John 4:9 says, "In this the love of God was manifested toward us, that God has sent *His only* begotten Son into the world, that we might live through Him." To identify the Son as the *only begotten* means that God has a relationship with only one Person. Then to directly relate the only begotten Son to us by saying, "that we might live *through* Him," reveals that *His relationship* with the Father has now become *our relationship.*

Jesus is both the Son of God and the Son of Man. As the Son of

God, He is the One who has the relationship with God. As the Son of Man, He is the One who has the relationship with man. He is *the* representative man. Indeed, only one Man has a proper and approved relationship with God and man. That one Man is Jesus Christ. He represents the meaning of man. In Hebrews 2:6 the question is asked, "What is man?" The answer comes in verse 9: "We see Jesus." Jesus Christ is the one Man who has the one, unique relationship with God. Seek no further.

The address of Christ in us   **January 12th**

"The Lord Jesus Christ be with your spirit. Grace be with you. Amen." 2 TIMOTHY 4:22

Many Christians may know the *objective* truth concerning their identification with Christ, but they may not know *subjectively* His location within their being. To experience Christ as our relationship with everything, one of the most crucial things to know is that He lives in our spirit. Man's regenerated spirit is the address of Jesus Christ. In the above verse the personal pronoun makes the address clear — "The Lord Jesus Christ be with *your spirit.*" This identifies the place where Christ actually lives in us.

We need to understand that our spirit is as much a part of our constitution as are our other faculties. For example, our mouth is *our* mouth, and our eyes are *our* eyes, and our hands are *our* hands. I can close my mouth and I can open my mouth. I can close my eyes and I can open my eyes. I can squeeze my hands and I can open my hands. I can do all these things with my mouth, eyes, and hands because they are *my* members. In other words, we have the ability to do whatever we desire with our own faculties. In the same way, we have control over our own spirit (1 Cor. 14:32).

Have you ever observed how many personal pronouns there are in the New Testament related to the human spirit? For example,

"The Spirit Himself bears witness with *our* spirit" (Rom. 8:16). "For they refreshed *my* spirit and *yours*" (1 Cor. 16:18). "And we rejoiced exceedingly more for the joy of Titus, because *his* spirit has been refreshed by you all" (2 Cor. 7:13). "The grace of our Lord Jesus Christ be with *your* spirit" (Gal. 6:18). All these verses refer to our spirit, the deepest part of our being, which is joined to the Lord (1 Cor. 6:17). It is from this joined part that Christ is our relationship with everything. By walking according to our spirit, which we control, Christ becomes everything to us.

Discovering His address   January 13th

"But the one who joins himself to the Lord is one spirit with Him." 1 CORINTHIANS 6:17 (NASV)

The secret of Christ becoming everything to us is found in this *mingled spirit, where* the two spirits have become one. Our wonderful Christ, who is our relationship with everything, is dwelling in our spirit. Like the other parts of our being, our spirit is subject to us (1 Cor. 14:32). When we realize that exercising our spirit is as simple as squeezing our hand, it will revolutionize our daily life. We can enjoy Christ anytime, in any place, and under any condition. Joining ourselves to the Lord, the Spirit (2 Cor. 3:18), to be one spirit with Him, activates a oneness in which the integrity of the two spirits and the distinction between them is still preserved (Rom. 8:16).

When we know the address of Christ in us and learn to abide with Him in that place (John 15:4-5), we can consistently experience the unsearchable riches of Christ in our daily life. There is no need to wait for a "mountain-top" experience. Years ago when I went to retreats, I would always *feel* close to God in the atmosphere of the mountains and big trees. Then a few days later, after returning home, I would wonder what happened to those feelings. I would try to imagine how to recapture that mountain-top atmosphere in order to be close to the Lord. But one day I discovered the address of Christ in me. I saw from the Word that Christ is dwelling in my spirit; and from that time forth, I began to experience Him in a way that I had never known was possible.

Christ is the Christian life   January 14th

"For you died, and your life is hidden with Christ in God. When Christ who is our life appears, then you also will appear with Him in glory." COLOSSIANS 3:3-4

The oneness between believers and the practice of the church are both dependent on the centrality of Christ. Christ is the center. Indeed, Christ Himself is the reality of the Christian life and the church life. When Christ is my center, I am free from my self. I am free from self-consciousness. I am free from self-condemnation. I am free from anxiety. I am totally free because I died and my life is now hidden with Christ in God. "It is no longer I who live, but Christ lives in me" (Gal. 2:20).

Christ is our joy. Christ is our encouragement. Christ is our faith. Christ is our living. We interact with Him in everything in our lives. We interact only with Christ. Our interaction is not with ourselves — with self-reflection and self-condemnation. Christ is our righteousness (1 Cor. 1:30). He is "all and in all" to us (Col. 3:11). Jesus Christ is the Christian life. We need to look away to Him. Look away from yourself. Look away from your failure. Look away from your bad mood. Look away unto Jesus. Christ is the centrality of everything in our Christian life. He *is* the Christian life itself in every aspect.

"For as the body is one and has many members, but all the members of that one body, being many, are one body, so also is Christ." 1 CORINTHIANS 12:12

Not only is Christ the Christian life, but He is also the reality of the church life. Apart from Him there is no church. We must understand that the practice of the church issues from the centrality of Christ. Christ is our relationship with one another (Col. 3:11). Because He is in all of us, we are related to each other in Him. We do not need to "join" the church. We do not sign up to become members of the church. The church comes into our spirit when we receive Christ. The church is in all of us because the church is Christ. We recognize Christ! When we recognize Christ, we recognize the church! The reality of the church is a Person. It is not a doctrine. It is not a way. It is not a man. It is Christ Himself. So wherever Christ is, *there* is the church. The best we can do is simply to see it, acknowledge it, receive one another, and say "Amen."

We receive one another because we have all been received by God (Rom. 14:3). We have been redeemed by the same blood. We have the same one Father (Eph. 4:6). There is only one "Abba," one Father, and He is in all of us (Rom. 8:15; Gal. 4:6). So what do we do? We say, "We are in the same family!" This is the church. It is so simple.

There is something already existing between us. God put it into us. It is called the oneness of the Spirit (Eph. 4:3). We learn to recognize this oneness of the Spirit between us and to keep it in our relationships. This oneness is so precious because it is made up of the oneness of the Father and the Son. The oneness between the Father and the Son is now embodied in the Spirit. Thus, through Christ as the life-giving Spirit entering into us, we have been admitted into Their oneness! Because of Christ, Their oneness has now become our oneness. This is the church.

15

The inner movement January 16th

"But the anointing which you have received from Him abides in you, and you do not need that anyone teach you; but as the same anointing teaches you concerning all things, and is true, and is not a lie, and just as it has taught you, you will abide in Him." 1 JOHN 2:27

It is marvelous that when we are regenerated, the Lord Jesus comes into our spirit in such a way that there is a union where He can be the Savior. We are not the savior. We do not save ourselves. Jesus is the One saving us. This is not just initial salvation, but constant salvation. He wants to be the Savior in everything. Because we are in union with Him, we can open to Him, we can turn to Him, we can draw from Him, we can say "Amen" to the inner registrations of His life in us.

It is by those inner registrations, called the anointing, that we can know Christ. The Greek word for anointing is *chrisma* (χρῖσμα), the verbal form of the noun *Christos* (Χριστός), which means Christ. *Chrisma* refers to the movement of the person of the Lord within our spirit. The word "anointing" tells us the nature of the way Christ is in us — *how* He is in us. After you have received the Lord, it is simply a matter of discovering what is happening inside of you.

The anointing is not something external from us. Knowing the anointing is not a matter of trying to understand with your mind something that is apart from you. First John 2:27 is a description of what is in me and what is in you. It is not describing something new that we are going to receive, but what we have already received. It is describing how Christ is living inside of us. This verse says, "the anointing which you have received from Him *abides* in you." This means the anointing remains in you. It does not leave you. The anointing as the inner movement of Christ is always operating in our being. It is the inner surveillance of the Lord Himself within us.

When we speak a word with impatience in our tone, immediately the anointing is surveying our inner being. So the anointing is not merely a positive leading of the Lord. It is an inner registration of what is compatible with the divine nature. What we feel or sense is that something is not compatible with the life within us. Of course, we are not condemned, though these kinds of registrations could be a factor to spiral a person downward. When your nature rises up in some form or another, if you identify with that and live expecting those risings to change, or think that something better should come out of you, then you are on the road to condemnation. But thank God, when there is a registration within us, that is the anointing that abides in us. So whenever we say something that is incompatible with the anointing, there is a registration. There is a leakage of life and peace. You can sense it. That leakage of life and peace is God's way of saying "no" to what we just said or did. It is a registration that says, "That is not My nature." Obeying the registrations of the anointing is the practical way for us to abide in Christ.

Compatibility with the anointing   January 17th

"But you have an anointing from the Holy One, and you all know." 1 JOHN 2:20 (NASV)

The anointing is simply the movement of Christ, the anointed One, within us. The anointing abides in our spirit. So in our spirit we are living with Jesus, with His nature. In our spirit we are partakers of the divine nature and we are begotten of God. Thus, whenever our emotions are not compatible with His life and nature, there is movement in us. Many times we do not interact with the Lord in that movement, or anointing. Instead we go to our mind and reason. We make excuses, we push down the sense coming from God's life. We cope with it somehow. In other words, we handle it ourselves. Consequently, we may go for years in the same way, having little expression of Christ in our life.

We have received the anointing, and that means Christ is active in us. He has been active in all of us from the day we received Him. The anointing is not something special for certain Christians. It is what every believer has abiding within. That is why it is hard to really rebel against God. It is hard to turn away. It is hard to resist too long. It is hard to be stiff-necked for a long period of time, because the anointing remains in you. This movement in us is unhappy whenever we are incompatible with God's life. *We* are sad, *we* are grieved, *we* feel empty, and *we* feel dry. It is because of something we said, something we did, something we interacted with that was incompatible with Him. He is just waiting for us to become compatible again. The secret of the Christian life is simply to remain compatible with the anointing at all times. Just say "Amen" to His movements.

Something done outside of me January 18th

"Christ Jesus, whom God set forth to be a propitiation by His blood, through faith, to demonstrate His righteousness, because in His forbearance God had passed over the sins that were previously committed, to demonstrate at the present time His righteousness, that He might be just and the justifier of the one who has faith in Jesus." ROMANS 3:24-26

We see the scenery of God's righteousness at the cross, where God's way of dealing with and relating to man is demonstrated. This demonstration unveils the fact that God's procedure and way is embodied in His Son. Christ went to the cross to be nailed there representatively and substitutionally. He bore all our sins, replacing us and receiving the punishment for sin. The One who knew no sin became sin for us (2 Cor. 5:21). He shed His blood, pouring out His life in death. All of this was a demonstration of God's righteousness. The Father saw the suffering of His Son's soul and was satisfied (Isa. 53:11). He accepted the death of His Son for sin. He accepted the shedding of His blood on our behalf. He pardoned man for Christ's sake. This is God's way, or procedure.

Now I, as a sinner, simply need to look at Jesus, to look at the cross. Christ died for me. This look itself is faith and constitutes me righteous. I am righteous not because of what I have done — not because of my history, my potential, my promises and deals with God, or my resolutions to reform myself. God does not make me righteous because of any works of the law done by me. He makes me righteous because of *something done outside of me*. Wonder of wonders! Something outside of myself! Calvary was outside of myself! God accepted the death of Christ for my sins and made me righteous. It was all because of Calvary. Now I can look at that One who died for me. And in that look not only are my sins forgiven, but I am quickened and made alive by the life of God imparted into me. This is God's way of doing things. This is God's righteousness.

Christ — our relationship to ourselves   January 19th

"If One died for all, then all died; and He died for all, that those who live should live no longer to themselves, but to Him who died for them and rose again." 2 CORINTHIANS 5:14-15

It is wonderful to discover that once we have received Christ, He becomes our relationship to ourselves. Paul makes this clear in the above verses. When he says, "One died for all," according to our understanding, we probably would continue the sentence by saying, "then all are forgiven." Of course, this truth is found in other passages of Scripture — when Christ died for all, He died to forgive all. But here in these verses Paul is stressing another aspect of Christ's death. The statement "If One died for all, then all died" reveals a crucial fact about our relationship to ourselves. In verse 15 Paul opens up what the issue should be of our having died in Christ's death — "that those who live should live no longer to themselves, but to Him." In other words, our relating to ourselves has ceased. Christ is now our true relationship to ourselves. We do not live to ourselves any longer. We live to Him.

The death of Christ is not only for our forgiveness; it is also for our termination. The terminating of the self is very positive because it has one goal in view — the release of Christ living in us. When we no longer live to ourselves, we are no longer our point of reference in our daily life and affairs. Our point of reference is no longer the self, but Christ. To live *for* Him is to live *to* Him.

He will quiet you   January 20th

"The LORD your God in your midst, The Mighty One, will save; He will rejoice over you with gladness, He will quiet you in His love, He will rejoice over you with singing." ZEPHANIAH 3:17

This verse reveals the effect that God's unconditional love has on us. The effect of His love is to quiet us. So in any kind of condition — whatever our condition may be — we just need to be in His presence with His love, and He will calm our every fear.

Come into His presence with all the noise of your mind, your condemned feelings, your failures — with the noise of it all — just come, and He will quiet you in His love. This means we can simply enjoy being in His presence and opening ourselves to Him, knowing that His precious blood has been shed for us and is cleansing us from all sin. Because we know that we can never go beyond the reach of the love of God, we will always be secure in that love; and our whole relationship with the Lord will be characterized by His love. Regardless of what kind of condition we find ourselves in, our relationship will be characterized by security in His love.

This consciousness of the love of God will begin to pervade our heart more and more so that our relationship with the Lord is not characterized by fear. With fear, there is torment, there is agony. But

20

"perfect love casts out fear" (1 John 4:18). Then our whole relationship with Him is characterized by love, security, and the confidence that our one need is simply to make contact with Him by calling upon His name (Zeph. 3:9), and to enjoy that love that has been poured out in our hearts (Rom. 5:5). We will not take any fearful thoughts from the enemy or any kind of negative, self-condemning thoughts. We will be quieted and secure in His love.

Our most basic dealing   January 21st

"For of him, and through him, and unto him, are all things. To him be the glory for ever. Amen." ROMANS 11:36 (ASV)

We must see that God's most basic dealing in our lives is to bring us into Himself as our source. Every part of our being is destined to live *out of* God as our source. In this entire universe, God is reconciling all things to Himself through Jesus Christ. This means that God is seeking to have His rightful place in the universe as the unique source of everything. This is the meaning of reconciliation individually, corporately, and universally — that God would be the source and the spring from which everything proceeds. This is not only the basic revelation of the Bible, but also the present movement, or current, of history. The destiny of the earth is that the kingdom of God would come in reality, where God is all in all (1 Cor. 15:28). Everything in this universe is ultimately *unto* Him.

God is at work in our lives and in the church to make Himself our source. For example, He wants to be the source of our thoughts. He wants to be the source for us to deal with our wandering mind. It is not a matter of our attempting to handle our thoughts by ourselves, but of our coming to the true source of thought life — God Himself. Interacting with God as our source supplies us to deal with the maze of thoughts that spring from our independent thinking. God is at work in our lives to establish Himself as the very source of our thought life.

21

A full spiritual scholarship   January 22nd

"Blessed be the God and Father of our Lord Jesus Christ, who has blessed us with every spiritual blessing in the heavenlies in Christ." EPHESIANS 1:3

B eing exposed in God's light is always a signal to us to once again draw our supply from Him. The Christian life is a life that has already been lived for us. And now this life that has already been lived is *continuously* being supplied to us. The Greek word *epichoregia* (ἐπιχορηγία) in the New Testament depicts the Christian life as a supplied life. For example, Philippians 1:19 says, "For I know that this will turn out for my salvation through your prayer and the bountiful *supply* of the Spirit of Jesus Christ." In the ancient Greek world *choregia* was used to describe the person who was responsible for a chorus of singers or dancers. In brief, this person was responsible for supplying all the needs of all the members of the chorus. He was "the supplier." The Greek word meant that he was both a leader and a provider of all the needs of the chorus. Whether it was clothing, food, or money, he supplied everything; and he supplied it lavishly and abundantly, without rationing or restriction.

Today this New Testament word for "supply" can be likened to students who are at a university on full scholarships. They are very relaxed. They are free from anxiety about their needs. They do not have to work their way through school; they just receive all the benefits of their scholarships. All their practical needs are cared for. Their tuition is cared for. Their research needs are cared for. Everything is fully supplied. This is the thought behind the word *epichoregia*. When the apostle Paul applied this word to the Christian life, he was conveying that everything in the Christian life is provided for. The normal Christian life is like being on a full spiritual scholarship with everything provided for us. Paul surely had this in mind when he declared in Ephesians 1:3, "Blessed be the

God and Father of our Lord Jesus Christ, who has blessed us with every spiritual blessing in the heavenlies in Christ."

The proceeding Word   January 23rd

"But He answered and said, It is written, Man shall not live by bread alone, but by every word that proceeds out through the mouth of God." MATTHEW 4:4

What does it mean to feed upon the Word? To the Lord it meant having a living and fresh relationship with the written Scriptures. For example, in Matthew 4:4 when the Lord said, "It is written," He used the perfect tense in Greek (γέγραπται), which can be literally translated "It stands written." He did not say, "It was written," as though the Word was something merely recorded in the past without any present reality. The force of the perfect tense, "It stands written," indicates that the Lord's attitude toward the Word was that it was God's present speaking — living and fresh, not dead and old.

In fact, the written Scriptures were identified by Him as being the very word that "proceeds out through the mouth of God." In saying "proceeds," the Lord again used a tense that reveals His attitude toward the written Scriptures. "Proceeds" is a present participle (ἐκπορευομένῳ), which denotes that "every word" was presently proceeding out through the mouth of God. He did not use the past tense "proceeded," as though He was articulating a theory on the inspiration of Scripture. He used the present tense "proceeds" to reveal that the written Scriptures are living and fresh, even proceeding "out through the mouth of God." This proceeding word, according to the Lord's view, is good for man not only to study and read, but to feed upon as bread and to live by. This was the Lord's realization concerning the Scriptures. Consequently, our relationship to the Scriptures should be characterized by feeding upon words that are presently proceeding out of God's mouth.

Purpose means one thing   January 24th

"But we do know that all things work together for good to those who love God, to those who are called according to purpose." ROMANS 8:28 (*A New Translation,* J. N. Darby)

In most translations of the Bible, the phrase "called according to purpose" is rendered "called according to *His* purpose," with *"His"* in italics. The translators supply the word "His" because purpose here obviously refers to God's purpose. But *His* is not in the original language. Neither is there a definite article before the word purpose. It is not "according to *the* purpose." It is simply "according to purpose." Then we might ask, what purpose? In God's thought there is only one purpose — Christ. This means that if you and I are not calibrated to Christ in our lives, in our experience — with every detail from morning to night — then we are not living according to purpose. We are in vanity.

In this universe everything apart from Christ is vanity. Only Christ gives purpose to all things. Christ alone is the reality and meaning of life. This is why, when we turn to Him in the middle of all things in our life and begin to identify with Him, we have such a sense of significance in our being. But if we are indifferent to Christ, if we try to figure things out on our own, then notice what it does to our insides. There is a sense of emptiness, the sense that we have nothing of Christ to share with others. But if we allow all kinds of environments to press us into the Lord, then we are filled with so much meaning, there is so much significance, and there is so much to share. This spiritual phenomenon happens because the one sure purpose of our human life is to be conformed to the image of God's

Son. By letting all things shape us into the form of God's Son, we have a deep sense that we are living according to purpose.

The meaning of your shortages   January 25th

"For whom He foreknew, He also predestined to be conformed to the image of His Son, that He might be the firstborn among many brethren." ROMANS 8:29

In our daily life, everything is significant because we know we have been predestinated. We have been marked out ahead with a destiny, which is to be conformed to the image of God's Son. So turning to Jesus and interacting with Him, calling upon Him, touching Him, is the meaning of my life. It is the meaning of every shortage I find in myself.

Do you understand that the meaning of your shortages and weaknesses is Christ? Your shortage is not just something for you to overcome, to get through, to be rid of. That is not what it is for. It is for Christ to make His home in your heart (Eph. 3:17). We think that for Christ to make His home in our hearts, we need to "clean up the house." But this means that we would be the savior. We would work to present ourselves to God in a perfect condition, as though we were the ones doing it. However, this is not the way Christ makes His home in our hearts. Instead, we bring our rickety, broken-down house — with the messes, with the clutter in the closets — we bring it to Him and say, "Jesus, now *You* live here. *You* cleanse my heart. *You* come in and do all the work, Lord." This is the purpose of all our problems. It is about Christ taking over the job and making home in our hearts. It is not arriving at a perfect state that I have accomplished by my own energy. It is a perfect touch, a perfect interaction, with a perfect Person who is my supply.

25

Not having or not fulfilling?

"For the flesh lusts against the Spirit, and the Spirit against the flesh; and these are contrary to one another, so that you do not do the things that you would." GALATIANS 5:17

The "lust of the flesh" in Galatians 5:16 refers specifically to the lust to bite and devour others (v. 15). These lusts are *desires* to strike out at someone by speaking in a way that would cut and hurt. They are feelings of being extremely unhappy with others. These desires manifest themselves in all of us from time to time. Paul says that the way to deal with them is to walk by the Spirit. Notice, however, that in walking by the Spirit he says that you shall not *fulfill* or *carry out* the lust of the flesh. We usually understand this to mean that you will not *have* the lust of the flesh; that is, you will not feel any negative reactions within your being. In other words, we think that if we are really walking by the Spirit, we will not be bothered by the slightest problem.

Many of us have the concept that to be in the Spirit means to experience a total absence of anything contrary within us. According to our thought, to be in the Spirit is to soar like a bird, without any opposing factor. Thus, if we still have contrary feelings and reactions while contacting the Lord, we conclude that our fellowship with Him must be defective. We reason that if we had really touched the Lord or were really in our spirit, we would not have any ugly thoughts or feelings. This kind of thinking ends in accusation and discouragement, and frustrates us from the full enjoyment of the Lord.

Contrary to what we think, Paul says that to walk by the Spirit means that we do not *carry out* or *fulfill* the lust of the flesh. This implies that we may feel the lust of the flesh *while* we are in the process of following the Lord. The key point is not that we do not *have* the lust of the flesh, but rather that we would not *fulfill* it. Therefore, the basic need in our experience of Christ is to remain continually in the realm of the Spirit so that we automatically deprive the flesh of its power over us and consequently do not carry out its lusts.

Our personalized cross   January 27th

"And he who does not take his cross and follow after Me is not worthy of Me." MATTHEW 10:38

The cross should become very personal. It must become in our experience a personalized cross. What do I mean by a personalized cross? The above verse indicates that if a man is going to follow the Lord, he has to deny himself and take up *his* cross — *his* cross — and follow the Lord. It is always *his* cross. Brothers and sisters, the Lord Jesus had His cross. He had the Pharisees and the Sadducees, the religious people 2,000 years ago. He had His Judas. He had His environment that was against Him, that was ordered before the foundation of the world (Acts 2:23).

The Lord had his own personal set of circumstances, His own trials, which were sent by God. He accepted everything, without exception. Watch Him when He was under the fiery testings, under the environments. And now the Lord tells us to follow Him. Each person has to take up his cross. It must become personalized. We must see our environment in the same way the Lord saw His environment. For God's plan to be worked out in us requires death and resurrection. We have to have *our* cross and know it in a personal way.

In Mark 8:34 the Lord said, "Let *him* deny *himself,* and take up *his* cross." This means the Lord has allowed certain situations. He has allowed certain troubles and insults. He has allowed a certain kind of husband, wife, or children. Each of these is a certain kind of environment. And for each, we have to take up the cross in a personal way. Let a man take up his personalized cross. To take up our cross means to embrace what God allows in our lives. It means to embrace our environment as the outward cross the Lord has sent to us. The cross must become that personal. But have we really personalized it? For example, when you complain about your husband, when you have an issue with your wife, when you are hoping that the other person will change — he or she is too hard on you and it is too difficult — when you have a blaming attitude, wanting to change the situation, it indicates that you are a person who has not embraced your cross. The Lord says to such a person, "Let him take up his cross, and follow Me."

The Word divides   January 28th

"For the word of God is living and powerful, and sharper than any two-edged sword, piercing even to the division of soul and spirit, and of joints and marrow, and is a discerner of the thoughts and intents of the heart." HEBREWS 4:12

A believer's greatest need is to get into the Word of God regularly and to go to the Lord day by day, especially in the mornings. Open up to the Lord and begin to pray over the verses. Reading the Bible must be more to us than a routine or academic pursuit. We need to actually contact God while we are in the Word. By getting into the Word in this way, we find it is "living and powerful." It begins to operate; it begins to speak. A word will stand out, a verse will stand out, or a phrase will stand out, and then you begin to pray with what touches you. That word entering into your heart clears you up inwardly. "The entrance of Your words gives light" (Psa. 119:130). You begin to see that you have been in your self — in your emotions, in your reactions, in your pride and hardness. You have been in your hurt feelings or in your reasoning mind about someone. You have chosen your own will. Light begins to dawn upon you, and you become inwardly clear about where you have been. You get divided. You begin to see how you have sinned, how you have lived in your soulish life, how you have lived out of your impulses, or how your motive for saying something was altogether impure. The word divides your soul and spirit, and discerns the thoughts and intents of your heart.

With this dividing and discerning, you begin to repent and confess to the Lord your lack of living out from Him. As you confess, your spirit rises to the surface of your being (cf. Eph. 5:18-19 with Col. 3:16), and everything becomes crystal clear. What originates from your soul is exposed to you, and what originates from your spirit is manifested. There is the realm of the soul and there is the realm of the spirit, and it is the living and active word of God that discovers for us which realm we are living in.

Qualified to participate   January 29th

"My little children, these things I write to you, that you may not sin. And if anyone sins, we have an Advocate with the Father, Jesus Christ the righteous." 1 JOHN 2:1

We have the privilege of calling "Jesus." This call is not a work to establish something with God. This call is a direct participation in His life. Of course, no human being dares to participate in God's life unless he is qualified. What then qualifies us to participate? We are qualified by the blood of Jesus (Heb. 10:17-20). Knowing this truth sets us free from trying to establish our own righteousness. Being in this reality takes away all pretense. Without this reality I will be trying to establish my own righteousness. For example, I may be in a bad mood and want to get to the Lord. My getting to the Lord can be like a little ritual that I go through. I have to call ten times before I can feel accepted by God. So even my calling upon the name of the Lord becomes a work of attaining to something, rather than a participation in the Lord's life through the merit of His blood.

First John 2:1 says, "And if anyone *sins,* we have an Advocate with the Father." It does not even say, "And if anyone *repents,* we have an Advocate with the Father." This means that the moment sin enters the picture and breaks our fellowship with the Lord, there does not need to be any time lost in restoring that fellowship. "We have [present tense] an Advocate with the Father." When sin occurs, in that moment we can turn and look to our Advocate who is before the blood-sprinkled throne.

Then it also may follow that the Holy Spirit will move within you concerning your sin. He will pass through you, and you will weep and weep. But your weeping will be tears of joy because you are a forgiven person. Yet at the same time you will find that you loathe yourself. Ezekiel chapter 36 indicates that when we have "a new spirit," indwelt by the divine Spirit, we will spontaneously loathe ourselves (vv. 26-27, 31). This loathing of ourselves is the activity of the Spirit. It does not come from morbid introspection and shedding many tears over our poor condition. Martin passed through this kind of introspection in his own experience. He shed tears, thinking that this would wash away his sins. But he discovered that his tears did not work to cleanse his conscience. Then one day from Romans 1:17 he saw Christ as his total righteousness and became a new man. The sight of Calvary releases our spirit to participate in Him.

"For we are not as the many, corrupting the word of God: but as out of sincerity, but as out of God, in the sight of God, speak we in Christ." 2 CORINTHIANS 2:17 (ASV)

Here the apostle Paul gives us a practical example of a person living out of God as his source. The three special phrases in this verse — *out of God, in the sight of* [or, *before*] *God,* and *speak we in Christ* — are all ways of describing how Paul's speaking was out of the source of God, and not out of himself. His ministry was proceeding *out of* God, *before* God, and *in* Christ.

When we are redeemed and regenerated, we are ushered into the realm of the new creation, where God begins a process in which experientially the old things start to pass out of our lives. The old things are related to our *self* as our point of reference. We lived out of our own impulses, our own choices, our own thoughts. But now we begin to live by revelation, that is, by what God has revealed to us in His Word. It is when we live by revelation that God becomes our source. He reveals to us the purpose of our human life. We no longer take man's views and concepts as the basis of our human existence.

Revelation unveils to us God's eternal purpose, which is the purpose behind the created universe. This revelation causes me to be a person who is living to be conformed to the image of God's Son, with the many brothers in the church (Rom. 8:28-29). Thus, we are squarely planted in the church life, with Christ as the focus and reality of our daily life. We do not live by our own thoughts — what we think we should do. We live by the unveiling of God's heart's desire for His Body, the church, where Christ is all and in all. It is by this unveiling that God becomes our source. The Spirit teaches us, through the Word, to be persons who are living a life in complete accord with God's heart's desire. Our daily life begins to proceed out of God as we learn to live out of Him as our source.

All things out of God

"Therefore, if anyone is in Christ, he is a new creation; old things have passed away; behold, all things have become new. Now all things are out of God." 2 CORINTHIANS 5:17-18

In the new creation, "old things have passed away." This means that my old existence, which was *apart from* God as my source, has passed away. "All things have become new" means that now "all things are *out of* God." He is now my source. When God reconciled us to Himself through Jesus Christ, He produced a relationship that makes *Him*, not *ourselves*, the source of our lives. He has the rightful place because He has imparted His Son into us. Now, the source of everything in our lives is the Spirit of His Son sent into our hearts crying, "Abba, Father!"

To be "in Christ" in the new creation is to be in the source where all things are out of God. His Son lived a human life on this earth for 33 1/2 years. In all His living, He did nothing apart from the Father. Whatever He spoke and whatever He did, He did *out of* the Father as His source. He was wholly dependent upon the Father's life as the source for His daily life. We must see that *the Son's life* lived out in the Gospels is now *in us*. As the Spirit, He is operating to produce His dependent life in us, and to eliminate our independent living — a life of living to ourselves. Our life in the old creation has been an independent life, in which we have lived out of our self as the source. We have made our own decisions, done our own things, lived out of our own feelings and thoughts. In brief, *we* have been the source of our life. Thus, the Lord works in our lives to actually make Himself our source. Why are we passing through all kinds of experiences and various environments? They are designed by God to bring us into Himself as our source. What we are going through right now is another step toward the goal of working a realization into our consciousness that our life is out of God Himself.

February

Spend time cultivating

"And He was saying, Abba, Father, all things are possible for You." MARK 14:36

It takes time to cultivate a love relationship with the Lord. This was demonstrated by the Lord's own earthly life. He repeatedly spent time with the Father, enjoying the Father's love (Luke 5:16). In Mark 14:36 we find Him in the garden of Gethsemane, where it was His habit to go and be with the Father (Luke 22:39). Here He is once again pressing into the bosom of the Father while facing the critical hour of crucifixion. Mark records that the Lord was saying repeatedly, "Abba, Father." This means that even when He became obedient unto death, the death of the cross, He did it by enjoying the Father's love. To say "Abba" is to call upon the Father in the most sweet and intimate way.

Now we must see that this same "Abba, Father" love-life has been sent into our hearts. Paul declares, "And because you are sons, God has sent forth the Spirit of His Son into your hearts, crying out, Abba, Father!" (Gal. 4:6). What a joy! What a hope! The very prayer life of God's Son is in our hearts. The intimate love-life between the Father and the Son has been put into us. We have it! It is not a matter of trying to find it or longing to possess it. We have the Triune God's love-life within us. And by virtue of our being a born-again Christian, we are entitled to merge in our hearts with the love flowing between the Father and the Son in the fellowship of the Holy Spirit (2 Cor. 13:14).

The Lord's love-life with the Father simply needs to be cultivated and released in us. That life is in us twenty-four hours a day. The same life that cried "Abba, Father," the same life that withdrew so many times into the wilderness to pray, the same life that wanted to be with the Father alone — that life is in us. And that life in us needs time. The same life that took time to pray in the Gospels still needs time to pray in us. The Spirit of His Son is located within our hearts, waiting for us to join in and cry "Abba, Father." What an indescribable enjoyment — that we could merge with the Son's life which is ever pressing anew with equal intimacy into the bosom of the Father.

Perfection in the divine realm   February 2nd

"But the anointing which you have received from Him abides in you, and you do not need that anyone teach you; but as the same anointing teaches you concerning all things, and is true, and is not a lie, and just as it has taught you, you will abide in Him."
1 John 2:27

The fact that you do not need anyone to teach you indicates that there is an inward tutor, an inward Person, who is teaching you. The anointing is teaching us concerning all things. When we are oriented to the anointing and we touch the Lord by praying and calling on Him and get to God, there is a kind of surveillance going on in our being. Things get sorted out. You get divided: "That is my mind. That is my flesh. That is coming from my self." There is a dividing of soul and spirit. Then you can side with the Lord and stand with Him, even over against your self. You can be most objective about your self. You can so easily look at your wife and say, "Dear, I'm a wretch. I don't know how you could be married to me. I don't know how you could live for so many years with such a nature as mine." You can talk this way with inner glee because you are not one with that old nature. You are one with Christ, and you are a partaker of Him.

Consider what would happen on this earth if all of us as believers would live by the anointing. This does not mean that we would be perfect, in the sense of what *we think* perfection is. Perfection in the divine realm is our getting to God. It means that we touch His life in the midst of all our imperfection. That is what perfection is. It is living by the anointing and simply getting to God in the midst of what we pass through, even with our imperfections.

Absolute dependence reproduced February 3rd

"Then Jesus answered and said to them, Most assuredly, I say to you, the Son can do nothing from Himself, but what He sees the Father do; for whatever He does, the Son also does in like manner." JOHN 5:19

To fully appreciate the significance of having a change in the source of our living, we need to consider the example of the Lord Jesus. Consider the source from which the Lord lived, from which He did everything. His base of operation was constantly the Father. This means that the Lord Himself, in His humanity, did not take His self as His source. Rather, He was one with the Father. This oneness came out of His continual fellowship with the Father in the Word (Matt. 4:4), in prayer (Luke 5:16-17), and in crying "Abba, Father" (Mark 14:36). As He lived a life of fellowship with the Father, He lived a life of absolute dependence. The source of His life was exclusively the Father. He denied and terminated His soul-life, and He lived out the Father's life.

Now the Lord wants to reproduce this same dependent relationship in our experience. This dependent relationship proceeds from the source of our spirit. It does not proceed from the self-life. This dependency issues in the building of the church, the shutting of the gates of Hades, and the crushing of Satan. So it is crucial for us to see that God's goal is that we no longer operate out of the base of our independent self. Rather, we are dependent, reliant, trusting Him

35

moment by moment about everything, including our thought life, our reactions, our fears, our problems, our whole way of living. We are persons in whom the absolute dependent life of the Son of God is being reproduced.

The realm of life   February 4th

"For the mind of the flesh is death; but the mind of the Spirit is life and peace." ROMANS 8:6 (ASV)

In the realm of life there are feelings and sensations (Eph. 4:18-19). These sensations may also be identified as the consciousness of life. For example, when you are talking with someone out of the source of your self, you may have a consciousness of feeling awkward, restless, uneasy, and uncomfortable. There is something within you forbidding. If you do not know the realm of life, you will just ignore those sensations and proceed with your thought, your view, your argument, your words. This means you are living out of the wrong source. Instead of coming from the source of the spirit, being sensitive to the feelings of life, you override the realm of the spirit by the self. So the undealt-with, ignorant self does not know how to relate in life.

To be a person in the realm of life is to be one who progressively learns to take care of the spirit and the inner registrations of life and peace. It is not to pay attention to right and wrong according to the self, but to pay attention to life and peace according to the Spirit. This is to take care of the inner consciousness in our being. It is the same as paying attention to the registrations of the Spirit written on our heart and mind (Heb. 8:10). It is the same as taking care of the flow of life coming from our innermost being (John 7:38-39). And it is also the same as recognizing peace and joy in the Holy Spirit (Rom. 14:17). This is how we relate in life.

"For this is the covenant that I will make with the house of Israel after those days, says the LORD: I will put My laws in their mind and write them on their hearts; and I will be their God, and they shall be My people." HEBREWS 8:10

The Lord's voice infuses and supplies us with love for Him, godly desires, willingness to obey Him, and the ability to go along with Him. This reveals that His voice is like an inner inclination in our being. That is, He puts His inclinations into us. This is the meaning of the laws put into our mind and written upon our hearts. This is the nature of His speaking. It is not hearing an audible voice; neither is it waiting for a vision; nor is it reading some words that appear before our eyes in a ticker-tape fashion. Rather, the normal voice of the Son speaking in us comes as a supplied feeling of life written into our consciousness. This feeling is an inner inclination, or inner tendency. It may even be considered as an inner bias, or disposition. It is the bent, or leaning, of our mind, emotion, and will. For example, there may be an inclination or desire within you to spend more time with the Lord. You have a leaning in that direction. It is not an overpowering feeling; nevertheless you seem to be bent in the direction of desiring more time to spend with the Lord in your daily life. That inclination is the voice of the Son of God. He is not speaking audibly in your ears, but He is speaking in your inner consciousness by an infused tendency. The tendency carries with it a fresh supply of grace. Thus, whenever you go along with that tendency and obey it, you discover that the bountiful supply of the Spirit of Jesus Christ is present there with you, backing up that tendency with fresh and available grace.

A state of perfection   February 6th

"I in them, and You in Me; that they may be made perfect into one, and that the world may know that You have sent Me, and have loved them as You have loved Me." JOHN 17:23

When the Lord prayed, "that they may be *made perfect*," He used the perfect tense of the Greek verb. The perfect tense indicates that the effect of what happened in the past continues to be a present state and reality. This tells us that He was not referring to a *process* of being perfected. He was identifying a *state* of perfection that we are in. Kenneth S. Wuest, in his *Expanded Translation* of the New Testament, translates verse 23 in a way that expresses the significance of the perfect tense: "I in them and you in me, in order that they, having been brought to the state of completeness [or, perfection] with respect to oneness, may persist in that state of completeness [or, perfection]..." In other words, being brought to a state of perfection is simply equal to Christ indwelling us with the Father.

The "I in them" is inseparably linked to the "You in Me." "I in them" means that the Son is in us. "You in Me" means that the Father is in the Son. So we have the Father in the Son as the Spirit flowing into us as our state of perfection. This perfection is the perfection of the oneness existing between the Father and the Son. That oneness comes into us when Christ comes into us. Therefore, perfection is not what we attain; it is what we receive when we receive Christ. In every relationship in the Body of Christ, recognize the existing perfection, and then persist and continue in it.

Fire life up   February 7th

"Therefore I remind you to stir up the gift of God which is in you through the laying on of my hands." 2 TIMOTHY 1:6

There is a life in our spirit that has power to change us. That life has become a drink to us. It has become our food. As we enjoy that life, it flows and it operates. It has the ability to tear down our hardness. It has the ability to work in us to actually change our choice, change our attitude, and change our feeling. That life in us can do a complete work on our insides, because it has passed through human living and death itself. It has resurrected and ascended all the way to the throne, and now it has been dispensed into our spirit and is living and operating and working in us.

What we need to do is simply stir up what is already within us. Second Timothy 1:6-7 says, "Stir up [or, fan into flame] the gift of God which is in you. . . . [7] For God has not given us a spirit of fear, but of power and of love and of a sound mind." Resurrection power is in your spirit. You do not know the potential that is there! All you have to do is *fan into flame* the gift of God which is in you. The Greek verb literally means "to fire life up," to "fan" it. Fire up what is smoldering there. This means that you and I have a spirit that is joined to the resurrected, ascended Christ. And this resurrected, ascended One is just waiting for our spirits to be fanned. For example, when you come to a meeting of the church and you sing, pray, and praise, you are fanning. You are "firing life up." Then that life operates. Or during the day as you are going through some kind of trial, open yourself to call "Jesus." By speaking His name you are fanning the flame, causing that resurrection life to operate and work.

What do we bring?   February 8th

"Therefore you shall be perfect, just as your Father in heaven is perfect." MATTHEW 5:48

To be "perfect" here is to be perfect in our relationships with others. By using "therefore" at the beginning of the verse, the Lord links perfection with loving our enemies (vv. 43-47). This same passage in Luke's Gospel says, [35] "But love your enemies, do good, and lend, hoping for nothing in return; and your reward will be great, and you will be sons of the Highest. For He is kind to the unthankful and evil. [36] Therefore be merciful and compassionate, just as your Father also is merciful and compassionate" (Luke 6:35-36). Matthew says, "You shall be perfect, just as your Father in heaven is perfect." But Luke defines the meaning of perfection by saying, "Be merciful, just as your Father also is merciful." So Luke explains Matthew by defining what perfection is, and Matthew defines perfection in the context of love.

Together, these two passages show us that perfection is bringing the love of God into our relationships. What do we bring into our relationships? Do we bring an ideal thought? Or do we bring the love of God? What do we bring into our relationships with one another in the church? What do we bring into our relationship in our marriage? What do we bring? What attitude do we come with? What is our standard? Is it an ideal concept that we all must conform to or measure up to? What we bring into our relationships determines the reality we have between us. The divine standard of perfection is to bring the love of God into our relationships. What we bring is God's kind of love.

Processed in His process   February 9th

"For if we have been united together in the likeness of His death, certainly we also shall be in the likeness of His resurrection." ROMANS 6:5

The crucified and resurrected Christ has joined us to Himself organically. We are joined to His death and His resurrection. In Galatians 2:20 Paul testified, "I have been crucified with Christ; it is no longer I who live, but Christ lives in me." This is the crucified and resurrected Christ that Paul was joined to and experienced. So if we experience Christ, we experience Him as the crucified and resurrected Christ.

The Christ who was processed in incarnation, human living, crucifixion, resurrection, and ascension is living in us to process us. That is, this Christ is now processing us with all the elements of His own process. For example, He is processing us in crucifixion. Not only were we terminated objectively on the cross two thousand years ago, but subjectively, day by day, we are being terminated. Our whole being is now being processed in crucifixion. That means our mind, our emotions, and our will — with all the practices of our body — are being processed day by day in crucifixion in order to be processed in resurrection. Thus, our whole being is under a divine process of crucifixion and resurrection. Because we have been joined together in the likeness of His death, we will also be in the likeness of His resurrection. Our whole being is under the process of crucifixion and resurrection for the building of the church. This is our destiny.

Our life-union   February 10th

"A little while longer and the world will see Me no more, but you will see Me. Because I live, you will live also." JOHN 14:19

The basis of our being compatible with the Lord's voice is our life-union with Him in spirit. This union is expressed in the Lord's words, "Because I live, you will live also." We live because He lives. It is that simple. First Corinthians 6:17 reveals that this union with the Lord is in the realm of our spirit. We are joined to the Lord and are one spirit with Him. This joining is the basis of the Lord's utterance "Because I live, you will live also." He lives within us in our spirit, and we live in union with Him. This life-union issues in a life-consciousness. So we can know and experience the very consciousness of the Lord's life within us. It is by this life-consciousness that we learn to be compatible with His life-voice.

This experiential reality is also expressed in John 4:14: "But whoever drinks of the water that I shall give him will never thirst. But the water that I shall give him will become in him a fountain of water springing up into eternal life." When the Lord said, "the water that I shall give him *will become in him a fountain of water*," He was referring to our life-union with Him. When we receive Christ, an artesian well is established in the deepest part of our being — our spirit. When this life-union, or inner well, springs up within us, it produces the consciousness of His life in the many facets of our daily life — from our inner thinking and motives to our outward behavior and deeds. It is this life-consciousness that constitutes the Lord's voice. When we go along with this consciousness, we are being compatible with God.

Living to God in a Person   February 11th

"For I through the law died to the law that I might live to God. I have been crucified with Christ; it is no longer I who live, but Christ lives in me." GALATIANS 2:19-20

Here we see how God dealt with us in our relationship to the law — we died to the law in the death of Christ on the cross. When Christ died on the cross, we also died (2 Cor. 5:14). Indeed, Paul makes it clear in Romans 7:3-4 that when the body of Christ was hanging on the cross, we not only died with Him but we died *to the law* with Him. The law demanded that the sinner die for his sin (Ezek. 18:4). Thus, in our co-crucifixion with Christ, we legally and judicially died. We were all judged on the cross in His death. The law effectively put us to death in Him and dealt a final blow to our law-breaking flesh. This is the meaning of Paul's statement, "I through the law died to the law."

Now that we have died to the law in the death of Christ, we no longer have a relationship with the law in ourselves. Our relationship to the law is now Jesus Christ Himself. He is not only the end of the law for righteousness to us (Rom. 10:4), but He is also the fulfiller of the righteous requirement of the law in us as we walk according to spirit (Matt. 5:17-18; Rom. 8:3-4). We are no longer occupied with living to an impersonal law and demand that has no life in it. We are living to God in a Person who is life and who gives life! Christ being my relationship with the law means that it is no longer the law-keeping "I" who lives, but Christ who lives in me. This means I am forever delivered from slavery, bondage, legality, impotence, and fear. I am now living to God in the Person of Christ.

Receiving "the sonship"   February 12th

"To redeem those who were under the law, that we might receive the sonship." GALATIANS 4:5

The way we live to God is not out of ourselves or our efforts. We live to God in our relationship and fellowship with His Son. In the Son we have received the "sonship." Sonship in the New Testament means to have an existence of continually living before God as an object of His love because we are in the One who is continually being loved — the beloved One! This is sonship.

I live to God in the very relationship that Christ has with the Father (Eph. 2:18). Even though I am still in the flesh and can feel its tendencies and weaknesses, my relationship with God is never disturbed. This is because of a constant infusion of faith that comes from being so flooded with the personal love of my Christ for me. Paul says it in Galatians 2:20: "the life which I now live in the flesh I live by the faith of the Son of God, who loved me and gave Himself for me." Thus, "the faith of the Son of God" was coming to Paul because of his love relationship with the Lord (Gal. 5:6). This is the way faith operates — simply by abiding in His love.

43

Despite the presence of the flesh, and even its rumblings, we are not under the law to interact with the flesh or to have any kind of relationship with it. The only thing we do now is keep ourselves in the love of God (Jude 21). By this we allow faith to keep infusing us to be completely occupied with Christ. This is how the church is in the reality of Christ. It is by saints being freed from the tyranny of the law and having only one relationship in their lives — Christ!

Nothing from the self   February 13th

"Then Jesus said to them, When you lift up the Son of Man, then you will know that I am He, and that I do nothing from Myself; but as My Father taught Me, I speak these things." JOHN 8:28

God wants to effect in us a transfer of our source. We see this transfer in Romans 14:7-8: [7] "For none of us lives to himself, and no one dies to himself. [8] For if we live, we live to the Lord; and if we die, we die to the Lord. Therefore, whether we live or die, we are the Lord's." This simplifies everything. This makes everything uncomplicated. This keeps us in the enjoyment of Christ hour after hour. Then we no longer handle the self, consult with it, debate with it, or live it out. We just know one thing — how to enjoy Christ, fellowship with Him, handle everything with Him, and relate to our environment with Him. We find ourselves no longer living an independent, self-trusting life. But increasingly we live dependent on the Lord, just as He lived dependent on the Father. In John 8:28 He describes His own living: "I do nothing from Myself." He neither spoke nor acted from Himself. It is this dependent life that the Lord supplies to us in our spirit. This grace-wrought dependency is the goal of God's dealing with the self. It refers to a genuine transfer of source that takes place in us so that we live one spirit with the Lord.

Now the Lord wants us to become familiar with our spirit — to discover our spirit, use our spirit, and learn to take the initiative with our spirit. In the past, our soul has been so activated that we have been flooded with our own thoughts and enmeshed with our own feelings and choices. In Ephesians 2:3 Paul clearly defines our unregenerate state: "Among whom also we all once conducted ourselves in the lusts of our flesh, fulfilling the desires of the flesh and of the thoughts." "The desires of the thoughts" means that we have lived out Satan in our independent thoughts. This character-ized our old life, before we were regenerated.

Even after we are regenerated, we may still live out of the source of our self in many things. However, in regenerating our spirit, the Lord has imparted His own dependent life into us. He lived a dependent life, and that is the nature of His life in us. Thus, our dealings with the Lord in our daily life will come in the things and in the areas where we live independent from Him. Expect to be brought into an ever deepening dependence upon Him.

A new standard   February 14th

"For those who live according to the flesh set their minds on the things of the flesh, but those who live according to the Spirit, the things of the Spirit." ROMANS 8:5

The preposition "according to" in this verse signifies the standard by which we live. When God changes the source of our being, we discover that we have a new standard to live by. We no longer live according to the standard of the flesh. The flesh is not our point of reference anymore. We do not live out from the flesh, or according to the flesh. Our standard now is to walk according to spirit, which means to do things, conduct ourselves, and live accord-ing to the realm of the Spirit.

To live according to the flesh is to set your mind on the things of the flesh. This means that you take your self as your source and live according to it. Experientially, you are absorbed in your self. You live out of your self, considering your condemnation, your shortage, your condition, your situation. This is to mind the things of the flesh. Minding the things of the flesh means that your tendency is to bring up your whole history — your failures, your inability, your conflicting thoughts. When you begin thinking in this way, you get bent in this direction, and soon you are possessed with your self. Actually, you are susceptible to thinking the devil's thoughts (2 Cor. 2:11). Indeed, your soul-life is enmeshed with the demonic realm (James 3:15). You entertain demonic thought-life and patterns. Why? Because you have lived out of the wrong source — not according to spirit but according to flesh.

In contrast, when we live according to the spirit, we set our minds on the things of the Spirit. The new standard of the Spirit ushers us into a new realm with a new way of thinking and an entirely new set of values. We begin to value and prefer Christ above everything else. Consider what you value, and you will discover the standard by which you live.

Loved to the end   February 15th

"Now before the feast of the Passover, when Jesus knew that His hour had come that He should depart from this world to the Father, having loved His own who were in the world, He loved them to the end." JOHN 13:1

The statement "He loved them to the end" reveals that we do not possess a temporary love, but a kind of love that loves us to the end or to the uttermost. This love has its roots in eternity past according to John 17:24 and Jeremiah 31:3. It is the eternal love proceeding from the eternal life of God. From eternity past to eternity future, throughout time with all its battles and problems, this love-life remains constant. This means that nothing — neither sin, the flesh, the world, the devil, distresses, or human weakness — can separate us from that love. Praise the Lord! It is this love-life existing in the Son that we are called to partake of and constantly abide in.

We see the love-life of the Lord Jesus with the Father in eternity past. Also, when He was on earth, the Lord was abiding in the Father's love (John 15:9-10). His entire earthly life was lived out in the unalterable atmosphere of the Father's love. In John 17:4-5 the Lord prayed, ⁴ "I have glorified You on the earth. I have finished the work which You have given Me to do. ⁵ And now, O Father, glorify Me together with Yourself, with the glory which I had with You before the world was." These precious words imply that the Son will be restored to the state in which He existed in eternity past. And again in John 17:24 the Lord said, "Father, I desire that they also whom You gave Me may *be with Me where I am,* that they may behold My glory which You have given Me; for You loved Me before the foundation of the world." This request to the Father shows us how this love-life is concentrated in the Son. We all need to be touched with the realization that the love-life of the church, His bride, is nothing less than a participation in the very love that is concentrated in the beloved Son.

As He is, so are we   February 16th

"And we have known and believed the love that God has for us. God is love, and he who abides in love abides in God, and God in him. Love has been perfected among us in this: that we may have boldness in the day of judgment; because as He is, so are we in this world." 1 JOHN 4:16-17

The context of these verses indicates that at this very moment on the throne, in the heavenly life between the Father and the Son, there exists a continuous motion of love between Them. The Son is in a wonderful, constant love relationship with the Father. This is the meaning of the phrase "as He is." He is always and ever being loved by the Father. In the same way that the Father is presently loving the Son on the throne, He is loving us in this world. This is the meaning of the next phrase, "so are we in this world." The intensity of love that the Father has toward the Son is the same intensity that He has toward us, because we are in His Son, and His Son is in us.

The Son is not the only beloved one. We are also beloved in Him. We too are the objects of the Father's love. It is so important that we see how this love is concentrated in His Son. It was concentrated in Him during His earthly life. It is now concentrated in Him in His heavenly life. And it is concentrated in us by virtue of His indwelling life. Because of our union with Him, as He is loved, so are we loved. He cannot be loved without us getting the benefit.

Christ formed in you   February 17th

"My little children, for whom I travail again until Christ is formed in you." GALATIANS 4:19

When Paul speaks of Christ being formed in you, he uses the Greek aorist tense, indicating that it happens at a point in time. Most Bible teachers have interpreted the word "formed" as though it was in the present tense, giving the impression that it is a *process* happening over a period of time. However, the aorist tense for the word "formed" implies that Christ needed to be once again formed in the Galatians' experience. This did not mean they had lost their salvation. They were still born of God. But due to their being focused upon the law instead of upon Christ, they fell out of being supplied in the realm of grace. Christ no longer profited them. They were, as Paul says in Galatians 5:4, "discharged" from Christ living and operating in them, because they went to something else. Instead of Christ being formed in them, Moses was formed in them,

48

circumcision was formed.

Maybe due to your religious background, what is formed in your mind right now are your own thoughts about the way you are supposed to be. You feel like you cannot get to the Lord until you fulfill some requirement. You have so many things formed in you. Paul says, "I travail again . . . until Christ is formed in you," that is, until He again becomes your present enjoyment and fellowship. Out of this He will live in you. Out of this He will operate in you. Out of this you will grow with the growth of God. The principle of this verse is identical to Colossians 2:19, where Paul speaks of "holding fast the Head," or "seizing the Head." Your point of reference is the Head. Seize the Head. Do not seize ordinances or regulations such as "Do not touch, do not taste, do not handle" (Col. 2:20-21). Seize the Head and you will grow with the growth of God.

Christ, my point of reference   February 18th

"And not holding fast to the Head, from whom all the body, nourished and knit together by joints and ligaments, grows with the increase which is from God." COLOSSIANS 2:19

If I am not holding fast to Christ, my Head, if He is not my point of reference in relating to all things, then nothing "works" in my Christian life. Christ's work in me — His living and operating — comes to a halt. There is no growth, no sanctification, no conformation to the image of His Son, and no way to proceed in the Christian life. If I am not interacting with Christ, then I am interacting with the law, or what is formed in my mind. I am interacting with my feelings of discouragement or the reasonings of my mind. My point of reference when I go through things is not Christ, but something else. My point of reference is my feelings, the outward circumstances, the situation, the law, what I am supposed to be, or even what I am not — all these mental gyrations that go on within us. The principle is that I interact with whatever is formed in me. If Christ is formed in me crying "Abba, Father," I interact with Him. If something else is formed in me, I interact with that.

Christ formed in me does not mean that I am perfect, that I am a finished product. It means that my point of reference is always Christ — that He would have the first place in everything. So I do not know how to handle myself. I do not know how to handle sin. I do not know how to handle my reactions to my environment. But Christ has already handled all these things. By taking Him as my point of reference in all these things, I remain in fellowship with Him.

But we see Jesus   February 19th

"You have put all things in subjection under his feet. For in that He put all in subjection under him, He left nothing that is not put under him. But now we do not yet see all things put under him. But we see Jesus." HEBREWS 2:8-9

There are two things to take note of in these verses: first, the fact that "we do not yet see all things put under him"; and second, *"but we see Jesus."* These two things are going on simultaneously. This means that we may see many things in us that are not yet subjected to Him — things that are not under His feet, under His ruling. But even in such an unfinished state, we still see Jesus! Our heart can be positioned and focused on Christ, despite the existence of the unsubjected things. Do not be distracted by what you see in yourself. Keep your eyes upon Jesus and trust Him to subdue every unruly thing.

Paul says in 2 Corinthians 3:16, "Nevertheless when the heart shall turn to the Lord, the veil shall be taken away" (KJV). Then he continues in verse 18, "But we all, with unveiled face, beholding and reflecting as in a mirror the glory of the Lord . . ." These verses show us that to behold the Lord with an unveiled face, we need a turned heart, a heart positioned toward the Lord. Our heart has been turned in another direction, away from the Lord, and we need to turn it toward the Lord. Our heart may be distracted by many things, but our one and only need is to turn it toward the Lord.

Our tendency is to have our heart turned toward our problems, our defeated condition, or what we see in ourselves that is still not subdued by the Lord. But the most important thing in spending time with the Lord is to get our eyes off ourselves and onto Him. Regardless of how we feel or what we see in ourselves, we still need to keep our heart focused on the Lord.

Justification and regeneration   February 20th

"Even so through one Man's righteous act the free gift came to all men, resulting in justification of life." ROMANS 5:18

As a believer I may know doctrinally that there is "no condemnation to those who are in Christ Jesus" (Rom. 8:1). Yet why do I still feel condemned? Why do I feel out of sorts within? If I am not under the law but under grace, then why do I experience discomfort and awkwardness within when I take a certain course of action? These kinds of questions have troubled many believers for years. The answer to these questions is quite simple. Yes, we are positionally "in Christ," and therefore we are justified persons and there is no condemnation. Yet whenever we do things that are not in harmony with the Lord's life, *we feel* the responses and reactions of Christ within our being, because He is, in fact, *our life* (Col. 3:4). This is the significance of the phrase "justification of life." It means justification that issues, or results, in a life-consciousness within us.

God's salvation over us includes not only justification, but also regeneration. Justification refers to our secure standing before God based upon the blood of Christ. Regeneration refers to the life of God that we have received into our spirit, making us one spirit with the

Lord. Justification is positional, whereas regeneration is dispositional. Regeneration is a matter of the divine life entering into us and inwardly guiding us throughout our life. Whenever we pursue a course of action that is not compatible with the Lord's life, our regenerated state causes us to feel bothered. We cannot remain inwardly content, because we are at odds with His life. His life within cannot change its life-consciousness. We are simply incompatible at that point. Our standing has not changed, but our present condition is incompatible. This disturbance of our inward harmony *is* the Lord's voice in us speaking to us to get us back on course with the divine life. He is not condemning us, but rather He is loving us by inwardly steering us back to Himself.

The lack of rest   February 21st

"Furthermore, when I came to Troas to preach Christ's gospel, and a door was opened to me by the Lord, I had no rest in my spirit, because I did not find Titus my brother; but taking my leave of them, I departed for Macedonia." 2 CORINTHIANS 2:12-13

Sometimes we are faced with decisions of guidance related to what we should do or where we should go. Paul had an open door to preach the gospel, but in his spirit he did not find the rest to do so. This means *the lack of rest* in his spirit *was* the Lord's voice indicating to him that to preach the gospel in Troas at that juncture was not compatible with the Lord's mind.

Luke records a similar experience of Paul's in Acts 16:6-7: [6] "Now when they had gone through Phrygia and the region of Galatia, they were forbidden by the Holy Spirit to preach the word in Asia. [7] After they had come to Mysia, they tried to go into Bithynia, but the Spirit did not permit them." In both instances, the anointing of the Spirit spoke in a way to "forbid" and "not permit" as they were proceeding to preach the Word. No doubt, Paul's fellowship with the Lord was rich and deep, and his inward parts were sensitive to hear the Lord's voice manifesting itself not by outward words but by an inward restraint. This inward restraint is the lack of rest. Do not impulsively take steps and make decisions if you lack the rest in your spirit.

Breaking the stronghold of reasoning   February 22nd

"Then the Spirit told me to go with them, doubting nothing. Moreover these six brethren accompanied me, and we entered the man's house." ACTS 11:12

You cannot obey the Lord and be a reasoning person. This is because a reasoning mind will always find a reason why we should *not* obey the Lord. What if one day the Lord in your spirit told you to do something you had never done before? What if inwardly you were restrained by the Spirit from doing what you had always done? Would this not cause your mind to reel? Would you not begin to think and reason — Why should I not do this? What reason is there behind this? Why would the Lord be speaking to me this way? But a person who knows the Lord would not question if the Spirit spoke in such a way. For example, when the Lord wanted to pour out His salvation upon the Gentiles, He told Peter to do something that he had never done before. He spoke to him to eat unclean foods (Acts 10:11-16). Later, Peter testified that what he had done in going to the Gentiles was in obedience to the Spirit, without doubting or reasoning (Acts 11:12).

It is reasoning that prevents us from obeying. We have reasons why we do not obey, reasons why we do not deal with certain things. The Spirit has been speaking for years, but we have our reason, we have our proof, we have evidence, as to why we do not obey. We can even support our disobedience with spiritual successes in other areas of our lives, in which we have touched the spirit and obeyed the Lord.

We have all kinds of reasons for not obeying the Lord over the matter He has spoken about.

I remember one of my first experiences of the Lord's dealing with me over my reasonings. Specifically, He was touching me about the sermons I had prepared when I was in a denomination. These messages were all typewritten. They were even used to bring people to the Lord. They were biblical and expository. Yet the Lord told me to burn them. I discovered that with obedience, there is no room for reason. If the Lord said it, that is good enough. There does not have to be a reason, especially when the Lord is breaking the stronghold of reasoning in our lives. In our mind, we want reasons. But when He deals with us to overthrow strongholds, He does not give reasons.

Let the Spirit prevail

"Now when they had gone through Phrygia and the region of Galatia, they were forbidden by the Holy Spirit to preach the word in Asia. After they had come to Mysia, they tried to go into Bithynia, but the Spirit did not permit them." ACTS 16:6-7

The apostles were attempting to preach the Word of God in Asia, but the Holy Spirit was forbidding them. They then attempted to go into Bithynia, but the Spirit of Jesus did not permit them to do so. This means that the Spirit prevailed over the reasoning mind. For example, they could have reasoned, "Shouldn't we go to Asia? Shouldn't we go to Bithynia? Isn't it right to go?" But the Spirit prevailed and forbade them. This simply means that to overthrow the stronghold of our reasoning, we must let the Spirit prevail. When we follow the Spirit, when we go along with the Spirit, then our reasoning mind can be overthrown. Then we can be in a position to catch the thoughts.

One by one, we take captive every thought that comes in — even a right thought. A right thought may come, and then we surround that thought with reasons — more and more reasons. We just live by reasoning. Maybe concerning someone, you have a view, you have an opinion, you have reasons that affect the way you speak to each other and think about each other. When you speak, though what you say may be right, your self comes out. Your speaking does not taste like Christ, even though you are trying to help each other. It is because you are too enmeshed in your own thought, you are too mixed with your own view. So we have to let our spirit prevail to overthrow the reasonings in our mind.

The secret of His inner life   February 24th

"But He answered and said, It is written, Man shall not live by bread alone, but by every word that proceeds out through the mouth of God." MATTHEW 4:4

These words, quoted by the Lord from Deuteronomy 8:3, not only reveal how He handled the devil's attacks, but they also show us the secret of His inner life. It is clear that the strength of the Lord's inner life was maintained by His regular feeding upon the Word. He was not living on bread alone, but on every word proceeding out through the mouth of God. If the Lord felt the need to spend time with the Father, feeding upon the Word, how much more do we need this kind of practice. The Lord Jesus was intrinsically the living Word (Gk. λόγος), yet He took time to feed on the written Word; and He could testify to the devil that this was the way He was living. He was living on every word proceeding out through the mouth of God.

Our inner life is constituted with the same inner life that was in Christ Jesus. The apostle Paul makes this clear in 1 Corinthians 6:17: "He who is joined to the Lord is one spirit." Our human spirit, which has been regenerated through the new birth, is

55

mingled with the Lord Himself, who is the Spirit (1 Cor. 15:45). Thus, what was true of the Lord's life in the flesh is still true of His life in resurrection as the life-giving Spirit dwelling in our spirit (2 Tim. 4:22). Now we must come to know in our experience how our inner man needs and requires regular times to feed upon the Word (1 Pet. 2:2-3). This was one of the Lord's secrets in maintaining His supply to live out the Father's life, and it must become our secret as well (John 6:57).

Nothing outside of God   February 25th

"For to me, to live is Christ." PHILIPPIANS 1:21

The Lord Jesus only wanted the Father's will. Paul also only wanted what God had for him. But we so many times want something else. We want something other than what God is giving us. Because of this, the best fellowship that we can be given is "Draw a circle around yourself. Do not touch anything outside of that circle. Just deal with yourself and want God alone. Just take God. Just pursue God Himself." This is what it means to follow the pathway of the cross. If we do not come to this point in our experience, then we will have to settle for another level of Christian life, another kind of Christian life. It is a life in which you want a little bit of God, but you also want a lot of other things. So you eventually become shallow, empty, without any weight, because you have settled for another level of Christian life. You want something else besides God.

Taking the pathway of the cross and dealing with the Lord by the cross means that we do not want anything outside of God. I do not want a marriage outside of God. I do not want a happy family outside of God. I do not want finances outside of God. I do not want a good job outside of God. I do not want to be successful for the Lord outside of God. I do not want to do anything outside of God. I just want God. This was Paul's attitude in prison in Rome. There he was — bound. If he had wanted something other than God, he could never have testified, "For to me, to live is Christ." That means he did not want anything outside of God. So also in our own experience, it is crucial that we want nothing outside of God.

The Lord's habits   February 26th

"And He who sent Me is with Me. The Father has not left Me alone, for I always do those things that please Him." JOHN 8:29

Making time to be with the Father was one of the most marked features of the Lord's life. As we read the Gospels, we see that He not only lived in the Father (John 14:10) and had continuous fellowship with the Father, but He also practiced in a regular way setting aside special time to be with the Father and pray.

The following verses reveal the Lord's own habits in spending time with the Father: "Now in the morning, having risen a long while before daylight, He went out and departed to a solitary place; and there He prayed" (Mark 1:35); "So He Himself often withdrew into the wilderness and prayed" (Luke 5:16); "Now it came to pass in those days that He went out to the mountain to pray, and continued all night in prayer to God" (Luke 6:12); "Immediately Jesus made His disciples get into the boat and go before Him to the other side, while He sent the multitudes away. And when He had sent the multitudes away, He went up on a mountain by Himself to pray. And when evening had come, He was alone there" (Matt. 14:22-23); "And it happened, as He was alone praying, that His disciples joined Him, and He asked them, saying, Who do the crowds say that I am?" (Luke 9:18); "And it came to pass, about eight days after these sayings, that He took Peter, John, and James and went up on the mountain to pray. And as He prayed, the appearance of His face was altered, and His robe became white and glistening" (Luke 9:28-29);

"And it came to pass, as He was praying in a certain place, when He ceased, that one of His disciples said to Him, Lord, teach us to pray, as John also taught his disciples" (Luke 11:1); "And coming out, He went to the Mount of Olives, as He was accustomed, and His disciples also followed Him. . . . And He was withdrawn from them about a stone's throw, and He knelt down and prayed" (Luke 22:39, 41).

Taking control of our environments February 27th

"And when He had sent the multitudes away, He went up on a mountain by Himself to pray. And when evening had come, He was alone there." MATTHEW 14:23

By considering all the examples of the Lord's prayer life in the Gospels, we are deeply impressed that the Lord not only felt the need to spend time with the Father, but that He also, in His busy schedule and ministry, made time to do it. We see how the Lord took control of His environment for the sake of spending time in prayer. He compelled His disciples to go to the other side of the sea (v. 22), and He sent the crowds away in order to make time to be with the Father privately to pray.

Unless we take control of our daily schedules and environments for the sake of spending time with the Lord, our daily environments will take control of us! There is no easy, automatic way that we will fall into a habit of making time to be with the Lord. We must at times "compel" and "send away" in order to make time to be with Him. Transformation depends upon our spending time with the Lord beholding His glory. Therefore, we must cooperate with those mingled desires by taking the initiative to make the time to do it. Every effort spent in this direction will be greatly rewarded. The Lord Himself promises a reward to those who exercise themselves to make time to be with Him. He says in Matthew 6:6, "But you, when you pray, enter into your inner chamber, and having shut your door, pray to your Father who is in secret, and your Father who sees in secret shall reward you."

Inner rearrangement   February 28th

"To be strengthened with might through His Spirit into the inner man, that Christ may dwell in your hearts through faith; that you, being rooted and grounded in love." EPHESIANS 3:16-17

The Christian life is not merely a matter of receiving Christ and knowing that we have eternal life and will go to heaven. Although none of these matters are wrong, they are short of the divine thought. God's full thought when we receive Christ is that a new source be established within us for our entire being. This new source is our regenerated human spirit (John 3:6). Having a change of source is the most central thing in our regeneration. To have a source-change means that we no longer live to ourselves, but to God. We no longer live by the self, but by His life. What naturally follows the new birth of our spirit is a progressive transfer of source in our daily life. For this transfer, it is necessary to pass through experiences with the Lord in which the old source, the self, is dealt with, and the new source, our spirit, gains the ascendancy.

According to 1 Thessalonians 5:23, man's being is composed of spirit, soul, and body. Before regeneration, although our spirit exists within us as a potentiality, it is in a dead condition (Eph. 2:1). So the source of our living is not our spirit, but our soul, composed of our mind, emotion, and will. But when the Lord enters into us, our spirit is born and we have an inner rearrangement of our being. The mind, emotion, and will are no longer to take the lead to determine our living. The leading part of our being now becomes our regenerated spirit, where we are joined to the Lord (1 Cor. 6:17). It is from this Christ-indwelt center that all the parts of our soul will find their proper place and function. Formerly, we were an independent self that did our own things, thought our own thoughts, made our own decisions. But once our center changes, all this is transformed. Christ comes in to make His home in our hearts and rearrange all our inward parts.

The activity around the throne February 29th*

"If then you were raised with Christ, seek those things which are above, where Christ is, sitting at the right hand of God."
COLOSSIANS 3:1

This verse leads us all upward to the throne, where Christ has been seated at the right hand and where God's government and His administration and His economy are operating this very moment to consummate this age — human history as we know it — and to bring in the next age with our Lord's appearing and His kingdom for a thousand years over this old earth. And then the kingdom becomes the doorstep into the holy city, New Jerusalem, which comes down out of heaven from God as His habitation for eternity. From the throne, there is present administration in this universe. This throne is far above every power, every principality, every demonic rule, all the evil spirits, all the Satanic activity.

There is a throne far above all. And if I am a wise person, with a spirit of wisdom and revelation, I will want to be under that throne and around that throne and to live my moments in the light of that throne. Because the throne of God is what is controlling the whole universe this moment, we need to know what is happening at the throne (see the book of Revelation). We need to know the activity around the throne. Let us go to the top, the highest place in the universe. Let us find out what is happening at the throne. If we know what is happening there, we will surely come under the full knowl-

* Leap Year

edge of God. The full knowledge of God can be learned, can be seen, by being around the activity of the throne.

In Colossians 3:1 Paul points us to Christ at the right hand of God. Then in verse 2 he says, "Set your mind on things above, not on things on the earth." Have you ever considered coming out of the stream of traffic on this earth — your life, your plan, your goals, your desires? Stop yourself. Let someone tap you on the shoulder and say, "Come on up and let me show you what is really happening in this universe — what the activity is around the throne" (cf. Rev. 4:1-2). What are they talking about around the throne? Are there any purposes unveiled in their talk? Can we know? We can. There is an unveiling of the throne. God did not leave us wondering what we are living for. He wants us to stop ourselves and to take time to set our mind on things above, not on things on the earth. He wants us to be controlled not by human thought, human interpretation, philosophy, or speculation, but by revelation and an absolute opening of His heart.

March

Being acted upon

"But we all, with unveiled face, beholding as in a mirror the glory of the Lord, are being transformed into the same image from glory to glory, just as by the Spirit of the Lord." 2 CORINTHIANS 3:18

The need for spending time with the Lord should be considered from the viewpoint of the nature of transformation. The verb "transformed" is used four times in the New Testament: in Matthew 17:2; Mark 9:2; Romans 12:2; and 2 Corinthians 3:18. Every time this word is used, without exception, it is in the passive voice. When the Lord was on the mountain being "transfigured," or "transformed," on His part it was passive. It happened to Him. In Romans 12:2, again the word "transformed" is in the passive voice: "Be transformed by the renewing of your mind." This means that our transformation is something happening to us. In 2 Corinthians 3:18 "being transformed" is also in the passive voice.

On our part, the nature of transformation is passive. It is something that happens to us. We, as the subject, are being acted upon, not doing the acting. For example, the statement "I am baptizing" is in the active voice (the subject is acting); whereas, "I am being baptized" is in the passive voice (the subject is being acted upon). When we are beholding the glory of the Lord, we are being acted upon — we are *being* transformed — by the Lord Spirit. It is this passive process of being transformed that requires spending special time in the Lord's presence beholding Him.

The fact that the nature of transformation is passive reveals that there is no need to attempt to correct ourself, improve ourself, or change ourself in a religious way. Transformation is a process that happens to us. It is the spontaneous and automatic working of the

63

Lord Spirit within us and upon us. For the Lord to be able to do this transforming work upon us, we need to spend time with Him, using our spirit to behold Him. So in our daily life let us spend more time with Him beholding His glory, rather than spending time being occupied with our own efforts and energy.

Locating life-consciousness   **March 2nd**

"For God is my witness, how greatly I long for you all in the inward parts of Jesus Christ." PHILIPPIANS 1:8

When the divine life enters into us, it comes into us with a definite consciousness. In fact, because the life of God is the highest form of life, it has the highest consciousness. God's life is exceedingly rich in consciousness and feeling. If animal life and human life have consciousness, how much more does the divine life! Because the divine life is a Person in us and not merely an impersonal substance, we begin to experience the rich feelings of God. His love, His joy, His peace, and His compassions stir us from deep within. In the verse above, the apostle Paul clearly depicts these stirrings. With Paul, those "inward parts of Jesus Christ" were the compassions and affections of Christ that he experienced as a life-consciousness within him. Paul was indwelt with Christ as his life (Col. 3:4), and by his own personal experience he knew the rich feelings of Christ that came from His indwelling life.

Not only did Paul have this life-consciousness, but every born-again believer has such a consciousness as well. Romans 8:10 declares, "And if Christ is in you . . . the spirit is life" (ASV). First Corinthians 15:45 says, "The last Adam [Christ] became a life-giving Spirit"; and 1 Corinthians 6:17 says, "But he who is joined to the Lord is one spirit with Him." This means that Christ as the life-giving Spirit now dwells in our regenerated human spirit, making our spirit life. The life-consciousness within us is located in our mingled spirit. Our spirit is the source from which every kind of life-consciousness flows into our being.

A one-time crucifixion March 3rd

"And those who are of Christ Jesus have crucified the flesh with its passions and desires." GALATIANS 5:24

Concerning his own flesh, Paul had to admit, "For I know that in me (that is, in my flesh) nothing good dwells" (Rom. 7:18). Then in Colossians he warns the believers that if they relate to the evil flesh with a religious flesh, they will encounter certain defeat (Col. 2:18-23). How then can we be related to our flesh, if flesh cannot overcome flesh? The answer to that question is found in Paul's words, "And those who are of Christ Jesus have crucified the flesh with its passions and desires." The phrase uttered by Paul, "those *who are of Christ Jesus,"* tells us *how* we are to be related to the flesh. It is those who simply belong to Christ Jesus, who are one with Him in spirit, that have crucified the flesh. Are you one who is of Christ Jesus? This means you do not have a separate life from Him. You are wholly identified with Him. You do not have a separate relationship with the flesh in your flesh. You are *of Christ Jesus*, and as such, you *own* His relationship with the flesh. His relationship with the flesh is not a long, drawn-out battle with it; rather it is a one-time crucifixion to it. The word "crucified" in Galatians 5:24 is in the aorist tense in Greek, indicating a blow was dealt to the flesh in the past that is decisive, complete, and final. That blow was dealt to the flesh on the cross of Calvary two thousand years ago.

How we are related to the flesh is wrapped up in the answer to one question — *Are we of Christ Jesus?* That is all we need to answer. We do not need to examine whether or not we have any potential. Neither do we need a record or string of victories that we can boast in. Nor do we need to look at our condition to see whether or not we feel like a crucified person. We just need to answer one question: Are we of Christ Jesus? If so, then we have crucified the flesh. Paul says it — If we are of Christ Jesus, then *we have* crucified the flesh. This means that Christ is our relationship with the flesh.

Keeping in step with the Spirit   March 4th

"If we live in the Spirit, let us also walk in the Spirit."
GALATIANS 5:25

In Galatians 5:24 our relationship with the flesh is established as a fact in Christ Jesus. Then in the next verse, the application and experience of this fact is revealed by Paul. To "live in the Spirit" in this verse is equivalent to being "of Christ Jesus" in the preceding verse. Thus, Christ *in the realm of the Spirit* is our relationship with the flesh. But for this fact to become our experience over and over again in our daily life, we need to walk in the Spirit.

The Greek word for "walk" in Galatians 5:25 is a specific military word, rather than the more general word for walk used in other places in the New Testament. It has the sense of keeping in step with the Spirit. This could be likened to a group of soldiers marching down the street, keeping in step with the cadence of the drummer. Their steps are very deliberate and specific. It is the same when we walk in the Spirit. Christ is in us, in our mingled spirit. He has already dealt a blow to the flesh. Now we must keep in step with Him whenever our flesh rises up to be fulfilled. This means we take a deliberate and specific step in spirit at the moment our flesh manifests itself. When we keep in step with the Spirit, the Lord Himself is our relationship with the reacting flesh. We just say, "Amen, Lord, I love You!" Or call upon Him. By this we keep in step with the Spirit and execute the crucifixion over our flesh.

"But you have not so learned Christ, if indeed you have heard Him and have been taught in Him, as the truth is in Jesus."
Ephesians 4:20-21

By observing the Lord's life on the earth, we can become more familiar with the Lord's life within us. The one unique life that is described in the four Gospels is the very same life that is now living in us. By studying the Lord's life in the Gospels, we are not merely considering something objective to us, but something that is also subjective in our spirit. His life lived out in the Gospels is what is now being reproduced in us by His indwelling.

As Christians we can have the assurance that the Christ who was once outside of us is the same Christ who is now inside of us. Furthermore, the way Christ lived on the earth is precisely the same way He is living in us. We must see that the kind of life He lived in the flesh is not something different from the life He now lives in us. This is a basic biblical principle — learning how to apply the Lord's life in the flesh to our own experience of Him in the spirit.

To "learn Christ" is to learn Him by His example in the four Gospels. "The truth . . . in Jesus" means that Jesus lived a life of truth, or reality, by always doing things *in* the Father, *with* the Father, and *for* the Father. This was the truth in Jesus demonstrated and recorded in the Gospels. Now as believers having Christ as our life and being taught in the realm of our union with Him, we learn that the relationship He had with the Father in the flesh is the same kind of experience being repeated in us in the spirit. We "have heard Him and have been taught in Him." Thus, to adequately learn the indwelling Christ in our experience, we need two things: to study the Lord's example in the Gospels, and to watch how that same life is being worked out in us in the details of our daily life.

Christis becoming your talking   **March 6th**

"Since you seek a proof of Christ speaking in me, who is not weak toward you, but mighty in you." 2 CORINTHIANS 13:3

The consciousness of Christ being our center and point of reference will continue to spread in our daily life. For example, you will find it in your speaking. You say something, but in your saying it, you feel as though you have put on a suit of clothes that does not fit, that does not feel right. As you are criticizing and gossiping, you are going to inwardly feel, "O Lord, this language does not fit. Lord, You are my talk. You are my speaking. I used to speak so freely. But Lord, Amen." By contacting Him and experiencing Him in this way, you begin to feel the restraint in your words. Christ is becoming your talking.

Little by little, the Holy Spirit will begin to make Christ real in your speaking. You may fail, but you experience Christ in your failure. You touch the living One, because your point of reference has changed. You can no longer rearrange your thoughts, thinking "I shouldn't talk that way anymore." Nor can you replace bad thoughts with good thoughts. That does not work. You have to interact with God. You have to touch the Spirit. And when you touch the Spirit, you draw from Him and He changes you. Then you come to a church meeting and you make the meeting Christ, because you have handled Him. You have handled Christ as your portion in your speaking.

The new knowing of Christ   **March 7th**

"Therefore, from now on, we regard no one according to the flesh. Even though we have known Christ according to the flesh, yet now we know Him thus no longer." 2 CORINTHIANS 5:16

The deep significance that Paul opens up here is a new kind of knowing of Christ in contrast to his old knowing of Christ. What is this new kind of knowing of Christ? The obvious answer is in 2 Corinthians 5:17, where Christ is presented in an enlarged way by Paul. He no longer considers Christ merely alone, by Himself. He says, *"If anyone is in Christ,* he is a new creation." Here Christ is not just an individual man, but a corporate man. Other persons are "in Him." So the new knowing of Christ is knowing Him as the church (Eph. 5:29-30). It is the knowing of Him according to 1 Corinthians 12:12, where both the one Body and the many members form one whole Christ! It is also the same knowing of Him found in Paul's prayer for the believers in Ephesians 1:17-23. There, the full knowledge of God is to know Christ as the Head of His Body, the church, which is described as being "the fullness of the One who fills all in all."

It is the church as Christ which is the new kind of knowing of Christ in 2 Corinthians 5:16. The church described as "the new man" in Colossians 3:10-11 is also the new kind of knowing of Christ. The church as the new man of the new creation is the realm where Christ is all and in all. It is also the realm where old things have passed away and all things have become new! In this realm we know each other as members of Christ. We no longer regard or know each other according to the differences and distinctions of the old creation (Gal. 3:27-28). In the new creation we always prefer Christ in one another.

What the church is   March 8th

"Therefore, if anyone is in Christ, he is a new creation; old things have passed away; behold, all things have become new."
2 CORINTHIANS 5:17

To say "old things have passed away" and "all things have become new" means that old relationships have passed away and all things in our relationships with each other have become new. We have all been newly created together in Christ as one new man, and have all been reconciled in one Body to God by the cross (Eph. 2:15-16).

Christ as our relationship with each other is what the church is. In other words, the church is just Christ between us. If Christ is not our mutual fellowship, then the reality of the church is lost. So to know the church is to know Christ as our relationship with each other. It is not a matter of knowing each other in a natural way, according to race or background. Neither is it formally joining a church to become a member. No. We are joined to the Lord in one Body, and His relationship with all His members becomes our relationship with every member. So we freely receive one another the way Christ received us (Rom. 15:7). This is what the church is.

The depths and intimacy of Christ as our relationship with one another can be seen in Paul's relationship with the Philippians. In Philippians 1:8 we read, "For God is my witness, how greatly I long for you all with the inward parts of Jesus Christ." Here Paul so identifies his feelings with the Lord's that he is not merely saying, "I am burdened for you" or "I am thinking of you." The Lord Himself with His inward parts became Paul's relationship with the Philippians. Paul was a man who embodied the Lord's own feelings and intimate care for the saints. This demonstrates the extent to which Christ becomes our relationship with one another. My relationship with you and your relationship with me is Christ. How precious this is. The more there is an increase of Christ in us, the more there will be an increase of Christ in our relationships.

Christ formed in us by the Word   March 9th

"But what does it say? The word is near you, even in your mouth and in your heart (that is, the word of faith which we preach)." ROMANS 10:8

A s we come under the hearing of the Word, it becomes the agent that forms Christ in us. This Word brings us under the hearing of faith, and Christ is formed in our heart. He is formed in me because someone spoke Him into me by means of the Word. For example, Christ was formed in the Corinthians by means of Paul's speaking the gospel. He implies this in 1 Corinthians 4:15: "For though you might have ten thousand instructors in Christ, yet you do not have many fathers; *for in Christ Jesus I have begotten you through the gospel.*"

Paul says, "The word is near you, even in your mouth and in your heart (that is, the word of faith which we preach)." How does the Word get into our mouth and into our heart? By being formed there as we sit, relax, and hear the Word. This is called "the hearing of faith" (Gal. 3:2, 5). Hear the wonderful words of life. Hear that Christ loves you. Hear that He died for you. Hear that He was raised for you. Hear that He will do everything in you. Just hear it. And the moment you say, "Lord Jesus," He is in your heart. He is formed there. How was He formed? He was formed by the spoken Word. So the way Christ is formed in us is not by works of law, but by the hearing of faith.

Justified vertically and horizontally   March 10th

"Therefore receive one another, just as Christ also received us, to the glory of God." ROMANS 15:7

If you and I do not know the joy of justification, and how to catapult ourselves immediately out of false feelings of the enemy and the flesh, and how to stand before God in the righteousness of Christ in boldness by the blood of Jesus, then our relationship with one another is going to feel the repercussions. The lie you believe about yourself is going to be projected on others. Then, of course, there will be no receiving of one another. This shows how crucial it is to know the joy of justification.

What an enjoyment it is when we sing songs about our justification, about how God "saved a wretch like me." What a blessedness

— to know that He saved this wretch and clothed this wretch in righteousness. When we relate to ourselves in this way, the love of God just beams out of us toward all the saints. In that love we experience the receiving of one another, just as Christ also received us. Justification affects both our vertical relationship with God and our horizontal relationship with one another.

Paul's main burden is that the saints would be established by receiving one another. In order that this could happen, he writes in the wisest way. He begins by bringing all of them to their common level of being sinners. Then he brings them all to the same righteousness, the same cross, the same blood — the same justification. In short, he brings them all into a marvelous feeling about themselves in their justification. Paul knows that these truths will be the solid factors between the saints.

Are you in your self or in Christ Jesus?   March 11th

"There is therefore now no condemnation to those who are in Christ Jesus." ROMANS 8:1

Christ is our relationship with condemnation. Has it ever occurred to you what your relationship with condemnation is? Many times we live under a stream of condemning thoughts from the enemy in our mind. We relate to these thoughts by coping with them in some form or another. Sometimes we try beating them away in a fly-swatter fashion. Or we attempt to replace them with new resolutions and promises to God that we will not fail again. Or we just sink into depression. We live always feeling condemned.

God's answer to this spiritual disease is found in Romans 8:1. Not being under condemnation has nothing to do with your past record or your present performance. Nor is it dependent on your ability to cope with your thoughts. It is strictly a matter of *where* you are. Where are you? Are you *in your self* or are you *in Christ Jesus?*

72

If you are in Christ Jesus, then you can shout "Hallelujah!" You can tell condemnation that you are now related to it in Christ. If Christ can be condemned, then you can be condemned. But since you are included and hidden in Christ (1 Cor. 1:30; Col. 3:3), all the arrows of condemnation have to go to Him. Of course, that is unthinkable.

Only answer with Christ   March 12th

"Who is he who condemns? It is Christ who died, and further-more is also risen, who is even at the right hand of God, who also makes intercession for us." ROMANS 8:34

When our religious flesh is alive, trying to be justified by the works of the law, we unwittingly set ourselves up for a condemnation situation. But if our flesh is terminated, and the law-keeping "I" is crucified with Christ (Gal. 2:19-20), then there is not even a possibility of receiving any condemnation. We do not even have a chance to be condemned anymore. We died with Christ, and it is "no longer I who live." Thus, Christ is now my relationship with condemnation.

Paul is so clear about being a person in Christ who cannot be condemned that he begins to boldly challenge everyone in the universe. It is as if he was saying, "Are you (whoever you may be) going to condemn me? Are you going to bring a charge against me? Come and listen to me!" He declares in Romans 8:31-34, [31] "What then shall we say to these things? If God is for us, who can be against us? [32] He who did not spare His own Son, but delivered Him up for us all, how shall He not with Him also freely give us all things? [33] Who shall bring a charge against God's elect? It is God who justifies. [34] Who is he who condemns? It is Christ who died, and furthermore is also risen, who is even at the right hand of God, who also makes intercession for us." Hallelujah!

Paul totally ignores the possibility of being chargeable, or of whether or not the condemnation is perhaps legitimate. He does not give any ground for anyone to say anything against him. He does not answer the charges with himself, his record, or even his victorious Christian life. He only answers with Christ Jesus. It is Christ who died! It is Christ who is risen! It is Christ who is at the right hand of God making intercession for us! It is Christ who is our relationship with condemnation!

The Heart-Knower   March 13th

"I, the LORD, search the heart, I test the mind, even to give every man according to his ways, and according to the fruit of his doings."
JEREMIAH 17:10

Who do we live to? Our orientation in our fallen nature is to live to ourselves — to our own reasoning mind, to our feelings, to our reactions, to our own analysis of ourselves. In the past the self has been our point of reference. When the self is our point of reference, we really do not know ourselves as we should in God's light. In fact, according to the Scriptures, apart from Him we are prone to being deceived about ourselves. The self cannot accurately know the self. No one really knows himself without God's light. Jeremiah 17:9 says, "The heart is deceitful above all things, and desperately wicked; who can know it?" Who can know their own heart properly? We may think we are fine, when we are totally off. Or we may think we are off, when we are fine. Brothers and sisters, we are unable to know our hearts. God says that our hearts are desperately wicked, whether or not we agree with His diagnosis. It is God who asks the question, "Who can know the heart?"

In Jeremiah 17:10 the Lord answers His own question. It is the Lord who knows and searches our hearts. He is even identified by a compound title in Greek — "the Heart-Knower" (Acts 1:24; 15:8). Thus, to know ourselves we must first come to know God. We may think we know ourselves by introspection, or by analyzing our own heart. We may imagine that we know ourselves rightly. But apart from being in fellowship with the Heart-Knower, we are prone to deception.

The faith-infusing scenery   March 14th

"I do not set aside the grace of God; for if righteousness comes through the law, then Christ died in vain." GALATIANS 2:21

To rely on a righteousness that is based on our own ability to keep the law is a direct insult to the cross of Christ. If it was even remotely possible for us to produce a righteousness acceptable to God, then Christ has died for nothing. Paul clearly declares that our self-achieved righteousness would set aside the grace of God. Righteousness does not come out of ourselves. Righteousness comes to us as a gift, based upon the death of Christ. To say *"Christ died in vain"* is a strong statement that exposes the consequence of anyone trusting in his own righteousness to please God.

In Galatians 3:1-2 Paul continues to describe the faith-infusing scenery: [1] "O foolish Galatians! Who has bewitched you that you should not obey the truth, before whose eyes Jesus Christ was clearly portrayed among you as crucified? [2] This only I want to learn from you: Did you receive the Spirit by the works of the law, or by the hearing of faith?" In these two verses we see the connection between *seeing* and *hearing*. In verse 1 the scenery of Calvary is clearly portrayed before our eyes; but in verse 2 what we see comes to us through hearing. The hearing *is* the seeing, and the seeing *is* the hearing. It is from this seeing and hearing that God's righteousness at the cross is made known. It is from this seeing and hearing that faith is both revealed *to* us and generated *in* us. From this seeing and hearing we believe that through Christ's death we are officially constituted righteous. Such a realization keeps us from looking to ourselves as the source of anything. When we know that our righteousness is wholly the Lord Himself, then we can only live from Him as our source.

The love in us   March 15th

"Whoever confesses that Jesus is the Son of God, God abides in him, and he in God. And we have known and have believed the love that God has in us. God is love, and he who abides in love abides in God, and God in him." 1 JOHN 4:15-16

One of the great discoveries in our Christian life is to continually know the love that God has not only "for" us, but "in" us. In the passage above, the apostle John brings out two perfect tenses, "have known" and "have believed." This means that we know and continue to know, and we believe and continue to believe, the love which God has *in* us. It is a love apart from ourselves. This love is a gift. This love is God's Son. This love is a love-life that is installed right into our being. We need to realize that there is a well in us, not only of living water, but a well of love. There is a well of love-life, and this love-life is available in the Son.

We do not know the love which God has in us until we begin to tap into it a little bit. Then we discover there is a flow of love in our spirit and in our heart, loving and praising Him. We do not have a straitjacket religion. No! We possess a love relationship that is not only available to us but is waiting to be enjoyed by us!

The nature of our spirit   March 16th

"Therefore, my brethren, you also have become dead to the law through the body of Christ, that you may be married to another, even to Him who was raised from the dead, that we should bear fruit to God." ROMANS 7:4

The Lord wants us to know that all the dealings with our self, all the many blows it receives, are to effect a transfer of our source experientially. By this transfer we become persons actually living one spirit with the Lord. For example, at home with your family, you live one spirit with the Lord—regulated and controlled by the Spirit. You are living out of the source of Another life, rather than living loosely, freely, and independently. Rather than rebelliously speaking what we want to speak, we actually experience a transfer. Everything He allows is for the process of bringing us into this wonderful transfer of our source.

Second Corinthians 5:15 reveals the experiential result of our transfer: "And He died on behalf of all, that those who live . . . " To "live" here means not just to humanly exist on this earth, but to be living in union with the Lord. This is how we live. We live joined to this crucified, resurrected Christ. This is the truth. Everything else is a lie. The fact is that in regeneration we have been joined and married to Christ. And because we have been crucified with Him and raised together with Him, the very nature of our spirit is crucifixion and resurrection — crucifixion for the flesh, the self, the old man, and resurrection life for us to live one spirit with Him.

Christ as our righteousness   March 17th

"But of Him you are in Christ Jesus, who became to us wisdom from God — that is, righteousness and sanctification and redemption." 1 CORINTHIANS 1:30

Through God's demonstrated righteousness on the cross, Christ becomes our imputed righteousness to transfer us out of the source of ourself to live to God. It is enlightening to see the distinction between *God's righteousness* and *Christ being our righteousness*. Although they are distinct, they are interrelated. First, God's righteousness is related to God's method, or procedure, in doing things. Indeed, it was through God's righteousness demonstrated at the cross that He could officially constitute us righteous. The cross was God's righteousness at work, making it possible for God to freely bestow upon us the gift of righteousness (Rom. 5:17). Second, the gift of righteousness is Christ Himself as our righteousness (1 Cor. 1:30). This gift gives us the same standing and relationship with God that Christ has, because this gift *is* Christ Himself.

With God's righteousness, we are justified according to God's way of doing things. With Christ as our righteousness, we are clothed with Christ as our robe as we stand before God (Isa. 61:9-10). Paul wanted to be found having Christ as his righteousness in order that he could know the Lord in a deeper way (Phil. 3:9-10). God's righteousness is what establishes our relationship with God (Rom. 3:21-26). Christ being our righteousness is what keeps our relationship with God on the proper basis. Our relationship with God is apart from any merit of our own and outside any reflection upon our own subjective condition. Christ as our righteousness becomes the solid foundation for us to live to God exclusively in Christ (Gal. 2:19-21; Rom. 6:11). In this way God becomes the source of our life.

Free from care and secure   March 18th

"In His days Judah will be saved, and Israel will dwell safely; now this is His name by which He will be called: THE LORD OUR RIGHTEOUSNESS." JEREMIAH 23:6

The Lord as our righteousness is mentioned in the Old Testament in several passages. These verses clearly reveal that Christ the Lord is our righteousness. They also reveal that we have been transferred out of the source of ourself into the Lord Himself as our "Branch of righteousness" (Jer. 23:5). When the prevailing condition among God's people is that the Lord is their righteousness, they will dwell safely. The Hebrew word for "safely" includes the thought of absolute security to the point of our feeling free from care. We are free from care in the sense that we do not worry or feel anxious about anything. When the Lord is your righteousness, you are secure. It is like going to sleep at night peacefully because your security system is on. You are released from taking anxious thought. In the same way, when we know the Lord is our righteousness, we are safe and secure. We are free from care in a good sense. We are no longer preoccupied with our condemning self, with all its thoughts and morbid introspection. Praise the Lord, we have been delivered from that realm. We have been transferred out of the source of our self into THE LORD OUR RIGHTEOUSNESS.

Led into a new reaction   March 19th

"As it is written: For Your sake we are killed all day long; we are accounted as sheep for the slaughter. Yet in all these things we are more than conquerors through Him who loved us."
ROMANS 8:36-37

The self-life does not know how to properly relate to environment. It blames circumstances. It blames the wife, the husband, the boss — whomever. But in the verses above, we see how Paul related to his environments. He was living out of another source, and from that source he gathered up all his environments as raw material for the self to be terminated, for the self to be crossed out once again, so that resurrection life could come forth.

An undealt-with self does not properly relate to environment. Rather, it is confused. It is frustrated. It is hurt. It is hoping for a better day. It does everything but deal with the Lord. It does everything but allow itself to be terminated. In its ignorance it does not know how to relate to environment, how to relate in life, or how to relate in the truth. These are all characteristics of an ignorant and undealt-with self, and expose that we are still coming from the wrong place. We do not yet come from life. We do not meet our environments with God's view. God's view of our environment is that all day long we are just being led to put to death the practices of the body (Rom. 8:13-14). This means we are being led into a new kind of reaction — led to put to death, led to react with the cross. We are being led into another circumstance for more of the self to surface so that it can be interrupted and terminated. In this way all things are working together for good — for our conformity to Christ (Rom. 8:28-29).

Getting into another realm   March 20th

"But He turned and said to Peter, Get behind Me, Satan! You are an offense to Me, for you are not setting your mind on the things of God, but the things of men." Matthew 16:23

The Lord was talking about realms when He identified that Peter was not setting his mind on the things of God, but the things of men. What Peter needed to do was to get into another realm! He needed to leave the realm of his opinion and set his mind on the things of God. To set our mind on the things of God, we have to do what Colossians 3:2 says: "Set your mind on things above." This happens by spending time with the Lord, opening to Him, seeking Him. And then, by being supplied in fellowship with Him, we are enabled to set our mind on the things of God. So we deal with opinion by getting into another realm.

When we get into the Spirit, we get into another realm, and we touch the cross. When we touch the Spirit, the Spirit is composed of a crucifying power that puts us to death, that cuts off the opinion, that denies the self, and that does not allow the self to make any provision for itself. The Spirit ushers in the cross to deal with our opinion, to execute crucifixion over our opinion. We need the exposure and the failures to humble us and open us up to the Lord so that we will lose all confidence in the self and simply trust in the Spirit. We trust in His divine operation to deal with our opinion, which is just the expression of the self.

Oh, brothers and sisters, this is critical, life-changing fellowship. We need to expose this horrible thing called opinion, which is actually Satan sitting in the church. Opinion is what destroys the church. It disintegrates, damages, insulates, divides, and immobilizes us! How crucial it is that we all target this opinion — good opinion, right opinion, opinion about your husband or wife, or the brothers and sisters. Just say, "Lord, crucify my opinion! Cut off its head! You are the Head. I am not the head. I do not like to hold any view. I only like to love You, to enjoy You, to be a person freed from opinion." We just want to be one spirit with the Lord and not hinder the Lord's movement among us in the church.

Looking at yourself in His light   March 21st

"For with You is the fountain of life; in Your light we see light."
PSALM 36:9

James says, "Draw near to God and He will draw near to you." Then immediately he adds, "Cleanse your hands, you sinners; and purify your hearts, you double-minded" (James 4:8). The religious way of understanding these verses is that *first* you cleanse your hands and try to purify your heart. You try to make things seem right, according to your thought. *Then* you draw near to God, as though you are the savior and the one who cleans yourself up — as though you are the one qualified to know the duplicity in your heart and to know when your heart is divided, as though you can do the work yourself. You think that after you have done what you could, then you can draw near to God. But James does not say it that way. He says to come as you are and draw near to God. As the well known hymn says, come just the way you are, without one plea, but that His

81

blood was shed for you. Blood has been shed. You can come the way you are, and God will draw near to you. Then you get in the light: "In Your light we see light" (Psa. 36:9). In God's light your hands are dirty, and you say, "O Lord, look at the dirt on my hands." And yet, when you are looking at your hands, you are not looking at them with yourself as the point of reference. You are looking at yourself in *His* light. And in His light the blood is cleansing. You can weep and you can repent and you can shed tears. And all the time that you are weeping and repenting and shedding tears, it is not at all ascetic or religious. You are actually participating in the grace of God.

God loves failures   March 22nd

"But God, who is rich in mercy, because of His great love with which He loved us, even when we were dead in trespasses, made us alive together with Christ." EPHESIANS 2:4-5

Ephesians 2:1-3 says, [1] "And you He made alive, who were dead in trespasses and sins, [2] in which you once walked according to the course of this world, according to the prince of the power of the air, the spirit who now works in the sons of disobedience, [3] among whom also we all once conducted ourselves in the lusts of our flesh, fulfilling the desires of the flesh and of the mind, and were by nature children of wrath, just as the others." These verses describe us as failures, perfected in sinning, rotten and corrupted, living under the dominion of the devil, living out the drives of the flesh, and being by nature children of wrath, even as the rest of mankind.

Then verses 4-5 say, [4] "But God, who is rich in mercy, because of His great love with which He loved us, [5] even when we were dead in trespasses . . ." Even when we were in that situation, God loved us. Here again is God loving people who are failures, perfected in their failure, and who are spoiled and corrupted to the uttermost.

And verses 5-6 show God demonstrating His love: ⁵ "He made us alive together with Christ (by grace you have been saved), ⁶ and raised us up together, and made us sit together in the heavenlies in Christ Jesus." This unveils the nature of God's love toward us.

We usually live in the realm and on the level of *our* worthiness and *our* condition. In this realm, whether God loves us depends very much on whether *we* feel we are lovable. If we think we have "measured up" a little bit — we have had a better week, or have done a few extra good things — then we feel that we can receive the love of God. Many times our perception of God's attitude toward us is based on our own feelings about ourself. God's love is far beyond our human concept or idea.

Victims of God's love   March 23rd

"Then the LORD said to [Hosea], Go again, love a woman who is loved by a lover and is committing adultery, just like the love of the LORD for the children of Israel." HOSEA 3:1

The phrase "loved by a lover" may be translated "loved by a husband." This indicates that Hosea loved his wife, Gomer, who was committing adultery. So he took this wife of harlotry, and she bore children to him and then continued in that same kind of harlot living. This can be likened to your becoming a believer and knowing the Lord for a period of time, and then turning away from Him and going back to your old life-style, or manner of life, and committing spiritual adultery with many other things. Let me say to you categorically that God's love to you is still unconditional, because you are the object of His love. It is eternal love based upon an eternal choice, and can never be destroyed or eradicated.

So, in a sense, we are the victims of God's love. We are the objects of His love. The Lord tells Hosea, "Go again, love a woman who is loved by a husband and is committing adultery, *just like* the love of the LORD for the children of Israel." These two words "just like" are the key words that reveal the nature of God's unconditional love. Humanly speaking, that woman did not deserve a thing but to be cast off. Yet God says to love that woman *just like the love of the LORD for the children of Israel."* This is what the love of the Lord is like. This is how God loves you, and how God loves me.

Grace flows from the cross   March 24th

"For if by the one man's offense death reigned through the one, much more those who receive abundance of grace and of the gift of righteousness will reign in life through the One, Jesus Christ."
ROMANS 5:17

Standing upon Christ as our righteousness is the key to enjoying God as our source. The verse above shows the relationship between righteousness, grace, and life. Righteousness is the basic factor for grace to reign. In other words, the supply of grace to us is based on the righteousness of God demonstrated at Calvary. Grace flows from the cross. In Romans 5:17 grace is *linked with* righteousness. In verse 21 grace reigns *through* righteousness. Both verses reveal that grace flows out of righteousness and issues in life. Life is the goal. Life refers to God Himself ruling and reigning from within as the source of our living. Thus, grace, or supply, reigns through righteousness, that we may enjoy God Himself as the eternal life being our source.

For our practical experience, it is important to know that grace does not come to us in a haphazard way. Our ability to stand in grace for God's supply is solidly based on God's righteousness at the cross (Rom. 5:1-2). Grace is not without a basis. Even if God wanted to give us grace, He could not do it apart from righteousness. Because God's character is one of righteousness, whatever He does is within the limits of His righteous nature and character.

In our experience we do not need to be concerned about whether we are lovable or whether we have potential so that God would receive us. It has nothing to do with that. It has to do with this: Has God righteously dealt with all the sins of all men? First John 2:1 answers with a resounding Yes! — "My little children, these things I write to you, that you may not sin. And if anyone sins, we have an Advocate with the Father, Jesus Christ the righteous."

Fresh supplies   March 25th

"And there is no creature hidden from His sight, but all things are naked and open to the eyes of Him to whom we must give account . . . Let us therefore come boldly to the throne of grace, that we may obtain mercy and find grace to help in time of need." HEBREWS 4:13, 16

When you see your shortness and realize you do not have a fervent love for the Lord — your heart is not inclined toward Him and His Word that much — God's desire at that point is to supply Himself to you. He wants to be your love for Him and that necessary desire for His Word. So never be troubled, never be fearful. Every new juncture in our Christian life, no matter what it is, is simply another occasion for fresh supplies from the throne of grace. For example, you may be reacting toward someone. What you need supplied to you is Christ to be lived out toward them. Or you may be anxious about your financial situation. So, what you need supplied to you is a life of trusting the Lord, taking one day at a time, and seeking first the kingdom of God. That very life is equally supplied. Or you may be exposed to a sinful and worldly environment, and you need the power to resist temptation. The life that overcomes sin and the world will also be supplied to you.

We must continually realize that we are vessels receiving the bountiful supply of the Spirit of Jesus Christ. Our whole understanding of the Christian life must be renewed in this way. The Christian life is a supplied life. Thus, spending time with the Lord is prime time in our daily life to get connected with the supply.

Unconditional kind of love   March 26th

"As it is written, Jacob I have loved, but Esau I have hated."
ROMANS 9:13

The objects of God's love are simply those He has chosen to love. Jacob was the object of God's love regardless of his condition — regardless of his rebellion, his conniving, his deceiving. Despite all that, the Lord followed him as "the hound of heaven." Wherever Jacob went, the Lord was there alluring him, seeking him, winning him. This is an example of God's love toward His people, and it is absolutely an unconditional kind of love. In the same way, there are no conditions to meet in the book of Hosea. Gomer, symbolizing God's people, has forgotten the Lord. She has gone to idols. Because this is her state, the Lord says that He will bring her to the wilderness and speak to her heart tenderly. He will do things in order to allure and win her.

Then in Hosea 2:19-20 the Lord says, [19] "I will betroth you to Me forever; yes, I will betroth you to Me in righteousness and judgment, in lovingkindness and mercy; [20] I will betroth you to Me in faithfulness, and you shall know the LORD." Though His people are in a rebellious condition, the Lord says, "I will betroth you to Me forever." This definitely tells us that He has plans for them — plans for a future marriage and union with Him. He is going to betroth; He is going to enter into a contract, a pledge, like a covenant, to love and to win them. Here we see the nature of God's love. Each time His love is revealed, it is toward ones in a rebellious condition, a fallen condition, a sinful condition — conditions that merit absolutely nothing, that deserve nothing but judgment and hell. But all the while, God keeps coming and revealing Himself.

Grace is guaranteed

"And we know that the Son of God has come and has given us an understanding, that we may know Him who is true; and we are in Him who is true, in His Son Jesus Christ. This is the true God and eternal life." 1 JOHN 5:20

G race and supply are reigning through righteousness. God's righteousness is the basic factor for our being qualified to be fully supplied. No one can touch this basic factor. Satan cannot touch it. The ones bringing a charge against God's elect cannot touch it. Our feeble thoughts cannot touch it. Even our present defeat cannot touch it. If righteousness is guaranteed, then grace is guaranteed. We can tell the Lord, "Lord, whether You love me or not, whether You feel good about me or not, You have to forgive me because Christ died a righteous death on the cross." God is now obligated to forgive sinful man for the sake of Jesus Christ the Righteous. Now grace can reign over us through righteousness. If we feel under-supplied, then we simply need to come back to our position of looking to Him so grace can reign.

Grace reigning through righteousness is *unto* something. It is *unto* eternal life (Rom. 5:21). God being man's source is all wrapped up with eternal life, and we know that the substance of eternal life is a *Person* — a Person who has become our source. Grace reigns through righteousness *unto* life. Because righteousness has done its work, and grace has done its work, we are brought into eternal life which is God Himself.

Reschedule your life

"But you, when you pray, go into your room, and when you have shut your door, pray to your Father who is in the secret place; and your Father who sees in secret will reward you openly." MATTHEW 6:6

With the eyes of our heart and with our spirit, we can cultivate our beholding of the Lord with songs, with the Word, and with prayer. This is the way to enjoy and behold the glory of the Lord passing before our spiritual vision. We need to nurture this kind of spiritual exercise. We have our home life, our family life, our school life, and our work life. We meet people, we talk to people, we are occupied daily with many things. Although we have this kind of life outwardly, we also need to preserve a secret life in a private room with the door shut, spending time with the Lord. Here there is no one else but ourself and the Lord. Here we can behold His glory by praying, by singing, and by reading the Word.

Spending time with the Lord is revolutionary in our experience. We may think our need is a little more gritting of our teeth to say, "Lord, this time I am going to make it through as a victorious believer." This kind of resolution, no matter how sincere, is nothing but our own energy and effort. Actually, we only need one thing — time with the Lord in a private place. Take the initiative and reschedule your life to go along with that still small voice within you that is prodding you to spend time with the Lord. And then just position your heart before the glory of the Lord. Simply expose yourself to this transforming element. Do not worry about what is not yet under His feet (Heb. 2:8-9). We see Jesus! Just let the Lord's Person and work pass before your eyes. You can behold Him because you are in the cleft of the rock, in the crucified One. You are under the precious blood. So you and I can enjoy all that the Lord is. Then we will be transformed into the same image from glory to glory (2 Cor. 3:18).

Find a hymnal and sing, making melody in your heart to the Lord. Take the verses of the Bible and pray with them. At other times just open yourself to the Lord and tell Him you love Him. Get acquainted with the blood of the Lamb in the book of Revelation and how everyone is singing about it in the heavens (Rev. 5:9-12; 7:9-14; 12:10-11; 14:2-4). Join in with the heavens and sing about His precious blood. Speak to the Lord about His wonderful Person and work. Your beholding and enjoying of Him in this kind of way will become your transformation.

Oh, may the Lord give us such a personal, secret, and intimate life with Him. Then we will be solid, then we will grow, then the devil will be defeated, then we will discover that the Lord will take us up into His own intercessory life to carry out His purpose and His plan. All of this issues from our spending time daily with the Lord and letting the glory of His Person and work pass before us.

Fresh consecration   March 29th

"And those who are Christ's have crucified the flesh with its passions and lusts." GALATIANS 5:24

Every consecrated person is a crucified person. He is crucified to the flesh with its passions and lusts. When we are consecrated, it means we apply specific crucifyings to the specific passions and the specific lusts. We inwardly apply the cross to those emotions in our being, those movements within us — the evil desires, the passions, the sinful stirrings, the unclean thoughts, the evil imaginations — the whole realm that Paul talks about in Galatians 5. In this way our being is drastically dealt with by the cross. We need to inwardly and specifically apply the cross to any evil passion that is toward some person or some thing. Apply the cross specifically to every individual lust that rises up within you. Those who are of Christ Jesus know that they do not belong to themselves. They are consecrated freshly: "Lord, I am Yours today. My mind is Yours today. My ears are Yours today." With this fresh consecration, you have consecrated the flesh with its passions and lusts to be crucified. This implies fellowship with the Lord.

In my time with the Lord every morning I am freshly consecrating — "Lord, today I give You myself. I love to touch You this morning, to have fellowship with You." Today is a new day. We need to apply the cross today. So we need to have an up-to-date, fresh consecration and fresh fellowship with the Lord. There is a way to live a life inwardly applying the cross. It is by being a person who is in the freshness of consecration and fellowship.

Him, not ourselves   March 30th

"And he showed me a pure river of water of life, clear as crystal, proceeding out of the throne of God and of the Lamb."
REVELATION 22:1

The Lord is working in our lives to make Himself our source. Why are we passing through all kinds of experiences and various environments? They are designed by God to bring us into Himself as our source. So what we are going through right now is another step toward the goal of working a realization into our consciousness that our life is God Himself. When God reconciled us to Himself through Jesus Christ, He produced a relationship that makes *Him*, not *ourselves*, the source of our lives.

This entire universe is destined to be consummated in God as the source of all things. The pure river of water of life is "proceeding out of the throne of God and of the Lamb." As God's eternal habitation, the holy city, New Jerusalem, is fully supplied with God as the source. The river of water of life proceeds *out of* the throne of God and of the Lamb. The source of supply is the Triune God flowing out and watering every part of the city. This vision of the consummation of all God's work in eternity future unveils Him as the unique source of the universe.

To be redeemed and regenerated is to be ushered into the realm of the new creation, where God begins a process in which experientially the old things start to pass out of our lives. The old things are related to our *self* as our point of reference. We lived out of our own impulses, our own choices, our own thoughts. But now we begin to live by revelation, that is, by what God has revealed to us in His Word. It is when we live by revelation that God becomes our source. He reveals to us the purpose of our human life. We no longer take man's views and concepts as the basis of our human existence. Revelation unveils to us God's eternal purpose. This revelation causes us to be persons who are living to be conformed to the image of God's Son.

The cross is in the Spirit   March 31st

"For if you live according to the flesh you will die; but if by the Spirit you put to death the deeds of the body, you will live." ROMANS 8:13

I have no existence apart from Christ. I am in Him. I am in the beloved One. I do not have a history outside of Him. I dare not consider myself outside of Him, not even a millimeter outside. Everything that is true of Him is true of me. Hallelujah! I relate to myself in the realm of the Spirit of Christ. I can now by that Spirit put to death the deeds, or practices, of the body. I am no longer left to myself to handle those practices.

If however we do not remain in our union with Christ (Rom. 8:9-11), and we instead indulge in the practices and conversation of the flesh, eventually not only will we be relating to ourselves from our flesh, but we will also be relating to others in the same way. In other words, when we do not exercise ourselves to remain in the realm of the Spirit, we are left to the realm of the flesh and the self. In this realm there is no capacity to receive ourselves or one another. But through many failures in the realm of the flesh, we learn to quickly get to the Spirit. We learn to quickly get through all the mire of thoughts and feelings. We go directly to our spirit-union with Christ. We do not solve problems. We are not concerned about answers. We do not stay on that level. We go directly to Jesus.

Satan wants to have long, drawn-out conversations. He likes to talk things out, to reach a compromise — whatever allows him room to live in us, nullifying the cross. That is his realm. But God's realm is the realm of the Spirit where the cross is. You always know when you are in the reality of the cross, because the cross is always quick. It works fast. If what you are doing is prolonged, if you yourself are trying to live a crucified life, it is probably not the cross. The cross is in the Spirit, and when you touch the Spirit, there is a quick cutting off of the flesh. It just happens. A quick circumcision of the flesh takes place. When we identify with Christ's death in the Spirit, we will live.

April

The exclusive relationship April 1st

"Jesus said to him, I am the way, the truth, and the life. No one comes to the Father except through Me." JOHN 14:6

God established a relationship with His Son, and then He took that relationship and put it into our heart. Now, Christ is *my relationship* with the Father. This is the meaning of John 14:6 where Jesus revealed that *no one* can come to the Father except through Him. In other words, He is the One who exclusively has a relationship with the Father. Christ being my relationship with the Father is also the meaning of Galatians 4:6, where the Spirit of *His Son* is sent forth into *our hearts*, crying, "Abba, Father!"

Based upon these facts, we need to reevaluate the source of our relationship with God. Is Christ the source of our relationship with God? Or are we the source? Instead of considering how *our* relationship with God is and how well *we* are doing, we need to consider how *His* relationship with God is, and how well *He* is doing. To look at *our* feelings, *our* condition, *our* day, *our* history, or *our* prospects for the future is to be in the wrong realm. As long as we remain in the realm of *our self* and *our relationship* with God, we will invariably fall into the pit of discouragement and condemnation. Our relationship with God is not in the realm of ourselves. Our relationship with God is Jesus Christ.

Relating by life April 2nd

"And do not be conformed to this world, but be transformed by the renewing of your mind, that you may prove what is that good and acceptable and perfect will of God." ROMANS 12:2

The way to relate to one another in the Body of Christ is by having a thorough dealing with the world and not being conformed to this age. How do you relate in the Body? The Body is one hundred percent a matter of life. It is organic, and it only responds to life. It only receives life. Anything that is not life, it rejects. So if there is anything of the world in us, any conformity to the age, then to that degree we will not know how to relate in the Body. The Body is not something organized. It is not something we merely mentally grasp. We apprehend the reality of the Body by experiencing Christ as our life.

To relate in the Body by life, our mind needs to be renewed. Our thoughts need to be renewed. The renewal of our mind and our thoughts is related to our dealing with the world and not being conformed to this age. Whenever there are dealings with the world, dealings with this present evil age, dealings over what our hearts are riveted to, there is a quickening among us concerning the reality of the Body. However, if the Body is not that real to us, it may be due to our lack of dealing with the world. If we have not dealt with the things that possess us, and instead have closed out light and life, the Body will not be that real to us.

The real dealing with the self will issue in relating properly to one another as members of the Body. Thus, dealing with the self issues in the Lord's building of the church. May the Lord do His work of exposing this self so that we can deny it and terminate its tyranny over us (Matt. 16:23-24). By this dealing we shut the gates of Hades and cast Satan out so that the Lord has a way to build us together and spread His economy on the earth (Eph. 1:10; 3:9; 1 Tim. 1:3-5).

Redirected from ourselves   **April 3rd**

"And if Christ is in you, the body is dead because of sin; but the spirit is life because of righteousness." ROMANS 8:10 (ASV)

Christ is life in the realm of our spirit. So our spirit is the focus in our experience of God being our source. God made our spirit to be a part of us that cannot be disturbed or shaken. Our spirit can *always* be the life-center and life-source for our whole being, because our spirit is backed by righteousness. The Lord Himself as our righteousness is what guards our spirit hour by hour to be the source from which we live. Our spirit is like Fort Knox, a place that is constantly and heavily guarded. Indeed, it is guarded by God's righteousness. My mind might be distracted, my feelings might be distraught, but in me is a regenerated spirit protected by righteousness, where God has set Himself up in my being to be my source. God Himself in the Person of His Son is dwelling in our spirit. From this life-center God now wants to become our source.

Again, our spirit being life is connected with Christ being our righteousness. This has practical implications for how we experience God as our source. When Christ is our righteousness and we have no righteousness of our own, then we are spontaneously redirected from ourselves to God as the source of our being. We are no longer expecting anything from ourselves (2 Cor. 3:5). We have no illusions about our potential, no hidden hopes of making it on our own.

Torn away from ourselves   April 4th

"We judge thus: that if One died for all, then all died; and He died for all, that those who live should live no longer to themselves, but to Him who died for them and rose again."
2 CORINTHIANS 5:14-15

For God to be our source, we need to see that God is not going to improve us. He is not going to mend us or even upgrade us. We may upgrade our computer software, but when it comes to improving the self, there are no upgrades in God's arrangement of things. God is not going to improve me, nor is He going to render some help to me, as if I was the source of my life. Christ becomes our righteousness in order that we might be torn away from ourselves and catapulted into Another life and source. God does things in absolutes. He crucifies the self and terminates it. He does not even give it a chance to try to work out its own righteousness. The fact that we "all died" in His death deals with the matter of source. A dead person can no longer live *to* himself. Christ comes to replace us. He comes to be the very source of our being. He comes to exchange our life for His life. He does this by joining Himself to our spirit, so that we become one spirit with Him (1 Cor. 6:17).

God's goal is to come into my spirit to become my source. The way He does this is by first taking me completely out of the realm of my self by crucifying me outright. This co-crucifixion with Christ quickly ends my religious history. God terminates me in one realm that He might resurrect me in another. The experiential effect of this co-resurrection, where Christ Himself is now my righteousness, is that I become completely reoriented. It is truly no longer I, but Christ in me, who is living to God. Because Christ is my life, God is now my source.

Under a hearing   April 5th

"Therefore, my beloved, as you have always obeyed, not as in my presence only, but now much more in my absence, work out your own salvation with fear and trembling." PHILIPPIANS 2:12

In the first part of this verse, Paul mentions the word *obey*. In Greek this is a compound word formed by the two words "hear" and "under." Thus, to obey means "to be under a hearing." Hearing the Lord's voice is integral to obeying or following Him, even as He indicated in John 10:27: "My sheep *hear* My voice, and I know them, and they follow Me."

To hear the Lord under the new covenant means to recognize

promptings within our heart. The prompting is God Himself operating within us. It is this prompting that Paul refers to in Philippians 2:13: "For it is God who works in you both to will and to do for His good pleasure." When we respond positively to the prompting, we are actually obeying Him. It is at the point of obeying Him that we need to see the difference between Old Testament and New Testament obedience. Old Testament obedience is man responding to the outward law of God without the supply of life that is necessary to carry it out (Gal. 3:21). New Testament obedience is man responding to God from the very responses and promptings inwardly produced by God Himself out of the riches and supply of His grace.

Responding to His inner prompting   April 6th

"And of His fullness we have all received, and grace for grace." JOHN 1:16

It is by grace that God authors and produces within us the promptings to Himself. Then He supplies grace once again at every point that we obey His voice and respond to His inner promptings. This is what is meant in the phrase "grace *for* grace" (or, "grace *in exchange for* grace" — Gk: *anti* / ἀντί). When we obey by saying "Amen" to His speaking, we are not carrying out an act of obedience from our own energy or strength. We are exchanging the grace of His promptings for a fresh supply of grace to work out those promptings in our practical experience. Obedience under the new covenant is a step of faith to open ourselves to the flow of God's grace to once again supply us with Himself. Thus, to hear His voice is not to come under a demand of the law. Rather, it is to hear a call to enjoy a fresh supply of grace.

The Lord's voice is located in the region of our heart. Hebrews 3:7-8 tells us, [7] "Therefore, as the Holy Spirit says: Today, if you will hear His voice, [8] do not harden your hearts as in the rebellion, in the day of trial in the wilderness." The voice of God speaks in our hearts. When the Lord is speaking, we can either constrict and harden our heart so that it is not soft and pliable to His voice, or we can hear His voice and soften our heart and go along with that voice. This is the way we interact with the Lord's voice under the new covenant.

Participation, not imitation   April 7th

"Let the same disposition be in you which was in Christ Jesus."
PHILIPPIANS 2:5 (Weymouth)

The Christian life is not imitation. It is participation. God has not called you to imitate Christ as if you were a person detached from Him. God has called you to participate in Christ as one attached to Him. "The one who joins himself to the Lord is one spirit with Him (1 Cor. 6:17, NASV). To join ourselves to the Lord is to merge with Him. It is merging our mind, emotion, and will with the Lord, who is the Spirit (2 Cor. 3:17). This merging is for our mind, emotion, and will to have direct participation in His life, nature, and disposition.

Paul does not mean to imitate Christ's disposition. He means to let or allow yourself to merge with Christ's disposition. There is a big difference. To imitate depends on coming up with "the goods" to perform. To merge is the exact opposite. It is receiving "the goods" by direct participation in them. For example, if an actor tries to play the part of a drunk, that is imitation. However, if he actually drinks wine and feels its effects, that is direct participation. In Ephesians 5:18 Paul says, "And do not be drunk with wine, in which is dissipation; but be filled with the Spirit." In the same way that there is direct participation in wine, there is direct participation in Christ as the Spirit. This participation in Christ is for us to live Christ by merging with His disposition. Paul says in Philippians 1:21, "For to me, to live is Christ." This is the one unique goal of all our participation in Christ — to merge with Him and live Him.

98

"Fill full my joy by thinking the same thing, by having the same love, joined in soul, thinking the one thing. " PHILIPPIANS 2:2 (Wuest)

At the end of this verse, Paul says something very unique: "thinking the one thing." Although some versions translate this phrase as "having the same mind," the Greek construction is properly translated as "thinking the one thing." Thus, from the supply of the encouragement in Christ in verse 1, something happens to us. There is the harmony of the Spirit between us to the extent that we think the same thing, have the same love, are joined in soul, and think the one thing. We are thinking *the* one thing. It does not simply say, "thinking one thing." There is a definite article before the word "one." Thus, it is translated properly "thinking *the* one thing." That means there is one unique thing to think. This is the burden Paul opens up in Philippians. It is that in the supply of the Spirit we are reduced to being saints who have a common factor between us — we think the one thing.

What is this one thing that we are thinking? To answer this we must understand something about the Greek word for "thinking," *phroneo* (φρονέω). This word, used primarily in Philippians and Romans, is one of the most spiritually rich words in the New Testament. First, this word means *a supplied kind of thinking*. It is not something we come up with on our own. It is a thinking supplied to us by the Spirit (Rom. 8:5-6). To think the one thing is something that God enables us to do. He dispenses into our being an inclination to think the one thing.

Second, *phroneo* is a word that includes the thought of direction, tendency, and being focused on an object. Thinking the one thing means focusing the mind, emotion, and will on one object with one direction. In the book of Philippians that one thing is Christ! The one object being focused on is Christ! It is being supplied by Christ (1:19), magnifying Christ (1:20), living Christ (1:21), having the mind of Christ (2:5), confessing Jesus Christ as Lord (2:11), boasting in Christ (3:3), counting all things loss for the excellency of the knowledge of Christ (3:8), gaining Christ (3:8), being found in Christ (3:9), knowing Christ (3:10), having a mind to pursue Christ (3:12-14), and more. Thinking the one thing is thinking Christ. It is to be a person always interacting with Christ to experience something more of the riches of Him (4:19). This is the one thing.

A mind-set to experience Christ   April 9th

"For all seek their own things, not the things which are of Christ Jesus." PHILIPPIANS 2:21

W hat is often behind the anxious attempts to solve *our* problems is a self-life and flesh that is chronically dissatisfied with everything. It is only occupied with its preferences, desires, and self-centeredness. Paul alludes to this in Philippians 2:19-21: [19] "But I trust in the Lord Jesus to send Timothy to you shortly, that I also may be encouraged when I know your state. [20] For I have no one like-souled, who will genuinely care for your state. [21] *For all seek their own things, not the things which are of Christ Jesus.*" We can be one of two kinds of persons — one who seeks his own things, including being centered on solving our problems for the sake of self, or one who seeks the things of Christ.

A supplied mind asks, Where is Christ in this? What is Christ in this? What is my portion of the Lord in this? The more there is the supply of the Spirit to the mind, the more our attitude, thinking, disposition, inclination, tendencies, even our reactions, are reduced to one thing — to gain Christ. This is a mind-set that is furnished and produced in us by the inner operation of God (Phil. 2:12-13). It is the mind-set to experience Christ, rather than a mind-set to solve problems. We all have problems. We all encounter problems. We will never get away from problems. However, we may be "otherwise minded" in our problems. That is, we may not be pursuing Christ in some areas of our life. Yet Paul assures us in Philippians 3:15 that God will reveal even this to us. Thank God for His condescending mercy. He meets us right where we are.

Only one love   **April 10th**

"And because you are sons, God has sent forth the Spirit of His Son into your hearts, crying out, Abba, Father!" GALATIANS 4:6

There is only *one* love in this universe. It is not *your* love, *his* love, *their* love, or *my* love. It is the love of the Son for the Father, and the love of the Father for the Son, in the current of the Spirit! In the Godhead there is one reality of love flowing, and that one love is poured out into our hearts! We love with *that* love. So none of us have to look at ourselves — at our own potential and ability to love — because it is all a matter of receiving Jesus Christ, who is the concentration of the love of God. It is having this Person live in you, crying, "Abba, Father."

There is only one love, and that love is *in* us. This relieves us from all the strain and struggle with the inner turmoils that we may go through. We say to ourselves, "I just don't have any love toward the Lord. I don't love the Lord that much." The more we say this to ourselves, the worse we feel, and the more we are in the pit of despair. But, oh, that we would begin to recognize the love dwelling in us. There *is* a love in our heart — the very love of the Son of God.

Your teachers   **April 11th**

"And though the Lord gives you the bread of adversity and the water of affliction, yet your teachers will not be moved into a corner anymore, but your eyes shall see your teachers. Your ears shall hear a word behind you, saying, This is the way, walk in it, whenever you turn to the right hand or whenever you turn to the left." ISAIAH 30:20-21

Often in our experience the Lord's voice in us encounters a deaf or indifferent ear. When this occurs, the Lord has a way to turn up the volume of His speaking. According to the Scriptures, His way is to use our environment and circumstances to intensify His inner speaking. This is the spiritual principle of discipline and chastisement in the lives of all God's children (cf. Heb. 12:5-9). The effect that God's discipline has on our ability to hear the Lord's voice is clearly seen in the verses above.

When the Lord gives us the bread of *adversity* and the water of *affliction,* He does it to get our attention, that we may hear His voice. Adversity and affliction are described as teachers that are not hidden in a corner anymore. Indeed, our eyes will see our teachers. These teachers are different from brothers and sisters giving us outward instructions. They are like personal tutors that are able to get our attention so that we will listen to the Lord. They are sent by God when all else seems to fail. Under God's sovereignty, the environments of adversity and affliction are used by Him to attain one end — our hearing of the Lord's voice.

Disciplined to hear   **April 12th**

"Your ears shall hear a word behind you, saying, This is the way, walk in it, whenever you turn to the right hand or whenever you turn to the left." ISAIAH 30:21

The effectiveness of environmental discipline in our lives is evidenced by the fact that we eventually do hear a voice behind us saying, "This is the way, walk in it." This voice keeps us on the straight and narrow way of experiencing Christ. Our tendency is to be side-tracked, turning aside either to the right or to the left. The right and left represent evil, the flesh, the world, or our own independent way (cf. Prov. 4:23-27). If we have learned from our teachers of adversity and affliction, when we are again tempted to turn off the road to the right or left, *we will hear* the Lord speaking through our consciousness, "This is the way (Christ), walk in it (Him)" (cf. Col. 2:6). All of God's discipline in our lives has this one goal — that we would hear the Lord's voice and follow Him.

In the New Testament, Revelation 3:19-20 reveals this same principle of discipline used by God to secure our inner attention to hear His voice. The Lord says, [19] "As many as I love, I rebuke and discipline. Therefore be zealous and repent. [20] Behold, I stand at the door and knock. If anyone hears My voice and opens the door, I will come in to him and dine with him, and he with Me." The Lord gives a little rebuking and a little discipline to turn up the volume of His voice. He has already been speaking in us, even standing at the door and knocking; but we have not heard His voice. Now He knocks a little harder through rebuke and discipline. When He says, "If anyone hears My voice," He is saying, "I spoke to you in a whisper, in a still small voice, but you closed your ears to Me by your reasoning mind. Your own self-centered desires deafened and muffled My voice. But now, through discipline, I have secured My goal in your life. You hear My voice and are opening the door, and I am coming into your heart to set up an inner table where we can feast together — you with Me and I with you."

Solving problems or experiencing Christ   April 13th

"For to me, to live is Christ, and to die is gain." PHILIPPIANS 1:21

To understand the spiritual nature of the New Testament, we need to ask a question: Did Paul solve problems or did he lead people into experiencing Christ? Where in the New Testament letters did Paul solve problems? What problem did he solve as an end in itself? What issue did Paul get involved in to solve? Have you ever considered this question? We all should go back to reread the New Testament and ask, What problems did Peter, John, Paul, and the other apostles solve? Did they solve people's problems or lead people to experience Christ? Of course, we know there were many problems among the Corinthians, but when we investigate how Paul solved the problems, we discover that he did one thing — he led them to experience Christ.

In our natural life we are prone to solve problems. We are looking for answers. We are seeking solutions. We want things to be cleared up and go away. We want to "right" what is "wrong." We are hoping for our environments to change for the better. We live in our imagined expectations. We want situations to be such that our soul would be at ease and find relief. Our souls are enmeshed in solving problems in many things in our daily life. In our natural life we are in the realm of solving problems. But with the supply of the Spirit in our spirit, we are in the realm of thinking the one thing — to experience Christ.

Paul's burden with the Philippians was not merely to solve their problem of disharmony, but to lead them to be supplied to think the one thing, Christ. To think the one thing is our greatest need. The way we can tell we are a supplied person is that we relate to matters and environments not by merely solving problems, but by experiencing a deeper, richer Christ.

Two things equally true

"And if Christ is in you, the body is dead because of sin; but the spirit is life because of righteousness." ROMANS 8:10 (ASV)

In our Christian life, as we pursue the Lord, it is important to understand that we have an intrinsically corrupt nature in our flesh. Pursuing the Lord while feeling the corruption of our flesh seems paradoxical, yet Paul puts these two things together in the verse above. We might think that when Paul says, "If Christ is in you," he would conclude with, "you are forgiven of your sins, you have full joy and happiness, and you do not have a problem in the world." But instead Paul says, "If Christ is in you, the body is dead because of sin." Here Paul is stating a fact about our actual condition while we are in this mortal body. Even though Christ is in us, there is still a part of us in a state of deadness, or utter weakness. This part has been smitten with total inability in relation to the things of God. So with our "dead" body, we do not have the ability to perform what we desire to do or even what we will to do. There is something dragging in us, and we can feel the pull of it. That pull is the feeling of death due to sin in the flesh, or indwelling sin.

The last part of Romans 8:10 says, "but the spirit is life because of righteousness." Most Bible versions translate "spirit" with a small "s" because here Paul is contrasting the human body with the human spirit, not the Holy Spirit. Two things are equally true of us as believers: on one hand, the body is dead because of sin, and thus we feel our weakness; on the other hand, the human spirit joined to the Lord is life because of righteousness. If Christ is in you, these two things are true. This helps us understand the actual situation of our Christian life.

Go directly to Jesus April 15th

"For the death that He died, He died to sin once for all; but the life that He lives, He lives to God. Likewise you also, reckon yourselves to be dead indeed to sin, but alive to God in Christ Jesus our Lord." ROMANS 6:10-11

In these verses we see how to relate to ourselves in our identification with Christ. We are absolutely identified with Him. So we reckon ourselves to be dead to sin. This means we live inwardly not identifying with condemning thoughts or those whispers of the "old man" trying to engage us in conversation. When you and I immediately shift to our real person, we are reckoning ourselves to be dead indeed to sin.

To reckon is to count on reliable facts. Let me give an illustration: $2 + 2 = 4$. This equation always holds true. It never changes, regardless of when, where, or why you use it. In the same way, your identification with Christ never changes. Do not look at your feelings. Do not think about your history. Just reckon $2 + 2 = 4$. Your person is Christ. You have been baptized into Him. You are one with Him. So reckon yourself to be dead indeed to sin, but living to God. Inwardly you quickly make a transfer. You do not bargain. You do not reason. You do not get on that level. You identify yourself with Christ in His death and resurrection. You are living to God in Christ Jesus. This is what is true.

So we see how this Christian life works — it is through justification, identification, and the resulting inward transaction of throwing off falsehood, and dealing with God. Now you learn to quickly get to the spirit. You learn to quickly get through all the mire of thoughts and feelings. You go directly to your identification with Christ. You do not solve problems. You do not get answers. You do not stay on that level. You go directly to Jesus.

106

"A little while longer and the world will see Me no more, but you will see Me. Because I live, you will live also." JOHN 14:19

We are not here preserving or protecting the self. Neither do we desire to save it. Our remaining open to hear the Body when the fellowship is transparent (Gal. 4:16) is a mercy from the Lord. And the consequence of such fellowship is that the Lord can do something. By our being open to the Body and not preserving our self, we can receive help from the saints. We are helped to be a person who relates in life rather than relating from the tree of the knowledge of good and evil. So this is our prayer — that the Lord would bring us out of the realm of knowledge and into the realm of life.

With the realm of life there is a flow and a supplied consciousness in our very being. This supplied consciousness is God Himself as life (John 14:19-20). This is also the way the Lord manifests Himself to us (John 14:21). In other words, life is experienced in the form of a consciousness. Life is God Himself in our very being. So when we fellowship with the Lord, it brings in the consciousness of His life (Rom. 8:16), and we treasure that consciousness because it is God Himself operating within us (Phil. 2:12-13). Out of this fellowship the Lord may restrain us from speaking something that may seem right, logical, and good. We are restrained by a feeling within, a consciousness. If we follow that consciousness and go along with it, we relate in the realm of life, not in the realm of knowledge. By this kind of experience we are led out of the ignorant self that does not know how to relate in the realm of life.

What are you doing here? April 17th

"And there he went into a cave, and spent the night in that place; and behold, the word of the LORD came to him, and He said to him, What are you doing here, Elijah?" 1 KINGS 19:9

Sometimes the Lord's voice comes in the form of a question, such as, What are you doing here? or, Where are you going? For example, one day the prophet Elijah was sulking because Jezebel was seeking his life (1 Kings 19:2-4). Yes, Elijah was truly a mighty man of God. He had already caused fire from heaven to come down and consume an offering, thus exposing the falseness of the prophets of Baal and exonerating and vindicating the living God (1 Kings 18:19-39). But when he heard the report that Jezebel wanted to kill him, he ran for his life. Eventually, his flight ended with his hiding in a cave.

In 1 Kings 19:9-13 we read the details of Elijah's encounter with the Lord's voice: [9] "And there he went into a cave, and spent the night in that place; and behold, the word of the Lord came to him, and He said to him, What are you doing here, Elijah? [10] So he said, I have been very zealous for the LORD God of hosts; for the children of Israel have forsaken Your covenant, torn down Your altars, and killed Your prophets with the sword. I alone am left; and they seek to take my life. [11] Then He said, Go out, and stand on the mountain before the Lord. And behold, the LORD passed by, and a great and strong wind tore into the mountains and broke the rocks in pieces before the LORD, but the LORD was not in the wind; and after the wind an earthquake, but the LORD was not in the earthquake; [12] and after the earthquake a fire, but the LORD was not in the fire; and after the fire a still small voice. [13] So it was, when Elijah heard it, that he wrapped his face in his mantle and went out and stood in the entrance of the cave. And suddenly a voice came to him, and said, What are you doing here, Elijah?" This story illustrates how the Lord is in the still small voice. In the original Hebrew language it means "a delicate whispering voice." The Lord was in that whisper. God's speaking was in that still small voice, and it was in the form of a question, "What are you doing here?"

Maybe you have found yourself in "a cave" at some time. Perhaps you went to the cave of a movie theater, and while you were watching all the defiling things on the screen, there arose a consciousness within you in the form of a question, "What are you doing here?" You can be sure, that was God talking to you. That is the way His voice speaks — right inside of you, within your own consciousness.

The church — Christ's Person and work   April 18th

"And He put all things under His feet, and gave Him to be head over all things to the church, which is His body, the fullness of Him who fills all in all." EPHESIANS 1:22-23

The church is not an entity separate from the Person and work of Christ. We should not think of the church as something different from His Person and work. The church is a description of Christ with the fullness of His Person in His Body resulting in a testimony of all that He has accomplished in His work to produce us as His expression. So the church is simply a manifestation, an extension, of Christ's Person and Christ's work.

Coming from various backgrounds, we may have different ideas of what "church" means. The church is a building, or the church is an assembly of people, or the church is what we experienced for years and maybe were disappointed with. "Church" could mean many different things to us. But we need to see a simple and clear revelation of the church — it is nothing less and nothing more than the Person and the work of Christ embodied and expressed through His people. This is the way we need to consider the church.

Properly speaking, the church is an extension of Christ's Person and His work. When the Bible says that we are His Body, it adds, "the fullness of Him who is filling all in all." This is how we are Christ's extension. It is by His filling us. As we are being filled, there is an expression of all His riches. Look at His Person, look at His work. Then you know the church. The church is simply Christ Himself and all that He is dispensed into all of us, with all the riches of His Person and His work flowing from each one of us to express His fullness. What a marvelous realization of what the church is. It is just Christ and more of Christ filling all His organic members.

Releasing the Builder   April 19th

"And I also say to you that you are Peter, and on this rock I will build My church, and the gates of Hades shall not prevail against it." MATTHEW 16:18

With my spirit I can participate in Christ as the Son of the living God. Based on this the Lord says, "Now you release Me and I will relate you in My building. Your participating in Me as the Son of the living God is the rock upon which I will build." There is fellowship, there is something in us that automatically happens, when we are together enjoying Christ, the Son of the living God. Participating in Him causes us to be gregarious in the spirit. We want to be together, to sing together, to fellowship, to forgive. It is His Person and His work that releases Him as the Builder. You cannot build yourself. You cannot relate yourself to anyone, including those closest to you. But touch Christ, interact with Him, let Him be your portion, your person. Take Him, eat Him, drink Him, turn to Him, and see what happens to your insides. Watch your insides change — you want to be with other brothers and sisters, you want to fellowship, you want building, you want to drop everything just for the dwelling place of God.

This shows us that Peter was under revelation when he saw that the church is a participation in the Christ, the Son of the living God.

When we participate in Him, He says, "I will build. I will connect you. I will fit you. I will frame you." It is in this realm that it happens. This is the reality. So the church is not something we can perform. It is not something we can organize, set up, or even agree about. It cannot happen apart from people participating in this Person.

Cooperate with God's operation   April 20th

"Work out your own salvation with fear and trembling; for it is God who operates in you both to will and to do for His good pleasure." PHILIPPIANS 2:12-13

We need to understand, from God's point of view, what it is to take the initiative. It is our response to and cooperation with God's operation in our being. Let me say that if you are born again and Christ is living in you, then there is present within you a divine working that is one-hundred percent bent on beholding the Lord. There is something already in you that matches the Word of God concerning spending time to behold Him. You do not have to produce something in yourself in order to take the initiative. Check with your inner man. Look for the hidden desire within you, and see if there is not a corresponding burden and feeling about your spending time with the Lord.

If you are honest with your deepest sense, you will realize that there is a still small voice within you day by day speaking to you about spending time with the Lord to enjoy Him and to behold Him. In fact, on the negative side, it feels like something nagging you. When you live neglecting your time with the Lord, there is something within you that spontaneously feels dissatisfied. You sense an incompleteness in your daily life even to the point of an inner protesting. Also, on the positive side, there is a desire and a longing to be with the Lord in a definite way — to wait upon Him, behold Him, and enjoy Him. This desire and longing is God working in you.

111

Taking the initiative simply means to cooperate with what God has already put within you. The Greek word translated "work out" in Philippians 2:12 and the word "beholding" in 2 Corinthians 3:18 are both in the middle voice. This means Paul was emphasizing that believers need to take the initiative to actively be involved and participate in the working out of their own salvation. However, the basis for taking this initiative is clearly defined by the following words: "For it is God who operates in you." This means that the initiative we take is actually our going along with the operating God within us. This is a crucial point in all our experiences of the Lord. God works and operates in us to a certain extent; then we need to take the initiative to complete and finish what He is working in us.

That inner ruling   April 21st

"And He is the head of the body, the church, who is the beginning, the firstborn from the dead, that in all things He may have the preeminence." COLOSSIANS 1:18

This verse reveals Christ's headship and administration. He is the Head of His Body, the church, showing that the church is a part of His administration. He is the Head of something. If you are a head, you have to have something to be head over. Christ is the Head of His Body, the church. His position as the Head over the church gives Him the position to head up the whole universe and to consummate this age and bring in the kingdom. This is why the church is so critical to God — because it is the unit of His administration.

In His work, Christ is the Head over His Body, the church. As members of His Body, the church, we are just an extension of His administration. This is not merely theology to us. It means that we do not have choices in our daily life. We are a ruled person. Are you ruled in your inner being by Christ? Am I ruled? Perhaps we have felt free to talk, free to do many things. But one day, as we are participating in Christ, we realize, "Lord, I have no life apart from You. My life is to be ruled by You inwardly." In that inner ruling is the ruling of the universe. Christ heads up the universe not in an organizational way, but in a hidden, silent way. As He is gaining us, He gets the ground on this earth and in this universe to come back and to exercise His government and His headship as the Lamb to consummate the age. How awesome is our life, participating in the Person and work of Christ in His administration.

His soul-life in the blood   April 22nd

"For the life of the flesh is in the blood, and I have given it to you upon the altar to make atonement for your souls; for it is the blood that makes atonement for the soul." LEVITICUS 17:11

Have you ever wondered why the blood is so meaningful to God? Why is the blood the God-appointed way to know Him and to fellowship with Him? Why did God not take another way? It is because in the Bible the blood signifies the soul-life: "For the life of the flesh is in the blood." The word "life" literally means *soul*. It is the Hebrew word *nephesh,* and is the equivalent of the Greek word *psuche.* Both mean soul. So the first thing this verse shows us is that the soul-life is in the blood. The second thing is that the soul-life is assigned by God to be the factor of atonement upon the altar.

Throughout the history of mankind, there was only one Man with a sinless, perfect soul — Christ Jesus. Thus, when He went to the cross, the blood locked up in His veins was precious blood. It was the blood of a perfect, sinless soul, the only kind of blood that would avail in crucifixion, in death, to satisfy the Father. There was no other blood in this universe that could avail for us except the blood in those veins, because it was coming from His sinless soul. There on the cross He died without sin, and that blood was shed and poured out.

113

Because the soul-life of the flesh is in the blood, in the Old Testament blood was sprinkled in the holiest of all before God, and was accepted there to make atonement for the sins of the people. That blood was a type of the blood of Jesus. Today His blood carries His soul-life. That is why you and I can drink the blood. And this is witnessed to by the Spirit. When we drink the blood, we have life in ourselves. This is because we are participating in the perfection of His thought life, His emotions, His will. His humanity was not left back there 2,000 years ago. His humanity is now in our spirit to participate in. To drink His blood is to drink the perfect soul-life of the Son of God, the last Adam who was made a life-giving Spirit for us to enjoy.

The precious blood   April 23rd

"Knowing that you were not redeemed with corruptible things, like silver or gold, from your aimless conduct received by tradition from your fathers, but with the precious blood of Christ, as of a lamb without blemish and without spot." 1 PETER 1:18-19

What Peter says here about the blood causes us to stop and consider its preciousness. We have been redeemed with precious blood. We need to appreciate the value of the blood from the divine point of view. All things have been cleansed by the blood. Even the heavens needed to be cleansed, so the Lord went there and sprinkled His blood. Everything was cleansed so that God and man could enjoy a mutual participation. Now we are directly participating in all that God is. There is nothing indirect or secondhand in our experience. Our participation is not through someone else, but directly with God — without any guilt and without any defilement.

The blood not only gives God a way to forgive us and not only takes care of our guilt, but the blood also cleanses us. Cleansing and forgiveness are two different things. Forgiveness has to do with guilt before God. We are guilty sinners. But the shed blood removes the guilt so that we are pardoned, we are justified. First John 1:9 says, "If we confess our sins, He is faithful and righteous to forgive us our sins." That is one thing — to be forgiven of our sins. But the conjunction *and* follows, telling us that there is something more — "*and* to cleanse us from all unrighteousness." Also 1 John 1:7 says that the blood is cleansing us from all sin. The blood is so precious. It not only cares for my guilt and my standing, but it also cares for all the pollution and the defilement as a result of sin, with its contamination upon my inward parts.

So the blood straightens me up inwardly. It lifts my head up. The blood brings me out of the realm of fear and intimidation that comes from a conscience that is pained because of residual defilement over my being from touching contaminated things. There is not only sin, but contamination from sin. There is accusation, there is condemnation, there are mixed emotions. There is all this turmoil within. But the blood cleanses my conscience to clear up my inner being so that my heart is a true heart. There is not any feigned faith, but only direct, bold contact with God! I have no second thoughts, I have no residual condemnation, I have no effects of contamination in my being, because the blood has reached my conscience! The blood cleanses me from all unrighteousness, all pollution, all contamination. The blood cares for that. Not only my guilt is gone but my pollution is gone.

Live to the Boss   **April 24th**

"For to this end Christ died and rose and lived again, that He might be Lord of both the dead and the living." ROMANS 14:9

G od wants us to keep coming forward and enjoy the grace that is ours. For this to happen, He gave us a new point of reference. Our point of reference is no longer ourself. It is Him. Romans 14:7-8 tells us, [7] "For none of us lives to himself, and no one dies to himself. [8] For if we live, we live to the Lord; and if we die, we die to the Lord. Therefore, whether we live or die, we are the Lord's." Then verse 9 tells us why Christ died and rose and lived again — "that He might be Lord" — the Boss — "of both the dead and the living." So live to the Boss. Live to the Lord. He died and rose again, not merely to become a ticket in our pocket for us to go to heaven when we die. He died and rose again to be Lord. This means we live now to Christ. He is our point of reference. We no longer live to ourself. We never refer back to ourself. Our whole source has changed, from ourself to Him. He is bringing us back to what He intended in the garden of Eden with the tree of life — that He would be our source.

Our relationship with ourself is Christ. This kind of understanding will come progressively in our experience. As our mind is renewed by the Spirit and by the Word, a consciousness of life will begin to permeate every area of our living. We will start linking the Word with our experiences.

"Out of" and "from" April 25th

"Now all things are out of God, who has reconciled us to Himself through Jesus Christ, and has given us the ministry of reconciliation." 2 CORINTHIANS 5:18

The preposition "out of" (*ek* / ἐκ) used in this verse reveals that our *starting place* is in God, and that everything proceeds out of God. Romans 11:36 also uses *ek* to show us that God is our source: "For *out of* Him and through Him and to Him are all things." God is the starting point for all things. For example, this morning when I woke up, I had a spontaneous feeling within me. It was as if the Lord was saying, "Don't move, don't think, don't allow yourself to do anything. Just sink into Me." We do not have a right to live. We are not the initiators in our lives. God is our starting place, because everything is *out of* Him. He has the first place in all things.

116

One of the clearest verses showing that the Lord Jesus lived from the Father as His source is John 5:30: "I can from Myself do nothing. As I hear, I judge; and My judgment is righteous, because I do not seek My own will but the will of the Father who sent Me." The preposition "from" indicates that, in His humanity, the Lord was not the source of his actions and words. Although He could have legitimately taken His own sinless soul as the base and source of His living, He lived exclusively *from* the Father.

First John 2:27 is a key verse in the New Testament that reveals how God is our source: "But the anointing which you have received *from Him* abides in you, and you do not need that anyone teach you; but as the same anointing teaches you concerning all things, and is true, and is not a lie, and just as it has taught you, you will abide in Him." God becomes our source experientially when we follow the movement of the anointing within us from Him. This indicates that the practical matters in our lives originate from Him as our source.

"Through" and "because of"   April 26th

"Thanks be to God through Jesus Christ our Lord! So then, on the one hand I myself with my mind am serving the law of God, but on the other, with my flesh the law of sin." ROMANS 7:25 (NASV)

The preposition "through" (*dia* / διά) reveals that Christ is the means through which we handle everything in our lives. For example, in the verse above Paul says, "Thanks be to God *through* Jesus Christ our Lord!" The context of this statement tells us that Paul could not handle his flesh by himself. He was a defeated, wretched, and miserable man. He had tried with good intentions to obey God's command, but apart from Him he was a failure. But then Paul breaks out with, "Thanks be to God *through* Jesus Christ our Lord!" Now it is *through* Jesus Christ. This indicates that He is my source to handle myself. He is the means through which I overcome my problems. He is the source I interact with when facing temptations. As my source, Christ is the One *through* whom I handle and touch everything in my Christian life.

The preposition *dia* with the accusative in Greek is translated "because of." The Lord uses this preposition in John 6:57 to show us that He is our portion: "As . . . I live because of the Father, so he who eats Me will live because of Me." By eating Christ, we take Him into us. He becomes the source of our spiritual nourishment and supply. We live because of Him. By our eating Him, He becomes the life-source of our daily lives. We can testify that we live *because of* Him. He is our source.

"Into" and "in"   April 27th

"For God so loved the world that He gave His only begotten Son, that whoever believes into Him should not perish but have eternal life." John 3:16

The preposition "into" shows how God becomes our source when we believe. This preposition even shows us the meaning of becoming a Christian. Based on John 3:16, our understanding of becoming a Christian is "whoever believes in Him." And many times, because of the way the gospel is presented, it issues in a kind of believing in Christ, but it is still objective: "Yes, I believe that story." And people do get saved, but they are left with a deficiency in their realization. The words that the Lord spoke in John 3:16 were according to the divine economy of God's operating from within man. Thus, He did not say "whoever believes *in* Him." He used the preposition *into:* "whoever believes *into* Him should not perish but have eternal life." This means that I move from being outside this Person *into* this Person. Paul also uses the preposition *into* when telling the Roman believers about their baptism: "Do you not know that as many of us as were baptized *into* Christ Jesus . . ." (Rom. 6:3).

The very words "into Christ Jesus" show us that from the beginning we have merged and become one spirit with another Person, another life, another source.

The preposition "in" reveals that I am *in* Christ. That is my position. My position is in Christ. And then Colossians says, "Christ in you." That is His position. His position is in me. I have a position, and He has a position. Many times we say, "Thank You, Lord, I am in You. I am outside the reach of condemnation. You are my righteousness." And we rejoice. But we also need the other side — Christ in you. That is His position. He is saying to us, "How am I in here? Are you letting Me live in here? Do I have freedom in here?" This is His position. We are in Christ, and Christ is in us. We have a position in Him. He has a position in us.

"To" and "toward"   April 28th

"And He died for all, that those who live should live no longer to themselves, but to Him who died for them and rose again."
2 CORINTHIANS 5:15

Here Paul is opening up another aspect of our inward posture in the Christian life. We are *to* the Lord. We are *toward* Him. That is our inward posture. Let me give an illustration. This life is like going to a boys' ranch, where you report to the director, and the director checks you in. Then he tells you, "You are going to be here for some time, and I am not going to give you a list of do's and don'ts. I want you to stay with me instead. I want you to be with me wherever I go. Every moment of the day, I will tell you what to do. You will not have a relationship with a schedule or a written program. You will have a relationship with me."

The Lord has come into us, not to be cheated by our religious living, but to be our source. He wants us to live moment by moment to Him. That means your eyes are looking at His eyes. You are looking at His face. Is He smiling? Is He happy in what you are saying right now, in how you are carrying on? Is He happy with your habits of life? Are you *to* Him? Are you willing to gather up your whole life and prove what is well pleasing to Him? Do you dare take every part of your life and live to Him? What about your relationship with others in the world? Can you prove that it is well pleasing to Him? What about your dress? How do you clothe yourself? Do you live somewhat naked? Can you prove yourself to be well pleasing in what you wear? Do you have a consciousness of what pleases Him in your dress? First Corinthians 10:31 says, "Whether you eat or drink, or whatever you do, do all to the glory of God." Eating and drinking is to be done out of the source of God. I am to eat to God. I am to drink to God. I am to dress to God. I am to talk to God. I am *to* Him. He is my source. This is the life that springs from within.

"With" April 29th

"The grace of the Lord Jesus Christ, and the love of God, and the fellowship of the Holy Spirit be with you all. Amen."
2 CORINTHIANS 13:14

Here Paul's use of the preposition "with" (*meta* / μετά) is related to our being *with* the Lord in a very experiential way. Whenever Paul ends his letters, he characteristically uses this preposition to convey an experiential emphasis. For grace, love, and fellowship to be *with* us from the Triune God means that we have more than mere head knowledge about God. It is a heart knowledge that supplies us with God Himself as our source.

Paul also uses another Greek preposition translated "with." It is *sun* (σύν). This preposition is characteristically related to our position in Christ. For example, it is related to our being crucified *with* Christ (Rom. 6:6), raised *with* Him, and seated *with* Him (Eph. 2:6). In Colossians it is used to show us that our life is hidden *with*

Christ in God (3:3). Positionally, everything about our life is *with* Him. Thus, we are *with* (σύν) Him positionally, in order that we might be *with* (μετά) Him experientially.

We are in the Son. And because we are in the Son, we are in the Father. He is the source. Now our life is *through* Christ. Now it is *because of* Him. Now it is *with* Him. Now it is *out of* Him. Now it is *into* Him. And it is *to* Him. We are joined to the Lord in our spirit. This reality is in our spirit. Now the Spirit is transmitting God as my source into my spirit. My spirit is joined to this source. Christ is my life. The Father is my enjoyment. So there is a pure source. Our source is God Himself joined to our spirit. Every one of us who is regenerated has a pure source from which to live.

Where are you?   April 30th

"Then the LORD God called to Adam and said to him, Where are you?" GENESIS 3:9

After Adam hid himself from the presence of the Lord, God came to him asking the question, "Where are you?" Of course, God already knew where Adam was, but Adam still had to admit to himself and to God where he was. Sometimes in our lives, when we are living for vanity, when we are in our own little world with our own self-centered goals and aims, there comes a consciousness within us with words that form in our own thoughts saying, "Where am I? What am I doing with my life? Where will my life end up?" It may seem like our own mind talking, but we must realize that God's voice comes to us as He is writing it into our consciousness — into our own thoughts and heart.

God is talking to us through our own consciousness. This way of speaking is according to the new covenant. He is not merely talking *to* us, but He is infusing and supplying into us the very thing He is speaking about. You probably do not realize how much of the

Lord's speaking you have in your daily life. For example, you may remember someone during the day. Perhaps as you are washing the dishes, you think about that person. Actually it is the Lord speaking to you, putting that person on your heart so that you would pray for him or give him a phone call. It is in these practical ways that Christ manifests Himself in us as our life.

May

Lingering with God

"As at the first time, I stayed in the mountain forty days and forty nights." DEUTERONOMY 10:10 *"So the LORD spoke to Moses face to face, as a man speaks to his friend. And he would return to the camp, but his servant Joshua the son of Nun, a young man, did not depart from the tabernacle."* EXODUS 33:11

Moses prayed to the Lord in Exodus 33:18, "Please, show me Your glory." Then he spent time in God's glory with an unveiled face (Exo. 34:34), and he was changed. In Deuteronomy 10:10 when Moses refers to his time with God, he says, "I stayed in the mountain." The original Hebrew word for stayed implies "I *lingered* in the mountain." This indicates that Moses realized the necessity of staying and even lingering with God on the mountain.

Exodus 33 and 34 provide the entire background of the New Testament word "beholding" (2 Cor. 3:18). Thus, for us to know what this beholding is, we need to be impressed with Moses' stay with the Lord. What stands out in Moses' experience of beholding the Lord and talking to Him, even face-to-face as an intimate friend (Exo. 33:11), is the time he spent — forty days and forty nights. It took this specific length of time for Moses to soak in the glory of God and to come down transformed. Of course, this transformation was only to the degree of the Old Testament glory. Nevertheless, there was a glory.

It is significant that Moses' record includes the amount of time he spent with the Lord on the mountain. This helps us to see that time is involved in the "beholding" mentioned in 2 Corinthians 3:18. We must realize that beholding the Lord to be transformed takes time. Being a person that makes time to be with the Lord is the sure way to be transformed into His image. Transformation does not happen superficially. It takes time. And not only so, it takes the right kind of time — spending quality time with the Lord.

Look and live   May 2nd

"For I am not ashamed of the gospel of Christ, for it is the power of God unto salvation for everyone who believes, for the Jew first and also for the Greek. For in it the righteousness of God is revealed out of faith into faith; as it is written, The just shall live by faith." ROMANS 1:16-17

Here Paul presents the truth about the source of faith. He declares that in the preaching of the gospel, "the power of God" is operating unto salvation to everyone who believes. "Tell me the old, old story of Jesus and His love." The author of this song knew what being under "the hearing" does. Tell me the good news. Tell me about the scenery. When you tell me about the scenery, a mysterious power is operating over me. It is the power of God unto salvation. Because in it — in the gospel — God's righteousness is revealed. Everyone's mouth is shut. The whole earth has to stop. Man's vain thoughts have to cease. Let us all stop and look at God's righteousness. There it is — on Calvary. None of us are righteous. Christ became *our* sin and we become *His* righteousness! (2 Cor. 5:21).

When we speak and sing about God's righteousness at Calvary, faith springs out of that message. This is the meaning of "out of faith into faith." It is a matter of looking and believing. The *believing* in John 3:16 is connected with the *looking* in John 3:14-15: [14] "And as Moses lifted up the serpent in the wilderness, even so must the Son of Man be lifted up, [15] that whoever believes in Him should not perish but have eternal life. [16] For God so loved the world that He gave His only begotten Son, that whoever believes into Him should not perish but have eternal life." The immediate context of John 3:16

includes verse 14, which summarizes the Old Testament account of the children of Israel being bitten by serpents due to their murmuring (Num. 21:6-9). At that time Moses prayed for the people, and the Lord told him to put a serpent on a pole, saying, "It shall be that everyone who is bitten, when he looks at the pole, shall live." Just *look* and *live*. The ones bitten by the serpent did not *do* anything; they did not cure themselves. They just turned from one direction to another to gaze at the brass serpent on the pole. The moment they looked, they lived. That is how fast deliverance came to them. In the same way, if you are not saved, just look at Christ and you will receive eternal life, not only initially, but continuously. It is all in the look at the scenery of Calvary that faith comes to us.

The blood and the new agreement   May 3rd

"But one of the soldiers pierced His side with a spear, and immediately blood and water came out." JOHN 19:34

In our experience, many times we have to get over the "guilties" before we feel that God can come and operate in us. But by the precious blood of Jesus, God holds everything in suspension in order that He can get His life into us. The blood holds all our problems in suspension so that there could be an impartation of life (signified by water). On the cross when the soldiers put the spear into the Lord's side, not only blood came out, but blood and water. The blood was for cleansing and for enacting a new agreement. What is the agreement? The agreement is that God Himself comes into us and does the work on us from the inside: "I am going to write My laws upon your heart. I am going to operate on your inward parts." The blood of Christ has made it possible for us to partake of God in a direct way.

While the blood is present over us, the life is being imparted. God is telling us, "In your condition, the way you are, I am writing My laws, I am writing My nature, I am writing Myself into you. And

125

all the time, your part is just to look at Me, partake of Me, and enjoy Me." This is the blood of the new covenant. This is the blood of Jesus that gives us boldness.

Prove how rich Christ is   May 4th

"To me, who am less than the least of all the saints, this grace was given, that I should preach among the nations the unsearchable riches of Christ." EPHESIANS 3:8

Paul begins here to explain some of the details of the church, the mystery of Christ — how this unique one Body is actually realized on the earth. It is realized by all the members together enjoying the unsearchable riches of Christ. It is realized by discovering in your daily life the unique answer for every situation that exists. This includes what exists in you inwardly — your inward problems and turmoils, your inward state. It also includes what you face outwardly — the things happening in your environments that affect you. The unique answer is that all your environments are to prove how rich Christ can be in you and to you. Instead of living in your moods and in your anxiety, you make a transfer. This transfer happens by calling that precious name, Jesus. When you call His name, you put yourself under a transmission of all the riches connected to your spirit. You activate your spirit and God begins to move in you. There is a flow. John 7:38 describes this flow: "Out of your innermost being shall flow rivers of living water" (NASV). This means we enjoy the unsearchable riches of Christ again and again in whatever we pass through.

Paul says that he is telling all the nations about these unsearchable riches of Christ. This is how the church happens. This is how the Body takes place on the earth. You do not organize it. You do not name it. You do not set up shop. You do not bring in entertainment. You do not set up programs — nothing like that. That is all a substitute for Christ, and a facade. Instead, you just find people — ordinary people, redeemed people — and gather them together and let the unsearchable riches of Christ flow out. This is the church.

Why I am alive   May 5th

"Having made known to us the mystery of His will, according to His good pleasure which He purposed in Himself." EPHESIANS 1:9

These are big words. These are lofty words. Yet, if I am a human being with common sense, I am going to take the time to position myself before this word. The mystery conceived in eternity past in the heart of God is according to the good pleasure of His will. If God has spoken about the meaning of my human life, then I should know what He said. If I have any sense, I will realize that it is worthwhile to consider this word, regardless of whether or not I am interested. This word has to do with the meaning of why I am alive.

God has *made known* to us the mystery of His will. What is the will of God in this created universe? It is a mystery. This means it must be revealed to us. None of us are going to come up with it on our own. God has made it known through the channel of the New Testament ministry. He unveiled it in the writings of the New Testament. This is God's way. He gave it to Paul, who was simply a steward handling this mystery. This was not Paul's philosophy of life. He was handling revelation concerning God's hidden desire conceived in eternity past and then made known in the New Testament. This is the proper understanding. Thus, it behooves us to take the time before the Lord in the Word to apprehend this mystery.

"To redeem those who were under the law, that we might receive the sonship." GALATIANS 4:5

When we are redeemed, we receive the sonship. Receiving the sonship simply means receiving the Son with all that He is and all that He has accomplished. We were redeemed to receive the sonship as a gift given by grace. The sonship is not something we work for or grow into. To receive the sonship is instantaneous when we receive Christ and are born again. It is not something we receive after a long process of being dealt with by God, or something we receive as a reward for work we have done.

What is the sonship? Galatians 4:6 tells us: "And because you are sons, God has sent forth the Spirit of His Son into your hearts, crying out, Abba, Father!" In other words, the sonship is the formation of Christ in us. He has been *sent into my heart* — not just into my spirit, but into my heart. Here it is not a matter of Him growing into my heart. Nor is it Him taking over my heart little by little. He has been *sent* (aorist tense / punctiliar action) into my heart. He has been instantly formed in me through regeneration.

The moment the Lord is formed in me through regeneration, I immediately begin crying, "Abba, Father." And my crying "Abba" is synchronized with His crying "Abba," and vice versa (Gal. 4:6 and Rom. 8:15). This crying is my direct participation in the sonship, which includes the Son's very own relationship with the Father. My orientation is the Son with the life of the Son (1 John 5:20). When I am weak, when I am "out of it," when I cannot make it, my focus is no longer on myself. I am now inwardly aligned with Christ. This is what it means to handle everything with Christ. I am one with Him. I am loving Him. Christ has been formed in my heart as the object of my love and attention.

Stay in the waiting room

"You have become discharged from Christ, you who attempt to be justified by law; you have fallen from grace." GALATIANS 5:4

In Galatians 5:3 Paul says, "And I testify again to every man who becomes circumcised that he is a debtor to keep the whole law." In other words, if you make one mistake, if you break one law, you are guilty of breaking the whole law (James 2:10). What does it mean that you have become discharged from Christ? You are not discharged from Christ in the sense that you lose salvation, or that you lose His indwelling in your spirit. But you have temporarily been separated from the benefit of having a present supply of grace from Him to change you. You have been separated because of what you are looking at and what you are oriented to. You are about to be discharged from Christ if you are looking at the law, expecting it to change you and perfect you before God.

The Christian life is not about changing and perfecting yourself. It is about coming to the Son the way you are, under the new covenant, by the blood. This gives Him the opportunity to come in as the Spirit to write on your heart and mind. By the blood of the covenant you keep coming to Him in a direct way, just as you are.

To fall from grace means you have fallen out of the supply that comes from enjoying Christ. In Galatians 5:5 Paul reminds the believers of the proper way to relate to the law: "For we through the Spirit eagerly wait for the hope of righteousness by faith." It is as if he was saying, "Do you want to know how we do it? *For we through the Spirit* stay in the waiting room." This is like a father remaining in the waiting room at the hospital, waiting and expecting the baby to be born. The Spirit is our waiting room for Christ to be brought forth in us.

129

God's estimate of things   May 8th

"For in Him dwells all the fullness of the Godhead bodily; and you have been made full in Him, who is the head of all principality and power." COLOSSIANS 2:9-10

If God's estimate of things is centered in His Son so that all the fullness of the Godhead dwells in Him, then who am I to challenge God about what is important in my life? I surely do not want to go after something other than Him. It is God who said that the fullness dwells in Him. Are we going to challenge God's interpretation of our life? Do we think we need something more than Christ? A better husband? A better wife? A better job? A better environment? Better security? Do not challenge God. God says, "In Him dwells all the fullness." And not only so, *"You* have been made full in Him." What contentment! What satisfaction! I might be deprived in my outward circumstances. I might even be tried to the limit, but I have a Christ in me who is rich and all-sufficient. He is my fullness and my satisfaction.

Because Paul knew Christ as his fullness and his satisfaction, he could be in prison and talk about always rejoicing (Phil. 4:4). He could pray, sing, and praise the Lord in the midst of suffering, because his understanding was so full and rich with Christ (Acts 16:24-25). The "full assurance of understanding" and "the excellence of the knowledge of Christ Jesus my Lord" were constantly ushering Paul into more and more experiences of Christ in his daily life (Col. 2:2; Phil. 3:7-8).

Put yourself aside   May 9th

"By putting off the body of the sins of the flesh, by the circumcision of Christ, buried with Him in baptism, in which you also were raised with Him through faith in the working of God, who raised Him from the dead." COLOSSIANS 2:11-12

In spending time with the Lord we must put ourselves aside. We have to say, "Lord, I put myself aside — all my distractions, all my fears, all my anxieties, all my condemnation, all my preoccupation with myself. Lord, I come to You and put myself aside." This is the practical significance of baptism and of praying. And in spending time with the Lord, this is an important factor. We have to learn to put aside the intruding thoughts that pop into our mind, such as, "I do not know how to spend time with the Lord. I have failed in the past. I do not think this is going to work for me." These kinds of thoughts must be put aside. Every distracting thought that enters into our mind must be put aside.

During the initial period of spending time with the Lord, it is good to take a little time just to put yourself aside in every dimension — put aside your feelings of failure, put aside your natural life, put aside your environment, put aside your present dealings, put aside what *you* think the Lord is speaking to you. Many times we imagine the Lord is saying something and doing something. Yet, it may not be Him at all. It may be our own thought. It is much better to remain in the principle of baptism. It is much better to bury everything, that is, to put aside our natural life, our religious life, and even our spiritual life. Just bury it. Absolutely put ourself aside. Tell Him, "Lord, I really do not know You that well. I know the doctrines of Christianity, I know many things about You, and I know what I am supposed to be. But Lord, I want to get to know *You*. So Lord, I put myself aside."

Poured-out love   May 10th

"Now hope does not put to shame, because the love of God has been poured out in our hearts through the Holy Spirit who has been given to us." ROMANS 5:5

This verse tells us that the love of God is a dispensed thing. It is not a worked-up thing. We do not try to find it in ourselves. The love of God is a poured-out reality. But what is the nature of the experience of that love in our hearts on a daily basis? How does it feel to have the love of God poured out in our hearts? To appreciate the nature of this poured-out love and what it is like to enjoy the Lord according to this love-life, we need to read the context of Romans 5:5. Verse 6 says, "For *while* we were yet weak" (ASV). This is the condition on which the love is poured out — not when we are strong, but while we are yet weak. Note the second part of this verse: "in due time Christ died for the ungodly." If you are ungodly, you are a prime candidate for the love of God. Maybe you are thinking miserable things about yourself — that you hate yourself for the things you have done. You wish you had not done them, but you did. You did some ungodly things that you would not want anyone to know about, and you hate yourself for it. But listen to what this verse says: "Christ died for the ungodly." You are the very kind of person He shed His blood for. Despite what you have done, He loves you! This shows us the nature of the poured-out love in our hearts.

God's buy-back   May 11th

"In Him we have redemption through His blood, the forgiveness of sins, according to the riches of His grace." EPHESIANS 1:7

In Christ we have redemption through His blood. We participate in the redeeming Lamb of God. But we must understand the word redeem. The English prefix *re* is derived from the Latin prefix *re,* which means to restore back or to recover. Thus, redeem literally means not just to buy, but to buy back. It means not just to purchase, but to repurchase.

The Lord died on the cross to redeem us. This tells us that we were not meaningless to God — people scattered, separated from God, that He decided to purchase on the spot. This would be like going to a second-hand store, looking at an item, deciding you like that item, and purchasing it. You buy it on the spot, without forethought. That

132

is not the depth of redemption. To buy back implies that we originally belonged to God. We were already in his heart. We were already His property. Before we were born, before the foundation of the world, we were God's own possession and property. We got lost as *His* property. But He found us and redeemed us. He bought us back.

Redemption takes on a whole new significance when we realize we have been redeemed by the blood. It is not merely a future salvation that we have — that we are going to heaven and not going to hell. Though we do thank God for our destiny, redemption is far deeper than that. We have been bought back, repurchased at the price of the blood of Jesus, in order to be restored back to the purpose for which we were chosen in Him before the foundation of the world.

Forget about yourself   May 12th

"While [Peter] was still speaking, behold, a bright cloud over-shadowed them; and suddenly a voice came out of the cloud, saying, This is My beloved Son, in whom I am well pleased. Hear Him!"
MATTHEW 17:5

God's eternal counsel concerning us is that we would share in the continuous flow of love between the Father and the Son (Eph. 1:4-5). Thus, we must put ourselves aside in order to cultivate this love that flows in the Triune God and that reaches out to take us up into Himself by making us organically the Body of Christ (Eph. 5:25, 28-30). From eternity past to eternity future God's love is over us and with us. In fact, nothing can separate us from the love of God which is in Christ Jesus our Lord. Principalities, powers, death, life — whatever realm — nothing can separate us. We are more than conquerors, not through our condition, not through our potential, but through Him who loved us. However, if we do not spend time with the Lord and put ourselves aside, we may be cheated from the daily enjoyment of this mighty flowing love.

Paul lived in the enjoyment of this love. And that was the realm whereby Christ lived in him. In Galatians 2:20 he said, "I have been crucified with Christ." That means I am put out of the way. I am terminated. "It is no longer I." I have been put aside. Now it is Christ who lives in me. "And the life which I now live in the flesh," that is, in the environment of my flesh — in the strivings of my flesh, the anxieties of my flesh, the depression of my flesh, all the things of my flesh — the life that I now live in this environment, I will tell you how I live. "I live by faith in the Son of God, who loved me and gave Himself for me." Not "loved us," but "loved me." This is how personal and intimate the Lord's love was to Paul, and this was what motivated him to enjoy this living Person.

In spending time with the Lord to cultivate a love relationship with Him, we must put ourself aside to hear God's voice speaking about His Son: "In Him I am well pleased." Forget about yourself. Just let the Lord speak that word to you, and then tell Him, "Lord, You are the Father's delight. I treasure this time that I could spend to enjoy You in prayer, the One who is the Father's delight." It is in this loving interchange in our spirit between us and the Lord, with the eyes of our heart gazing upon Him, that we are spontaneously being transformed.

A condemnation situation   May 13th

"For the flesh lusts against the Spirit, and the Spirit against the flesh; and these are contrary to one another, so that you do not do the things that you wish." GALATIANS 5:17

Here Paul is speaking a clear word about the intrinsic conflict between the flesh and the Spirit. It shows us that to have mixed emotions and to feel rumblings within us is a normal experience. We have this conflict because there are two natures within us that are intrinsically opposed to each other. That is why you cannot live "on the fence" as a Christian. You will be miserable. If you sometimes

134

go along with the Spirit and you sometimes go along with the flesh, eventually you will reach the point of saying, "I do not want to be a hypocrite anymore. I am going to give up the whole Christian life." And some people do give up the Lord because of this unresolved conflict within them.

The fact that you have inward turmoil indicates that the Spirit is in you and the flesh is in you. These two natures are intrinsically opposed to each other, and you feel the opposition. For example, if you turn your eyes a little bit and gaze on something that stirs up your flesh, you can feel opposition to God within you. At the same time, God in you is opposing sin and the flesh. He does not want to even be spotted by it through one glance (Jude 23). So both these natures are in us, each opposing the other.

Then Paul says in Galatians 5:18, "But if you are led by the Spirit, you are not under the law." Why does he add this immediately after verse 17? "Under the law" means that you are in a potential condemnation situation. Paul knows that when you feel the inward conflict between the flesh and the Spirit, you could potentially come under the law and be condemned. But you are led by the Spirit if you say, "Lord, I admit that there is something in me that has its lusts and its desires. But Jesus, I am coming to You. Thank You, Lord." As you touch the Spirit, as you go to the Lord, you are not under the law. You are not categorized as a condemned person when that intrinsically corrupt flesh raises its head and you feel it. Rather, you are led at that point by the Spirit.

Let your problems humble you   **May 14th**

"But He gives more grace. Therefore He says: God resists the proud, but gives grace to the humble." JAMES 4:6

Why did God leave us with conflicts and struggles? What is His intention? To answer this we need to know that God

135

originally created man to be dependent upon Him. But due to the fall, man became proud and independent of God. Now God is at work to humble us and make us dependent on Him. For this He uses everything, including our problems. When James says that God gives grace to the humble, it means that your conflicts and struggles are intended to humble you in order to receive fresh supplies of grace.

We can position ourselves for grace, even though there is a nature within us that is at enmity with God. James is speaking to believers who have wars and fights among them due to the warring pleasures in their members — all this conflict (4:1-5). Then he tells them that God is going to give more grace. How does God give more grace? It happens by our drawing near to Him and dealing with our sinful doings, dealing with our divided heart. When we admit we are wretched, when we admit there is nothing good in us — that is the best place to start. James 4:9 says, "Lament and mourn and weep!" The Greek word for lament is the same word Paul uses in Romans 7:24 to describe his inward condition of wretchedness: "O *wretched* man that I am!" So James is saying, "Be wretched!" Simply admit that in yourself dwells no good thing.

In James 4:6 we read that God gives more grace. Then in verses 7-8 we see how this can happen: [7] "Therefore submit to God. Resist the devil and he will flee from you. [8] Draw near to God and He will draw near to you." This is James' way of saying "The law of the Spirit of life in Christ Jesus has made me free from the law of sin and death" (Rom. 8:2). Paul uses the word "law" in Romans. This means that if you touch the Spirit, if you go to the Spirit, you are going to a higher law in you. The Lord lives in you 24 hours a day. He is in your spirit — deeper than your mind, your emotions, and your will. You have a spirit and I have a spirit. We are joined to the Lord. Our mind may be going one way, and our emotions another way. But that is okay. Simply stay in your spirit. Call "Jesus." Pray. Sing to the Lord. Open yourself to the Word. Share the gospel with others.

Fellowship with believers. By activating your spirit, you get into another law that frees you from the law of sin and death every time. This is Paul's way of describing the divine solution to our problems.

Our relationship with everything May 15th

"Likewise you also, reckon yourselves to be dead indeed to sin, but alive to God in Christ Jesus our Lord." ROMANS 6:11

Christ is our relationship with *all* things — both positive and negative. On the positive side, Christ is our relationship with the Father. He is also our relationship with all the saints, the members of His Body. On the negative side, Christ is our relationship with sin, the self, the flesh, the world, condemnation, the devil, and the law. So we must ask ourselves, How are we related to sin? How are we related to our flesh? How are we related to the world? Often we have tried to live the Christian life with ourselves as the source. But we must see that we have no life in ourselves apart from Christ (John 6:53). Our life is wholly wrapped up with Him. Our true life has been hidden with Christ in God. "Christ who is our life" in Colossians 3:4 means that we died to sin *in Him*. We died to the flesh *in Him*. We died to the world *in Him*. We defeated the devil *in Him*. And we died to the law *in Him*. Praise the Lord!

Our relationship with all these realms is Christ. Even in our encounters with sins, we need to be a person who reacts exclusively with the blood of Jesus (Heb. 10:17-19). Concerning our sin nature, we need to interact with what happened on the cross. Christ died to sin, and in Him we reckon ourselves to be dead indeed to sin. We are alive to God *in Him* (Rom. 6:8-11). When we are oriented to these facts, our partaking of Christ and our participation in Him become so rich and full. He supplies to us the victory. The victory over sin and death is just Himself. We do not strive to win the victory. We receive and participate in His victory!

God accepts only one Person May 16th

"But when it pleased God, who separated me from my mother's womb and called me through His grace, to reveal His Son in me . . ."
GALATIANS 1:15-16

Brothers and sisters, we are all on the same level, so we can all echo the familiar song, "Just as I am, without one plea, but that Thy blood was shed for me . . . O Lamb of God, I come, I come." This is exactly how we should relate to the Lord — always coming to Him *just as we are.* If you are thinking that you have to repair yourself or that you have to reach a point where you are stronger in yourself to be accepted by God, then you have it all wrong. There is nothing in ourselves that can stand before God (Rom. 7:18). In fact, if we would seek to clean ourselves up on our own and come to Him with some merit in ourselves, His analysis would be that all our righteousnesses are nothing but filthy rags (Isa. 64:6). God only accepts one Person — His *only begotten Son.*

When Christ is revealed in me (Gal. 1:16), I have a new relationship with everything. I no longer come from the source of my self. I am no longer trying to be the savior of my life. Christ Himself is my Savior. I no longer interact with matters and things apart from Him, as though I was on my own. As a man in Christ, I am in the realm of the new creation, where *"all things are out of God"* (2 Cor. 5:17-18). The new creation means that Christ is the center and spring of my life. Because of this, I now have a new relationship with all things.

A new center

*"And He died for all, that those who live should live no longer
to themselves, but to Him who died for them and has been raised."*
2 CORINTHIANS 5:15

No longer living to ourselves is experiential. The cross is a fact
that transfers the source of our lives. Now we are joined to
Christ through regeneration. What is the issue of this? What is the
purpose of it all? It is that we no longer live *to* ourselves, that we
no longer take ourselves as the point of reference for anything! We
no longer consult with ourselves or debate with ourselves. To live no
longer *to* ourselves, but *to* Him means that we have a new center, a
new source, a new base of operation. From this new source, we live
to Him who died for us and has been raised.

Based upon this transfer and its experiential effect of no longer
living to ourselves, verse 16 begins, "Therefore, from now on . . ."
Notice the words "from now on." In verse 15 it is "no longer," and
in verse 16 it is "from now on, we know no one according to the
flesh." This means we do not interpret people or relate to one another
in the way we did in the past. "From now on" is the outcome of "no
longer" living to ourselves. Because we have a new base of
operation, our whole attitude about one another and how we relate
to one another is changed. We no longer know each other according
to the flesh. This even includes the way we are related to the Lord,
to Christ. Paul testifies, "Even though we have known Christ
according to the flesh, yet now we know Him thus no longer" (v. 16).
We do not remain in our human concepts, ideas, views, and imaginations about Christ. But now we are firmly, solidly established in
spirit — our new base, our new source, our new center.

Remembrance and God's voice   May 18th

"I thank God, whom I serve with a pure conscience, as my forefathers did, as without ceasing I remember you in my prayers night and day, greatly desiring to see you, remembering your tears, that I may be filled with joy, when I call to remembrance the genuine faith that is in you, which dwelt first in your grandmother Lois and your mother Eunice, and I am persuaded is in you also."
2 TIMOTHY 1:3-5

Paul illustrates in these verses that the Lord's voice speaking to him is in and through his thoughts. It is in the normal avenues and channels of his being. The Lord's speaking to Paul came in the form of his remembrance. The remembrance of Timothy was a call to pray for Timothy. This example out of Paul's life corresponds to God's new covenant way of imparting His laws into our mind and inscribing them upon our heart (Heb. 8:10). When we understand this new covenant way of God's speaking, we must confess that we all have heard more of His voice in our daily life than we realized. For example, God's speaking has come to us many times in the form of desires within us. We may have a desire to go to the church meeting. That very desire within us is God's speaking in the form of an inclination inscribed on our heart.

Also, the Lord's voice often comes in the way of His bringing something to mind. For example, in Matthew 5:23 the Lord says, "Therefore if you bring your gift to the altar, and there *remember* that your brother has something against you . . ." In other words, while you are fellowshipping with the Lord, something comes to mind. You remember your brother. When it comes to mind, that is the Lord speaking to you. Thus, we can see how simple and intimate is the Lord's voice *to* us and *in* us under the new covenant. His speaking is imparted into our mind.

It's the blood!   **May 19th**

"How much more shall the blood of Christ, who through the eternal Spirit offered Himself without spot to God, purge your conscience from dead works to serve the living God?" HEBREWS 9:14

It is the pollution within that turns me in on myself. It is the pollution that makes me feel that I have to do something more. It is the inward contamination that causes a conscience to be uneasy. But how much more shall the blood of Christ cleanse my conscience from all those dead works to serve the living God! This means that there is a contamination in my being whenever I try to work out something religiously before God. But the blood cleanses my conscience from that. Here, it does not say "from sin." It says "from dead works." Because of this cleansing, we have instant, constant access to participate in God Himself.

What blood! It has done a work in the heavens to cleanse the heavens, and it has done a work in my heart to give me a true heart, so that I might be a participator in God Himself. The value of the blood is beyond our comprehension. To God it means so much. To the heavens it is the gathering factor of all the multitudes of saints through the ages. That is why, in the book of Revelation, those who are "out of every tribe and tongue and people and nation" are singing, "It's the blood!"

My grandfather through marriage knew the Lord in a real way. When he was over ninety years old, he became ill and was confined to his bed. At that time, some of the family members wondered if Grandpa was getting a little senile because he kept repeating a phrase — "It's the blood." These words just kept coming out of him — "It's the blood. It's the blood." When I heard that some of the relatives were wondering if Grandpa was losing his keenness of mind, I thought to myself, "No, I think Grandpa has one foot in the glory and one foot on the earth, and he sees that it's the blood. It's the precious blood of Jesus." And, no doubt, when we are in the heavens with that multitude in the festal gathering, we are all going to say, "It's the blood! You have redeemed us to God by Your blood."

An intensive saturation   May 20th

"For you did not receive the spirit of bondage again to fear, but you received a spirit of sonship, in which we cry out, Abba, Father." ROMANS 8:15

When we merge with God and allow Him to flow and pass through us, the first benefit we receive is that He imparts His life into our being. Romans 8:11 says, "But if the Spirit of Him who raised Jesus from the dead dwells in you, He who raised Christ from the dead will also give life to your mortal bodies through His Spirit who dwells in you." This indwelling implies an intensive saturation of the Spirit throughout our being, which results in life being imparted into us. Although prayer has its answer, even if there were no answer, by our allowing the Triune God to pass through us we obtain the greatest benefit — the divine life is imparted into us. When we exercise our spirit to cry "Abba, Father," two things take place in us — the Triune God passes through us, and while passing through, He imparts life into our being.

The second benefit of allowing the Triune God to pass through us is that we get cleansed and purified. James 4:8 says, "Draw near to God and He will draw near to you. Cleanse your hands, you sinners; and purify your hearts, you double-minded." This means that in our drawing near, God Himself draws near to us and begins to pass through us. This has the effect of cleansing and purifying our being. However, we should not think that this is merely an automatic thing that happens without our cooperation. "Cleanse" and "purify" are both in the imperative mood, indicating our responsibility to confess and deal with the Lord as God passes through us in an inward way. As we merge with God flowing in us, our sins are exposed and

142

cleansed, and our double heart is exposed and purified. If you want to get into the Lord's light, just spend time with the Lord and draw near to Him. Your hands will be cleansed and your heart will be purified. This is the effect of allowing the passing-through of the Triune God.

God's opportunity   May 21st

"But Jesus looked at them and said to them, With men this is impossible, but with God all things are possible." MATTHEW 19:26

The highest revelation of the church is to see that the church is Christ (1 Cor. 12:12). This is how the Father sees the church. This is how the apostles saw the church, and this is how we should see the church. The vision of the church as Christ is truly a heavenly vision. This vision reduces us to Christ and becomes the governing factor controlling our daily life. By this vision, we will be escorted to Christ over and over again.

We need to see in the Bible the divine principle of measurement that governs God's relationship with man. God works with fallen man on the basis of this principle. First, He measures man according to His standard. Then this divine measurement becomes a demand upon man. This demand, in turn, reveals man's shortness and failure. Finally, man's realization of his failure is intended by God to escort him to Christ. In other words, the measurement and the subsequent demand of God is for one thing — to lead us to Christ to experience Another life.

God desires to be man's life-supply. The way He fulfills this desire is by first measuring man to expose his shortness. By this measuring He escorts man out of his own resources into God Himself as his boundless supply. Thus, in God's economy the measuring Word of God is always intended to produce a standard beyond man's ability and capacity. Indeed, God's Word with its divine measurement and high demand, which far exceeds man's

143

natural capacity, is the same Word that escorts man to God Himself over and over again. It is this principle that we see governing God's relationship with fallen man, both in the Old Testament under the law and in the New Testament under the higher demand of the law revealed in Matthew 5—7. Indeed, *man's extremity* becomes *God's opportunity.*

The voice of conscience   May 22nd

"This being so, I myself always strive to have a conscience without offense toward God and men." Acts 24:16

Learning to follow the voice of conscience is the proper way for a believer to learn to hear the Lord's life-voice within. This is because our conscience is interrelated with our regenerated spirit (cf. Rom. 9:1 with 8:16). So, if our conscience is not clear, our spirit cannot properly function and be released. This is a crucial principle in our Christian life.

Our conscience may be regarded as the leading function of our spirit. In his own life, Paul maintained the principle of keeping a clear conscience. He testifies in Acts 24:15-16: [15] "I have hope in God, which they themselves also accept, that there will be a resurrection of the dead, both of the just and the unjust. [16] This being so, I myself always strive to have a conscience without offense toward God and men." Paul exercised himself to keep his conscience clear so that his relationship with the Lord would be up to date, and also so that he would be ready for the judgment seat of Christ at the resurrection of the righteous. Thus, it is important to have a relationship with the Lord that is governed by the voice of conscience.

The voice of conscience is God's appointed means for man to learn to be inwardly regulated (Rom. 2:14-15). The conscience approves or disapproves our actions and words (Rom. 13:4-7). The basic lesson of learning to live by the Lord's voice in us is to learn to listen to the voice of our own conscience (cf. 2 Tim. 1:3 with Rom. 1:9). If we do not practice this, how could we discern the requirement of the Lord's life in us? Therefore, in our daily life when the Lord is teaching us to hear His voice, the first lessons we learn are to pay attention to the voice of our own conscience. When we follow the requirement of our conscience by obeying it over matters pertaining to right and wrong, we will be inwardly genuine and exercised to learn the requirement of the Lord's life in other areas related to the intuition of our spirit (2 Cor. 2:12-13).

A life-part of Himself   May 23rd

"And He is the head of the body, the church, who is the beginning, the firstborn from the dead, that in all things He may have the preeminence. For it pleased the Father that in Him all the fullness should dwell." COLOSSIANS 1:18-19

The Body is central in the heart of God because it is the Body of Christ! As the Head, Christ is filling all the members of His Body, the church. Consider Paul's utterances: [22] "And gave Him to be head over all things to the church, [23] which is His body, the fullness of Him who fills all in all" and "He is the head of the body, the church . . . For it pleased the Father that in Him all the fullness should dwell" (Eph. 1:22-23; Col. 1:18-19). In other words, the way the fullness dwells in Christ is directly related to His being the Head of His Body. He has dispensed Himself into our spirit, making us an organic, life-part of Himself. Now the mystery of Christ is revealed, explained, and displayed through all His members. The life flowing from you and the life flowing from me is the life flowing from the Head. He is filling each one of us so that there will be a full, complete expression of how rich our God is.

In this universe there was something hidden in God, and that was His desire to have a Body for His Son. This corporate entity is also

145

described as the Father's house. We are the many abodes in that house, and we are His dwelling place (John 14:2; Eph. 2:22). He desires to live in us, walk in us, and move through us (2 Cor. 6:16). This is God's home. This is what He wanted in this universe — to have all His chosen and redeemed people indwelt with His very life. This was what God had in His heart when He thought about creating an earth. So we can say, "Earth, this is your meaning. Trees, grass, atmosphere, stars, moon, your meaning is for our God to have a dwelling place in man." This is the meaning of the universe — Christ with His Body, the church.

Do not waste your time   May 24th

"Unto an administration of the fullness of the times, to head up all things in Christ, the things in the heavens, and the things upon the earth; in Him." EPHESIANS 1:10 (ASV)

The mystery of Christ has had a gradual unfolding through the ages. It was conceived in eternity past (Eph. 1:4-5), it was produced through Christ's death and resurrection (Eph. 1:19-23; 2:14-16), it has been revealed to the apostles and prophets in spirit (Eph. 3:3-6), it is written in the Scriptures (Rom. 16:25-26), and now it is being made known to all the nations to evoke the response of faith. The phrase "unto an administration of the fullness of the times" means that it is time to have the church life on this earth. Once we see the church, it is time for us to be in the church. When light comes to us concerning the church, that is the time to rise up to have the church life on this earth. Once it is made known to us, that knowledge is *unto* the fullness of the times. In other words, do not waste your time anymore. Do not play with childish things anymore. The revelation of the church ushers in its administration and working out. It is time now! God wants to head up the universe. He wants to head up the heavens and the earth in Christ. This revelation is

146

waiting for "the obedience of faith" (Rom. 16:26, KJV). This means that once the revelation comes to us, that *is* the divine command and call, "Get into the church life." This is why we are human beings — to experience Christ and to assemble on the earth in cities where there is a testimony of Jesus until Christ comes back and sets up His kingdom over the whole earth.

The Head of the household   May 25th

"To be strengthened with might through His Spirit into the inner man, that Christ may dwell in your hearts through faith; that you, being rooted and grounded in love." EPHESIANS 3:16-17

To be strengthened into your inner man is to be strengthened into your spirit (2 Cor. 4:16). When you touch your spirit and experience the strengthening, the purpose of this is that Christ would move into your heart. And He does not take several months to move in. He immediately moves in and occupies every "room" of your heart. So when you are strengthened into your spirit, you begin to handle Christ as the One who has made His home in your heart. As you are in spirit, He is in your whole heart as the "Head of the household." This is *how* He is in us. As the Head He says, "This is My house. Everything about you belongs to Me. I give the orders here. I am doing the talking. I am going to supply. I am going to provide. I am going to do everything here." Let Him make home in your heart.

Christ making home in our hearts is not a gradual process. Paul uses the Greek aorist tense for the infinitive "to make home" or "to dwell." This means it is an instantaneous action. He just comes in and takes up His residence in every part of your heart as the Head of the household. He is doing everything. You refer everything to Him. He is Head of your house. You do not make the decisions there. From now on, He is going to tell you what to do.

147

The growth of God

"And not holding fast to the Head, from whom all the body, nourished and knit together by joints and ligaments, grows with the growth of God." COLOSSIANS 2:19

There is a proper growth and an improper growth in the Christian life. The context of the above verse alludes to an improper growth. The Colossian believers were being robbed of their experience of Christ and the proper growth of God. Paul describes this by saying, "Let no man rob you of your prize" (v. 18, ASV). Do you know what your prize is? Your prize and my prize is Christ Himself. Our prize is our present possession and enjoyment of Christ. Do not let anyone rob you of this. It is not merely that Christ will be our prize in the future. Christ is our prize right now as a present possession. The normal Christian life is that Christ is all to us at every stage of our growth. Nothing should replace Christ in our experience regardless of where we are.

Paul exposes the things that were replacing Christ and robbing the Colossian believers: a false humility, worship of angels, being vainly puffed up by a fleshly mind, and not holding fast to the Head. When Paul says, "and not holding the Head" (KJV), he is telling us that there is a way to grow and a way not to grow. The way not to grow is to be focused on your self, having a relationship with your self, your flesh, your own energy, the law, and man-made religion. That is the way not to grow. Growing comes from holding the Head. "Holding the Head" is in the present tense, which means that you are continuously holding Christ as your Head. Whenever you hold something, you handle it. The Colossian believers did not hold the Head. They were not handling Christ. Handle Christ *before* you handle anything, especially your self.

"Rejoice always, pray without ceasing, in everything give thanks; for this is the will of God in Christ Jesus for you. Do not quench the Spirit." 1 THESSALONIANS 5:16-19

These verses reveal how the Triune God is interwoven with the various ways we contact the Lord. Here we see the Trinity — the Father, the Son, and the Spirit. All Three are related to unceasing prayer, rejoicing, and giving thanks. This shows us that whenever we exercise ourselves in these various ways, we open the way for the Triune God to pass through us. It is by this passing-through of the Triune God that He sanctifies us. He sets us apart and saturates us with Himself. The apostle Paul declares in 1 Thessalonians 5:23, "Now may the God of peace Himself *sanctify* you completely, and may your entire spirit and soul and body be preserved blameless at the coming of our Lord Jesus Christ."

We receive life, we are cleansed, we are purified, and we are sanctified by allowing the Triune God to pass through us! Just let Him pass through. This is the benefit of praying and of spending time with the Lord — we are joined to the flow of the Triune God. When we pray we allow the Triune God to pass through us, to take care of every one of our needs — to impart life, to cleanse us, to purify us, and to sanctify us. This is the vision we need when we spend time with the Lord. Allow God Himself to pass through you. Just say, "Lord, I want You to pass through me now. I open myself to You from the depths of my being that You may flow in me." Stir up your spirit in this way, and the living water will flow (2 Tim. 1:6-7).

God's intentions in us   May 28th

"In whom we have boldness and access with confidence through the faith of Him." EPHESIANS 3:12

How much of God's intentions have passed through us? Do we know what it means to pray, "Lord, Your name be sanctified. Lord, Your kingdom come"? For this kind of prayer we need light and revelation. So we should pray in this way: "Lord, fill me with Your intentions." This is how Paul prayed. In his praying in Ephesians 3:9-11, he opened up the vision that controlled him: 9 "And to make all people see what is the fellowship of the mystery, which from the beginning of the ages has been hidden in God who created all things through Jesus Christ; 10 to the intent that now the manifold wisdom of God might be made known by the church to the principalities and powers in the heavenly places, 11 according to the eternal purpose which He accomplished in Christ Jesus our Lord." In these verses Paul brings to light God's intention in the universe — that which had its beginning in eternity past and will be consummated in eternity future, and which is now being made known to the principalities and the powers in the heavenlies. And what is God's intention? God's eternal purpose and intention is that His manifold wisdom would be made known through the church.

Immediately following the declaration that God's intention was accomplished, or carried out, in Christ Jesus our Lord, Paul says, "In whom." Paul knew exactly where he was. He was in the Second in the Godhead. In whom? Christ Jesus our Lord. He merged with the prayer life of the Triune God. And in this One, Christ Jesus our Lord, he had "boldness and access with confidence through the faith of Him." This means that Paul's boldness and confidence and access to pray issued from God's intentions pulsating in his being!

When Paul spoke in this way — "boldness and access with confidence through the faith of Him" — he was building one word upon another. It was as though he had mounted up to the heavens to command the whole universe to come under God's administration. Here Paul was not engaged in prayer to fulfill his own needs and desires. Although God does answer our personal requests, we need a higher vision so that we can pray with God's needs and intentions in our being. This is the way Paul prayed. He fully merged in his prayer with the eternal intentions of the Triune God.

God's desires   May 29th

"Therefore I exhort first of all that supplications, prayers, intercessions, and giving of thanks be made for all men."
1 TIMOTHY 2:1

Not only do we pray with God's intentions passing through us, but also with His desires passing through us. This is revealed in 1 Timothy 2:3-4: "God our Savior, who desires all men to be saved and to come to the full knowledge of the truth." This means that God's expressed desire is for all men to be saved. So when we pray, we not only touch the larger scale of God's intentions for the church and the kingdom, but we also allow God's desires for all men to pass through us. This includes God's desires for everyone in *your* life — coworkers, neighbors, classmates, the mailman, the checker at the grocery store, the person you met at the bus stop, as well as your family members and relatives. Paul says that first of all there need to be supplications, prayers, intercessions, and thanksgivings made for all men. In spending time with the Lord we can allow God's desires for others to pass through us.

Effectual prayer is made up of desire. For example, we may want to see someone saved. Yet, if in our prayer our own heart is not deeply moved for that one, such a prayer will never move the heart of God. If we ourselves do not possess the desire to see someone saved, how could God's desire ever be released in our prayer? Paul illustrated this principle when he said, "Therefore we

151

are ambassadors for Christ, as though God were pleading *through us: we* beseech you on Christ's behalf, be reconciled to God" (2 Cor. 5:20). This indicates that God's desires are not merely kept within Himself. They need a human channel to pass through. God's desire to see the lost saved must be located within our very being. God's desire must become *our* desire, culminating in our persevering in prayer for them.

An early-rising life   May 30th

"Now in the morning, having risen a long while before daylight, He went out and departed to a solitary place; and there He prayed."
MARK 1:35

It is encouraging to realize that the early-rising life has been received by us with much grace (1 Cor. 15:10). This means that spending time with the Lord by rising early is a matter of depending upon the energizing work of the resurrected Christ within us, and then cooperating with that grace by choosing morning by morning to rise up early to spend time with Him. Watchman Nee's testimony, in his book *A Living Sacrifice*, is very helpful. He says, "Let me quote the words of Miss Groves, a co-worker of Miss M. E. Barber, who has helped us greatly. She stated that the first choice giving evidence of one's love towards the Lord is the choice between one's bed and the Lord. If one chooses to love his bed more, he sleeps longer; but if he chooses to love his Lord more, he will rise up a little earlier. She spoke these words to me in 1921, but I still sense the freshness of them today. Yes, a man has to choose between the bed and the Lord. If you love your bed more, sleep on longer; but if you love the Lord more, you must rise up earlier."

We must accept the fact that the Lord's life within us is stated as being "our life," according to Colossians 3:4. Regardless of how we feel about it, when we received Christ we received an early-rising life (Mark 1:35), a prayer life (Heb. 7:16, 25), a love-life (Gal. 4:6), a fellowshipping life (1 John 1:3), and a feasting-upon-the-Word life (1 Pet. 2:2-3). These are the main features of this life which has now become "our life." If we follow this life every morning by rising a little earlier, we will discover that there is a special capacity early in the morning to enjoy the Lord.

Keep yourselves in the love of God   May 31st

"But you, beloved, building yourselves up on your most holy faith, praying in the Holy Spirit, keep yourselves in the love of God, looking for the mercy of our Lord Jesus Christ unto eternal life."
JUDE 20-21

Things are never as bad as we think they are. It is the devil that tells us all the negative things. He is the accuser of the brethren. He is a liar. He is a destroyer. He is a killer. He is a cheater. He usurps us. God surely does not feel that way about you. We believe lies about ourselves. If we will just pray in the Holy Spirit, open our mouths and call on the Lord, or sing with our hearts, we will discover that God's love *in us* is what is real.

We can keep ourselves in the love of God by praying in the Holy Spirit. The Holy Spirit is within us. The love of God and the grace of Christ will flow in us in the fellowship of the Holy Spirit (2 Cor. 13:14). And that fellowship of the Holy Spirit is ours simply by praying in the Holy Spirit. This is how we keep ourselves in the love of God. Oh, what a love-life! This is an encouragement to everyone. Even if you feel like the most pitiful person, you are a candidate for the dispensing of this love-life. Just let the Lord in. And then keep letting Him in. Pray in the Holy Spirit, and you will discover how you feel about yourself from God's point of view. You will say, "I am really in a wonderful condition! God loves me!"

153

June

A private time in a private place

"But you, when you pray, go into your private room, and when you have shut your door, pray to your Father who is in the secret place; and your Father who sees in secret will reward you openly."
MATTHEW 6:6

Without spending time with the Lord, there is no possibility for us to experience a solid transformation. And this time must be a private time with the Lord. The Lord makes this clear in Matthew 6. Beginning in verse 5 He says, "And when you pray, you shall not be like the hypocrites. For they love to pray standing in the synagogues and on the corners of the streets, that they may be seen by men." The Lord points out here that the Pharisees were hypocrites because the motivation behind their kind of praying was to be seen of men. Then in verse 6 He says, "But you, when you pray, go into your private room." The Greek word for private room can also be translated "inner chamber." The King James Version renders it "closet." All these translations — the private room, the inner chamber, and the closet — signify a personal, private time in a private place.

In the verse above the Lord gives still further detailed instruction. After you go into your private room, "shut your door." Shutting the door is a reinforcement of privacy, of aloneness with the Lord. And then He says, "pray to your Father who is in the secret place." There is a deep significance in having a private time in a private place, and that is, that our transformation would be genuine and not something hypocritical. It should not be a performance. In our private time with the Lord, no one else is there. We open ourself to the Lord deeply, without any pretense, without any hypocrisy, without being motivated by any onlookers. There is no one else there saying anything or knowing anything. This means our Christian life is taken out of the realm of man-pleasing and mere outward behavior, and is brought into the reality of an intimate, personal relationship with the Lord.

My heart is fixed   June 2nd

"My heart is fixed, O God, my heart is fixed; I will sing and give praise." PSALM 57:7

David's testimony in the Old Testament indicates that he had a heart that could remain fixed before the Lord. Like David, we can also fix our heart. When our heart turns to the Lord, the veil is taken away! A turned heart then becomes a fixed heart. As we spend time before Him, with our heart fixed and stationary, He can write His transforming life and nature into us.

To turn our heart means to stop our heart from all its preoccupations, from its endless stream of activity, and fix it on the Lord. Just as Moses brought the tablets of stone up to the mountain and spent time there in God's presence so that God could write on them, we too can turn our heart to the Lord and spend time being written upon by the Spirit of the Living God. When we turn our heart to the Lord, the writing Spirit (2 Cor. 3:3) is activated in us. This turning should not merely be a partial or shallow turn, but a deep turn that opens us up to the Lord and causes us to linger longer with the Lord for the Spirit to do His inner writing. It is this Spirit-writing that transforms us. As the Spirit writes upon us, we are transformed into the same image. And this image is the image of Christ Himself. So let us pay the price in our daily life to spend adequate time with Him. This is our greatest need.

The new covenant operating

"Who also made us sufficient as ministers of the new covenant, not of the letter but of the Spirit; for the letter kills, but the Spirit gives life." 2 CORINTHIANS 3:6

The new covenant is based on the divine operation of the Lord's life in us related to everything in our living. We are enjoying Him — His very life and nature, His soul-life with His thoughts. As we merge with Him, we find that our spontaneous reactions become just Himself. The fruit of the Spirit is love, joy, peace, and long-suffering. This is not something you are trying to be. It is something that has grown and manifested itself because you are dealing with the Spirit. Christ is operating and becoming the very content of the church in every member by our participation in His life — by eating His flesh, drinking His blood, staying before the tree of life. As we participate in Him, He operates. Apparently we are just common, ordinary people. Yet hidden within us is the divine life operating and the church becoming the expression of Christ Himself. This all happens by our participating in this Person.

In the new covenant God says, "I am going to write My laws within you." It is not going to be a ticker tape. It is not going to be something you read outside of you telling you to love the saints and to follow the Lord in your daily life. You are going to have an aversion within you to not touch that unclean thing. You yourself will have an aversion. That aversion is the work of Christ in your mind, in your emotion. Follow that feeling, follow that aversion. Just say "Amen." Just be one with that life, that little feeling of life. It is not a bolt of lightning. It is not going to overwhelm you. It is a little feeling of life. Follow that impulse. That is the new covenant operating in our being. And the more we follow the movement of God within us in our daily living — in our attitudes, in our thoughts — the more we are participating in Him. Then the church is just a Person. You meet a Person. You meet Christ in the saints.

157

"Looking unto Jesus, the author and finisher of our faith, who for the joy that was set before Him endured the cross, despising the shame, and has sat down at the right hand of the throne of God." HEBREWS 12:2

What do we see? What is our vision? What is our revelation? Without vision, there is no proper incentive to apply the cross, and there is no real application of the cross in its full significance. To experience the proper subjective application of the cross, we must be filled with heavenly vision.

To be a person with vision is to be a person under God's economy. It is to be one who lives according to the divine destiny over his whole being. This destiny is that we would be completely conformed to the image of God's Son. Even our bodies will be conformed to the body of His glory. Paul was under this vision of God's economy. We need the clear vision of God's economy over our being to apply the cross. I have to see that my being — my mind, emotion, will, and body — has only one destiny, which is to be saturated and filled with Christ Himself. By this saturating and filling, God becomes my portion.

Because my being has only one destiny — conformity to the image of God's Son — God is causing everything to work together to this end and goal (Rom. 8:28). This is God's economy. So if I am a person who is clear about God's economy, I will readily apply the cross inwardly to anything that challenges that economy, anything of this self that has a controversy with the Lord. This includes the self in any relationship with any person. This includes my private life, my daily living. My stubbornness, my impulsiveness, my mind — anything in my being that opposes God — has to bow. It has to be terminated, because I am under the vision that my being has a destiny to be conformed to the image of God's Son. My god is not my belly (Phil. 3:18-21). My God is God Himself.

A transcendent life

"So then death operates in us, but life in you." 2 CORINTHIANS 4:12

The context of this verse indicates that we need to inwardly coordinate with our environment (vv. 10-11), which means we need to exercise our spirit of faith (v. 13). How does death operate in you? Death operates by your coordinating the inward cross with the outward cross. When does it operate? It operates when you are handed over to someone's long face, and you want to react. But instead of reacting and carrying out your reaction to that long face with self-pity or vindictiveness, you call on the Lord and activate your spirit and do not agree with your kind of reaction. In doing this your focus is immediately shifted from the person who gave you a long face to your reaction to that long face. The fact that you could react in such a way is not Christ. So you are taken immediately out of the realm of right and wrong. You are not on the tree of the knowledge of good and evil. Your focus has shifted. The one thing that matters is that you put to death this self that would indulge itself in pity or hurt feelings. You put to death this thing that is not Christ, this thing that reacts in any other way than by turning the other cheek. This is how transcendent the Lord's life is. This is the life that is to be wrought into our experience. If someone hits you on one cheek, then turn the other cheek to him — not in a coping way, but in a crucified way. Then you are living another kind of life. You are not living just a good life, but a transcendent life (Matt. 5:38-48).

Thus, in the experience of coordinating with our environment, the outward cross must be matched with the inward cross. By this, a little more of the outer man decays, and a little more of the inner man is renewed. This is the proper vision for our daily living.

"For this is the covenant that I will make with the house of Israel after those days, says the LORD: I will put My laws in their mind and write them on their hearts; and I will be their God, and they shall be My people." HEBREWS 8:10

To experience Christ is to touch His willingness and zeal for the Father's house. Christ is in a perpetual state of building that house. He must always be about His Father's business. This is His nature. So whenever willingness surfaces in your heart — willingness calibrated to the church, God's house, His dwelling place — you have met Christ in your mind, emotion, and will. You meet Him as that disposition of willingness surfacing within you. The evidence that He is taking you over and possessing your heart is your feeling of willingness to lay down your life for the saints and for His house. When willingness springs up, you have met Christ. The Lord Jesus is not just a name on a piece of paper. The Lord Jesus is a Person, and He feels like willingness. This is how you know you are touching the real Person and not a mere concept or belief — you find God's disposition springing up within you. Our highest privilege and dignity is to participate in this willingness which is Christ Himself.

Christ works His disposition of willingness into us. He works with the grain of our being, not against the grain. Living the church life described in the New Testament requires willingness. Nothing is forced. Willingness springs up from within us and we pour ourselves out in a spontaneous way to meet the needs. This is because Christ in us is this way.

Willingness for the Lord, willingness for His interest, is not in you and me. This should relieve us. It should relieve the pressure that comes from being in a false position and taking condemnation because we feel unwillingness in us. Of course we are not willing. No one is naturally willing for the church life. This is an impossible life to live. But God has imparted the Impossible Life into our spirit. And now this willingness is being written into our disposition. He is writing His very nature and life into our mind and into our heart. So willingness is ours in the new covenant as we participate in and enjoy Christ.

An atmosphere of freedom   June 7th

"I delight to do Your will, O my God, and Your law is within my heart." PSALM 40:8

The very nature of God's move has nothing to do with the realm of coercing. It has everything to do with a group of people participating in the life of another Person who is absolutely willing — "I delight to do Your will, O My God" (Psa. 40:8; cf. Heb. 10:7). Willingness is not merely what is described in a dictionary — wanting to do something. No, that is the shell. The kernel and life-content of willingness is Christ. Just as all the virtues of the fruit of the Spirit are Christ, so also willingness is Christ. So whenever willingness is in you, you have met Christ in your being. You have met Him in the form of His disposition of willingness. That is His life. It is the nature of His life within us. It is the way He feels.

In the Old Testament, when the tabernacle was being constructed, it was done only by those who had a willing heart. Exodus 35:5 says, "Take from among you an offering to the LORD. Whoever is of a willing heart, let him bring it as an offering to the LORD: gold, silver, and bronze." To offer something to the Lord is not merely an outward act. "Whoever is of a willing heart" reveals the nature of the people's offering and the nature of God's corporate testimony. This is what makes God known on the earth. This is the way He is made known. He is not made known in a forced environment, but in an atmosphere of freedom, an atmosphere where willingness can spring forth. This is because love cannot exist without an atmosphere of freedom. Love freely gives. Love freely goes out. Love freely serves. If you put me under a demand to love by telling me, "You *must* love me" — that does not express an atmosphere of freedom. That expresses the law of Moses: "Thou shalt." It is the law. What expresses God is an atmosphere of freedom, willingness, and love. This atmosphere characterizes our relationships in the church life.

Organic union

"For if we have grown together in the likeness of His death, certainly we also shall be in the likeness of His resurrection." ROMANS 6:5

To help us understand the word "organic," let us read Frederick Godet's commentary on Romans 6:5. He is describing the Greek word *sumphutos* (σύμφυτος), translated as "grown together." Godet says, "This adjective, therefore, denotes the organic union in virtue of which one being shares the life, growth, and phases of existence belonging to another."

Organic union means that one being shares the life of another. This is the nature of the organic union in our spirit. In our spirit we are sharing the life of Another (Rom. 8:10). Our entire being is made up of spirit and soul and body (1 Thess. 5:23). Our spirit is the deepest part of our being, referred to in Ephesians 3:16 as "the inner man." It is in our spirit that the organic union is effected in us. It is Christ Himself, His very resurrected Person, the real Jesus, alive, the One who died, rose, and ascended, who is now transmitted directly into our spirit. Our human spirit is joined to His risen life (Rom. 7:4, 6).

In this spirit-union I am joined to a Person. He is the Person in my person. First Corinthians 15:45 describes the nature of Christ's Person: "The last Adam became a life-giving Spirit." "The last

Adam" means that He is the proper and genuine Man of all men, the proper Person of all persons. In the Gospels the Lord called Himself the Son of Man more than any other title. He is the representative man. He is the real man. He is the real personality. He is the real human being. He is the proper human life. He is the Son of Man.

This Person wants to be our person, so His Personhood became a life-giving Spirit who is now joined to our spirit. Thus, what we are joined to is the life of the last Adam, the perfect Person, who is God's wisdom to us, including righteousness, sanctification, and redemption (1 Cor. 1:30). Now *our* person is Christ living in our spirit. When we speak of the organic union, it means we share the life, the growth, and the phases of existence belonging to Him. In our spirit we are partaking of all that Christ is and has accomplished!

The organic "I" June 9th

"The Lord Jesus Christ be with your spirit. Grace be with you. Amen." 2 TIMOTHY 4:22

We are joined, organically united, to Christ in our spirit (2 Tim. 4:22). This organic union is revealed to us in John 15, where we are the branches connected to the vine, sharing the life of the vine. This means that the righteousness of the vine becomes my righteousness! Everything that the vine is, is for me as a branch to participate in. That is why my righteousness is not a matter of prayer, Bible reading, or what I do or do not do. My righteousness is a matter of the vine and of my being a branch supplied by participating in all the riches of the vine.

Frederick Godet comments on the organic relationship between the branch and the vine in his description of the words "grown together" in Romans 6:5. He says, "It is that the existence, prosperity, and decay of the branch are bound up with the state of the stem." In other words, how is the stem doing? That is the question. It is not about how the branch is doing, because the state of the branch is bound up with the state of the stem. So you ask me, "How are you doing today?" My answer is, "How is *He* doing today?" That is the real issue. My life is joined to this One. My life is a life of participation in His Person. This is the sense and meaning of something organic.

In regeneration we have a new "I," an organic "I," that is joined to the Lord. It is from this union that the Lord is building His church. So His words, "I will build" (Matt. 16:18), become exceedingly practical. The Lord will build, but He is not going to build apart from the organic union in our spirit. The "I" who will build the church is now the resurrected Christ joined to our spirit. It is from this spot that He will build. The building is a habitation of God in spirit (Eph. 2:22).

The inner inclination   June 10th

"For to be carnally minded is death, but to be spiritually minded is life and peace." ROMANS 8:6

To be carnally minded or spiritually minded is to be *inwardly inclined.* Many translations have attempted to capture this thought in different ways. The American Standard Version says, "For the *mind* of the flesh is death; but the *mind* of the Spirit is life and peace." *The Concordant Literal New Testament* translates it, "For the *disposition* of the flesh is death, yet the *disposition* of the spirit is life and peace." *The Emphasized Bible* by Rotherham says, "For *what is preferred by* the flesh is death, whereas *what is preferred by* the spirit is life and peace." All of these translations attempt to capture the depth of the Greek word *phronema* (φρόνημα) used here by Paul.

This New Testament word *phronema*, according to the Greek lexicons, means the *bent or direction of the mind, emotions, and will.* In other words, it refers to the inclination of all the faculties of our inner being. Romans 8:6 tells us that the very source of the bent and inclination toward life and peace is the Spirit. It is the Spirit that produces a Spirit-inclined disposition in us that registers the consciousness of life and peace. In fact, this is one of the major things the Spirit accomplishes in us — inclining our inner being toward the things of God.

The Lord's voice in daily life   June 11th

"Now hope does not disappoint, because the love of God has been poured out in our hearts by the Holy Spirit who was given to us." ROMANS 5:5

When we experience inclinations toward God and the things of God, it causes us to worship Him because we realize that the very thing He is inclining us to do, He Himself does. It is all grace! For example, He wants us to love Him, so He Himself imparts into us the love whereby we can love Him. We discover that the love of God is something poured out in our hearts through the Holy Spirit. Another inclination that we discover is a desire to share Christ with others. We gradually begin to realize that the inclination itself *is* the Lord's voice in us prompting us to preach the gospel. There are also the times when we wake up in the morning with a few words of a hymn or spiritual song. We are then inclined to go to our hymnal to find the rest of the words of that song. When we do, we are face-to-face with God's specific words or speaking to us for that day. How many times have you been inwardly directed to a devotional book, such as *Daily Light*, only to find the word, the line, or the verse that met your need at that moment?

To hear the sweet sound of the Lord's voice in our daily life, we need to look for and follow the Spirit-produced inclinations. Following these inclinations will issue in the sense of life and peace within. Under the new covenant, His speaking does not normally come to us as an audible voice. It comes in the line of a verse, in the words of a song, in fellowship with another member of the Body, in a message we heard from the Word, or in the growing burden we feel in our hearts. As we open ourselves to live out of the source of the Spirit (Rom. 8:4-5), we will increasingly be made aware of our heart's inclinations (Rom. 8:6). It is in those inclinations that we will find the Lord's voice for our daily life.

A constant participation in God   June 12th

"Then Jesus said to them, Most assuredly, I say to you, unless you eat the flesh of the Son of Man and drink His blood, you have no life in you." JOHN 6:53

The Lord Himself became the sacrifice so that now we can drink His blood to have life in ourselves. And what is this life? It is a participation in His very human life. His humanity is especially our portion. He is not only the Son of God but also the Son of Man. As the last Adam, He became a life-giving Spirit. So now in our spirit we can participate in and partake of all of His humanity lived out for 33 1/2 years. That is why there are no excuses. I do not care what your mind says to you. I do not care how you feel. You are no different from me, and I am no different from you. We all have our fallen flesh. We all have those things within us that are ugly. We are all in the same category, but we also all have the same portion to partake of. We simply need to interact with Him, and when we do we are partaking of the substance of His attitudes, thoughts, emotions, and reactions, so that we get life in ourselves. Not only do we get life in our spirit, but we also get life in our thoughts and in our feelings. So when people touch us, they touch Christ. He is on the surface of our being, because we have life in ourselves. He is not just in our spirit, but He is living out of us. This comes from drinking His blood, from participating in Him.

How precious is the blood of Jesus! Of what great value is this blood, because it represents the soul-life. What makes the blood so significant is that it was shed, poured out in death, in propitiation to satisfy the Father, in order that we might be pardoned and made right with God. We see the type of the Lord's blood in the Old Testament. When an animal was sacrificed, the blood was first poured out beside the altar. Then that same blood was picked up by the priest and taken into the holiest of all. There it was presented and sprinkled on the mercy seat. Hebrews 12:24 tells us that the blood of sprinkling speaks better things than that of Abel. This blood is speaking for us right now.

So the heavens themselves have been prepared. Come on in. Talk to God. Fellowship. Open up. Brothers, having boldness by the blood of Jesus, let us draw near. Come boldly to the throne of grace. Despite how you feel, despite your emotions, despite where you are, come forward! Draw near! That is the whole point. That is what the blood cries out. The blood is speaking for us to become a constant participator in God.

Escorted to Christ   June 13th

"Therefore the law was our escort to bring us to Christ, that we might be justified by faith." GALATIANS 3:24

The demand of the law pushes man beyond his capacity. It exhausts him of his own resources. When the law makes its demand upon the flesh, the flesh cannot do it. This failure results in a sense of discouragement within fallen man. He is discouraged because of his inability to measure up to the law of God. Of course, that is precisely what God intends to produce in man. That weak feeling of inability and our discouragement over it become God's way of escorting us to Another life!

The biblical principle of measurement is brought out by the

apostle Paul in Galatians 3:21-24: [21] "Is the law then against the promises of God? Certainly not! For if there had been a law given which could have given life, truly righteousness would have been by the law. [22] But the Scripture has confined all under sin, that the promise out of faith in Jesus Christ might be given to those who believe. [23] But before faith came, we were kept under guard by the law, kept for the faith which would afterward be revealed. [24] Therefore the law was our tutor [Greek: escort, or guide] to bring us to Christ, that we might be justified out of faith." We can see from these verses that the law has become our escort to Christ. The law could not *give* life, but it did *lead* and *escort* us to life.

Many times when we are being measured by the Lord, instead of being escorted to Christ, we are left in our discouragement. We are left with hopeless feelings of not making it and wanting to give up. Thus, it is imperative to see that the demand of the law is the principle of measurement that governs God's dealings with man. This demand is designed by God to produce a certain effect in man — feelings of failure and frustration. It is these very feelings that serve to escort us to Christ. God uses our frustration to lead us to Another source and life that we might learn to become a partaker of Christ, who is our life.

The cross and livingness   June 14th

"For if you live according to the flesh you will die; but if by the Spirit you put to death the practices of the body, you will live." ROMANS 8:13

One thing is guaranteed when you apply the cross in your life — "you will live." You cannot help but live. Everyone that applies the cross is a living saint. You cannot apply the cross and not be living. Resurrection life is spontaneous. When you touch the Lord and by the Spirit interrupt your murmurings, your reasonings

— all the activity of your flesh — you keep your self in death, you keep your flesh in death, and resurrection life bursts forth spontaneously. You come to a church meeting and you have a testimony. You meet someone and you have the gospel. You talk with the saints and there is genuine fellowship. You are just a living person. This is how you can tell if you have applied the cross.

How living are you? If you are dead, if there is no supply, no life, it may be that inwardly you have not cooperated with the cross in your environment, you have not activated your spirit. Or you have allowed unclean thoughts to go by unchecked, undealt with, so that your inward parts are defiled and you are deadened. Thus, the way to know if you have applied the cross is simply by your livingness. You are fresh and living. You are alive with God. This is the way you can tell the cross is operating in you.

Make the Body happy   June 15th

"Therefore if there is any consolation in Christ, if any comfort of love, if any fellowship of the Spirit, if any affection and mercy, fulfill my joy by being like-minded, having the same love, being of one accord, of one mind." PHILIPPIANS 2:1-2

The way you can tell that you have applied the cross is that others are happy with you. You may ask what this means. To fulfill my joy means to make me happy. And how are you going to make me happy? It is by being like-minded, having the same love, being of one accord, of one mind. This kind of oneness in the Body requires the cross.

In Philippians 2:6-8 Paul speaks of the Lord Jesus taking the way of the cross. Then he applies this cross-taking mind to the believers in the verses that follow. He speaks of God operating in us both the willing and the working for His good pleasure. This operation has to do with the inward application of the cross. And the way Paul

169

would know that the saints at Philippi had inwardly applied the cross is that harmony would be among them, the flow of fellowship would be between them. This would make his joy full. This would make him happy.

Sometimes in the church life we have not made the Body happy because we have been so "crossless" in our experience. So the joy in the church is not full. The Body is a barometer. Are we making the Body happy? Are the saints full of joy because of us? When the saints think about us, when the saints consider us, when they see our face, do they get happy, full of joy? This is a good way to tell whether we have applied the cross inwardly — do we make the saints full of joy? Paul was saying, "Make my joy full. Encourage me. Fellowship with me. Bring some consolation to me. Make me happy." Such an atmosphere comes from the inward application of the cross. Make your wife happy. Make your husband happy. Make the brothers happy. How do you do it? By inwardly applying the cross to murmurings, to reasonings, to right and wrong. Get out of the realm of the self and into the spirit. Be constituted with Christ, and the joy in the church will be full.

Occupied exclusively with the Son of God   June 16th

"Who is he who overcomes the world, but he who believes that Jesus is the Son of God?" 1 JOHN 5:5

The main point of this section of the Word is simply that we would be persons confessing that Jesus is the Son of God. This is to acknowledge that He is my life, He is the One who lives. It is His Person that is the object of my attention. I am riveted to Him. I am not something in myself. To say this, is not just a doctrinal confession. It is a deep release of our spirit with a clear focus on Him.

When our spirit is so focused that Jesus is the One — Jesus is the life, we lay our hand on Him — this activates life within us. The factor for life to flood us is our being occupied exclusively not with ourself, but with Jesus, the Son of God. You start your morning with telling Him, "Lord, You are the Son of God. You are the One living today. You are my thought today. You are my feeling. You are my choice. You are my life today." Jesus is the Son of God! It is this continuous fellowship and enjoyment that releases the life and brings forth the testimony, the proper witness, the proper response in our being. When we testify that Jesus is the Son of God, there is a witness within us that this is right. You are on course even when your feelings are on the floor, because you are saying, "Jesus is the Son of God. Lord, You are the Son of God. You are the One living today." Right away the Holy Spirit witnesses within you. You have the witness within yourself that everything is okay, because Jesus is the Son of God.

The category of revelation   June 17th

"By which, when you read, you may understand my knowledge in the mystery of Christ, which in other ages was not made known to the sons of men, as it has now been revealed by the Spirit to His holy apostles and prophets." EPHESIANS 3:4-5

The church is something hidden in God. This shows that the church is not in the category of man's invention, wisdom, or concept. The church is absolutely in the category of mystery. Mysteries in the Bible are not like the ancient Greek mysteries that you could not know. In the biblical sense, a mystery is something that cannot be known apart from God unveiling it, explaining it, revealing it. It is not something that comes up in man's heart (1 Cor. 2:9). It is unknown. We do not know "the mysteries of God" unless God reveals them (1 Cor. 4:1). The church is "the mystery of Christ." Thus, it is in the category of revelation (Eph. 3:3-6). We do not originate it, organize it, name it, or define how it meets. This is not under our jurisdiction. It is God's revelation. We must see that the church is in this category.

When Paul speaks of the mystery of Christ, he is speaking of the Body, a corporate entity. This corporate entity is made up of all kinds of peoples who have been baptized into Him and are parts of Him organically by the indwelling of His life (1 Cor. 12:13). When we as members of Him follow that indwelling life, we become a vital, functioning part of the Body.

Consecration   June 18th

"And those who are of Christ Jesus have crucified the flesh with its passions and desires." GALATIANS 5:24

The phrase "those who are *of* Christ Jesus" implies ownership. We belong to the Lord. Ownership, in turn, implies consecration. We consecrate our being without reservation. One day we say, "Lord, every single member belongs to You. My eyes belong to You, my ears belong to You, my hands belong to You, my feet belong to You, my mind belongs to You, my emotions belong to You. Lord, I present myself."

We have been purchased by the blood. Now, based upon that purchase, the Lord legally owns us. But He still does not force us. He waits for our consent. He waits for us to come to a point of seeing God's economy in our lives — that we are to be filled with Christ. For this economy to be effective in us requires our consent for God to take us over. This is consecration. It is a handing over of our whole being for Him to have the freedom to supply us, energize us, and so operate in us that all our members would be willingly and exclusively presented to Him for His full occupation of our hearts.

Consecration means that we have no more rights, no more choices. It means that we are devoted and consecrated for the one purpose of conformity. It implies the pathway of the cross — the

172

termination of the self, the flesh, and all that comes out of our self. This is consecration. A consecrated person inwardly applies the cross. But often we lose the freshness of our consecration. We may have consecrated to the Lord years ago, but what about today? Maybe we have backslidden from our consecration. We may have taken back our eyes so that we look at what we want to look at. We may have taken back our ears so that now we listen to what we want to listen to. But this is not the case with those Paul describes in this verse. "Those who are of Christ Jesus" belong to Him, are consecrated to Him, and "have crucified the flesh."

Murmurings and reasonings   June 19th

"Do all things without murmurings and reasonings."
PHILIPPIANS 2:14 (ASV)

To live a life inwardly applying the cross, do not rebel against God. You say, "What do you mean, do not rebel? I am not rebelling." Every murmuring is a rebellion, and every reasoning is a rebellion. Murmuring and reasoning are two words that describe how we rebel against God and against the cross. Paul uses these words in the context of talking about the inward application of the cross. In Philippians 2:6-8 the Lord Jesus is presented as the pattern of one who did not rebel against God. He emptied Himself, He humbled Himself, and became obedient unto death, even the death of the cross.

Then Paul applies this pattern to the believers in verses 12-14: [12] "Therefore, my beloved, as you have always obeyed, not as in my presence only, but now much more in my absence, work out your own salvation with fear and trembling; [13] for it is God who operates in you both the willing and the working for His good pleasure. [14] Do all things without murmurings and reasonings." This is the cross — to do all things without murmurings and without reasonings. This is how to inwardly apply the cross. Once I murmur or reason with the Lord's environmental dealing with me, I nullify the cross inwardly. This is why Paul gives us a most practical handle on how to apply the cross subjectively. Simply do not murmur and do not reason, because these are the two things that manifest rebellion to God and to His arrangement.

God's ways with us   June 20th

"Now when they came to Marah, they could not drink the waters of Marah, for they were bitter. Therefore the name of it was called Marah." EXODUS 15:23

Consider the experience of the children of Israel in the wilderness. God arranged everything. He brought them to Marah, where there was bitter water (Exo. 15:23). That means God's ways came in. God showed His *acts* to the children of Israel, but His *ways* to Moses (Psa. 103:7). Moses knew God's ways. God's ways with me are how He treats me. He treats me with my spouse. He treats me with my children. He treats me with in-laws. He treats me with a family. This is how God has treated me. These are God's ways in my life. For me to murmur when God is treating me a certain way is an outright rebellion against God and His ways with me. To do or say things expressing my dissatisfaction, expressing what I do not like, is murmuring. Murmuring is just expressing my complaint, maybe even under my breath. Speaking in this way is rebellion. We have to realize that every murmur is a rebellion and also an escape from the cross.

Reasoning is intellectual rebellion, the rebellion in our mind. God does not give reasons. God just does what He wants to. In the book of Job, Job eventually saw that God is God, and He does what He wants to do in the way He wants to do it, and there is nothing to

174

say. So when we begin to reason and question why an environment is happening, why something is the way it is, that is rebellion in our mind toward the Lord. We have to see that to live a life inwardly applying the cross, you just do not rebel. To not rebel means to do everything without murmuring and without reasoning. You lose *your* speaking, you lose *your* reasoning mind, and you are left with your spirit. Praise the Lord! By applying the cross, you are left with your spirit to enjoy God and to be renewed in the spirit of your mind.

Transferred   June 21st

"If you endure chastening, God deals with you as with sons; for what son is there whom a father does not chasten?" HEBREWS 12:7

It is important as a believer to see the goal of God's dealings in our life. God does not leave us to ourselves. He deals with us. The basic dealing for all God's sons is the dealing of the cross. What does God want to accomplish in us as we pass through the dealings of the cross? What goal does He have in view? The unique goal is that we would have a transfer of our source, that is, that we would be transferred from the realm of living in our soul to living in our spirit. This transfer means that subjectively we start living from a different source, or place. We relate to ourselves from a different place. We listen and hear others from a different place. We hear and read the Bible from a different place. Instead of coming from the source of our self, we come from the source of our regenerated spirit. Having this subjective transfer from our soul to our spirit is the goal of all dealings with the self. The outward cross in our environment always aims at practically terminating the self in order to effect a progressive transfer of our source from soul to spirit.

175

"That which is born of the flesh is flesh, and that which is born of the Spirit is spirit." JOHN 3:6

When we are born again, a new source is established within our being. The verse above reveals that there are two sources for our being, two places we can "come from" in the way we interact with things. We can come from the flesh, or we can come from the spirit. The flesh is the living out of our fallen self. In fact, if you drop the "h" in the word "flesh" and reverse the order of the letters, you have the word SELF. Both of these words, the flesh and the self, refer to another source for man's being other than the spirit.

The two sources that man can live by are revealed at the beginning of the Bible. In Genesis 2:8-9 God put man in a garden in front of two trees: the tree of life and the tree of the knowledge of good and evil. These two trees show that man can live by one of two sources. The tree of life represents dependence upon God in the realm of the spirit. To live by the tree of life is to live by God as our source. It is to take God Himself as our life, living in fellowship with Him and relying upon Him moment by moment. It is a life of believing and trusting in the Lord. It is a life of learning to draw from God as our supply and then following the impulses of that supply. It is a life that can be described as "living out of God." It is a life of not making our own decisions anymore or leaning on our own understanding (Prov. 3:5-6). It is a life of filtering everything through the divine life. It is a life of not making a move or doing anything apart from compatibility with our inner sense of abiding in the Lord. It is a life in which we can do nothing apart from Him (John 15:5).

A new base   June 23rd

*"And He died for all, that those who live should live no longer
to themselves, but to Him who died for them and rose again."*
2 CORINTHIANS 5:15

One of the main reasons that Christ died on the cross was to give
us a new base of operation in our spirit, that we would no longer
live to ourselves. Thus, the practical issue of the cross in our lives
is that we no longer live to ourselves but to Him. This means we have
a new center, a new point of reference, a new base from which we
operate, a new source from which we draw our resources. In
Galatians 2:20 our new base of operation is described: "It is no
longer I who live, but Christ lives in me." Our base of operation is
no longer our self. The cross has freed us from ever again having to
take the self as the source from which we live. Now we can deal with
everything *from* the Lord, *in* the Lord, and *with* the Lord.

We have to worship the Lord for coming to us by His mighty
hand in our environment, through the members of the Body, and
through the supply from the Word — all of which are to deal with our
self to effect a transfer of source. This transfer to a new base of
operation means that we no longer operate out of the self. When the
self is denied, we are a person enjoying the Lord as our source. This
denying of self is not the practice of asceticism; rather, it issues from
our enjoyment of Christ as the Spirit in our spirit. By the Spirit we
are putting to death all the practices of the body (Rom. 8:13). In this
way we are operating out of a new base. However, the less we allow
the Lord to deal with our self, the more we will crowd Christ out, not
allowing Him to be our source and center from which we handle
everything. If the self is not denied, we are just little "gods," doing
our own thing and operating our own lives. Our base of operation
and understanding is just the self. Thus, we can see that the goal of
dealing with the self is to effect a subjective transfer of source, giving
us a new base of operation.

The embodiment of love   June 24th

"And suddenly a voice came from heaven, saying, This is My beloved Son, in whom I am well pleased." MATTHEW 3:17

The word "beloved" in the New Testament always refers to the object of another's love. Thus, in this verse from Matthew, "beloved" refers to Christ as the object of the Father's love. Likewise, when we are called "beloved," it is actually an identification of us as individual objects of the love of God. We are the loved ones. We are the beloved.

Our affectionate relationship as the bride to the Bridegroom is embodied in Christ! So do not bother looking at *your* love. Look at the *embodiment of love* — look at Jesus! We need a kind of blessed detachment. Forget completely about yourself and your condition. Do not look at yourself or think about whether *you* have any potential in yourself to love the Lord affectionately as your first love. Forget about yourself altogether. What you have to see is that the unique embodiment of this love-life is in the Son. The foremost thing we need to see is that the love-life of the bride is entirely concentrated and embodied in the Son.

The Beloved   June 25th

"To the praise of the glory of His grace, with which He graced us in the Beloved." EPHESIANS 1:6

In the Gospels the word "beloved" is used mainly as an adjective. But here "Beloved" is not an adjective, but a participle (a verbal adjective). A participle is an action word, indicating that something is happening. This participle is in the perfect tense, describing a present state that is going on. Actually, it describes something that began to exist in the past, that exists in the present, and that will continue to exist in the future. Thus, when Ephesians 1:6 declares

178

that we have been "graced in *the Beloved,*" it refers to Christ in a state of actively being loved by the Father. In other words, this love is not a static kind of love, motionless, or unmoving. It is dynamic. It is constant. It is going on all the time. It never ceases. It is a radiating love that is in the Father all the time, just beaming out. When Paul says that we are graced in *"the Beloved,"* he is speaking of Christ as the present, living concentration and embodiment of the divine love. He is describing Him as continuously and perpetually being the object of the Father's love. There is a love-flow going on all the time between the Father and the Son, and we have been escorted by grace into this flow.

Conceived and produced   June 26th

"Having abolished in His flesh the enmity, that is, the law of commandments contained in ordinances, so as to create in Himself one new man from the two, thus making peace." EPHESIANS 2:15

After we see how the mystery of the one Body of Christ was *conceived* in eternity past, then we need to see how it was *produced.* In the first part of Ephesians 1, we see its conception. In the last part of chapter 1 and in chapter 2, we see how this mystery was actually produced. Ephesians 2:13-16 says, [13] "But now in Christ Jesus you who once were far off have been made near by the blood of Christ. [14] For He Himself is our peace, who has made both one, and has broken down the middle wall of partition, the enmity, [15] abolishing in His flesh the law of commandments contained in ordinances, so as to create in Himself one new man from the two, thus making peace, [16] and that He might reconcile them both to God in one body through the cross, thereby putting to death the enmity."

According to these verses, the mystery was produced by God through the death of Christ on the cross. When the Lord Jesus was on the cross, not only were *our sins* laid upon Him, but also *our divisions.* The *division* of humanity was abolished. Not only do I have the enjoyment of being freed and pardoned from all sin, but I am also freed from all the ordinances that divided us. The factors that have separated us and kept us in such individualistic ways were abolished on Calvary. When He died, He terminated not only sin, sins, the flesh, and the old man, but also our race, our national distinctions, our background, the old creation, and everything that separates man. He recreated us all in Himself, producing the new man, where He now is all and in all. That is what He did on Calvary! Division is over. It is gone forever. Calvary says so. This one Body was produced by the process of Christ's all-inclusive death and resurrection.

Watch the resurrection   June 27th

"And what is the exceeding greatness of His power toward us who believe, according to the working of His mighty power which He operated in Christ." EPHESIANS 1:19-20

On one hand, through Christ's death we see how our relationships in the old creation were terminated; on the other hand, through His resurrection we see how our relationships were recreated in Him to make us His one Body. In Ephesians 1 Paul describes how this one Body was produced in resurrection. He is praying for the saints to see something related to the resurrection. Watch the resurrection. Look at its process. Look at what is happening in this resurrection. Verses 20-21 say, [20] "and seated Him at His right hand in the heavenly places, [21] far above all principality and power and might and dominion, and every name that is named, not only in this age but also in that which is to come." Keep watching the resurrection. Verses 22-23 say, [22] "and He put all things under His feet, and gave Him to be head over all things to the church, [23] which is His body, the fullness of the One who fills all in all."

By considering these verses, we see clearly that the one Body, the mystery of Christ, was produced through death and resurrection. When Paul speaks of the resurrection, you have to follow it all the way out of the tomb, into the heavens, to the throne, to the descending of Christ as the Head into all the members, and to His baptizing us as an organic part of Himself to make us His Body. Now there is a Body of Christ. Christ has a fullness. Look at the church. Look at the saints. Look at their lives. Look at the expression of the Head in His members. That is Christ in His enlargement. That is Christ living, filling, flowing, expressing Himself. He is the One who is now filling all in all. This one Body was not only conceived in God's heart, but through Christ's death and resurrection it was produced.

Losing everything   June 28th

"But what things were gain to me, these I have counted loss for Christ." PHILIPPIANS 3:7

The single most important factor in the subjective application of the cross is vision. The question in all our trials is, What do we see? When you are tempted to talk back to someone in a way that would give vent to your flesh, what do you see in those moments? When you would like to strike out at someone — to either vindicate yourself or to say something in a cutting way — what do you see? What is your vision then? If our vision is on an earthly level, we will exchange words with others and live out the self. There will be no application of the cross to interrupt what we feel, to not carry out what begins to boil within us. So without vision we are a person who does not execute the cross from our spirit over our self in that kind of situation.

Many of our problems are solved very simply if we have vision, if we see that the meaning of everything is Christ, this Person gained by us subjectively. And the way we gain Him is by losing everything

181

— losing our opinion, losing our heated reaction. Not gaining it, but losing it. We lose our reaction by dropping it, by interrupting it. We are not suffering through it, but we are letting it be terminated. Just terminate it, gaining Christ in that moment. This must be our vision. If we are under this vision, everything is clear. You are clear about your marriage. You are clear about your job. You are clear about your problems. Because the Lord Himself had this vision before Him, He endured the cross. We have the same vision set before us, so in like manner we apply the cross in every situation.

Stimulate your spirit   June 29th

"For as many as are led by the Spirit of God, these are sons of God." ROMANS 8:14

The way to live a life inwardly applying the cross is by stimulating your spirit. This is the way to renew the vision of your sonship continuously in order to execute the cross over your self. This is exactly what Paul is saying in Romans 8. Let us consider verses 13-15 together, looking first at their structure. Verse 13 is the result of verse 14. That is, the putting to death of the practices of our body is the result of the leading of the Spirit. Verses 14-17 actually reveal to us what precedes the putting to death in verse 13. Paul says in verses 14-15, [14] "For as many as are led by the Spirit of God, these are sons of God. [15] For you did not receive the spirit of bondage again to fear, but you received a spirit of sonship in which we cry out, Abba, Father." In our experience verse 15 brings in verse 13. Verse 15 is the stimulation of our spirit by crying, "Abba, Father." You just consider — we have received a spirit of sonship in which we cry, "Abba, Father." And when we do something with our spirit, immediately "the Spirit Himself bears witness with our spirit that we are children of God" (v. 16).

By the stimulation of your spirit you freshly renew the vision of

182

who you are. Because this is a continuous experience, Paul uses present-tense verbs to describe it. We are *crying* "Abba, Father," and the Spirit Himself is *witnessing* with our spirit (vv. 15-16). Notice, the witness is that we are the children of God. And then in verse 17 Paul quickly adds, "And if children, then heirs — heirs of God and joint heirs with Christ, if indeed we suffer with Him, that we may also be glorified with Him." This is vision coming to you instantly when you stimulate your spirit. And it is vision with a consciousness — "What am I doing here arguing? What am I doing vindicating myself? What am I doing living out this flesh again? What am I doing here? O Lord Jesus! Abba, Father!" You begin to activate your spirit and get out of your reasoning mind and your fickle emotions. As you cry "Abba! Father!" out of that crying comes the sensation that you are a child of God. Then from that initial sensation comes a deeper sensation that you are an heir of God and a joint heir with Christ. The vision of God's economy over your life rises within you simply by stimulating your spirit to have contact with God.

Rising early   June 30th

"The Lord God has given Me the tongue of the learned, that I should know how to speak a word in season to him who is weary. He awakens Me morning by morning, He awakens My ear to hear as the learned." Isaiah 50:4

In spending time with the Lord, it is important to observe how the Lord practiced rising up early in the morning to be alone with the Father. In considering this we must read Mark 1:35: "Now in the morning, having risen a long while before daylight, He went out and departed to a solitary place, and there He was praying." The context of this verse indicates that at this particular time the Lord's responsibilities and ministry demands were quite heavy. Even His living situation was somewhat inconvenient. The night before, He had ministered to virtually the entire city after the sun had gone down (Mark 1:32-34). He was under the pressure of caring for others' needs and sicknesses. There was also the presence of demonic activity in the ones coming to Him. Besides this, He was not in His own home where He could have more easily found a private place to pray. Yet, despite His environment and unsettled circumstances, He rose up very early to spend time with the Father in prayer.

The Lord's earthly example of rising early to make time to be with the Father despite His full schedule should help us to discern the still small voice in our spirit. That voice, morning by morning, calls us to rise up and spend time with the Lord. That voice is the same life that in the Gospels practiced early rising to fellowship with the Father. Now that life is in our spirit still needing to spend time with the Father. The Lord was so definite concerning His time with the Father early in the morning. We also need to be definite in this matter if we want to be persons who satisfy the inner requirement of the Lord's life in us.

July

"But by the grace of God I am what I am, and His grace which was toward me was not in vain; but I labored more abundantly than they all, yet not I, but the grace of God which was with me."
1 CORINTHIANS 15:10

God's eternal goal over our lives is to transform us into the image of His Son. This goal is accomplished by spending time beholding the glory of the Lord (2 Cor. 3:18). The secret of learning how to behold His glory is simply discovering that we can take the initiative to do it. The Lord's desire to do His work of transformation over us is an ever present fact of His heavenly ministry (Heb. 7:24-25). Nevertheless, He still waits for us to draw near to behold Him in order to accomplish this work.

Taking the initiative does not mean that we are initiating something from nothing. In spiritual things, taking the initiative means we do something with a preexisting condition. Every Christian has this preexisting condition. It is *Christ in you* (Col. 1:27). Thus, Christ is the underlying factor of all your spiritual desires.

Take the initiative everyday. Go along with that little feeling within you. It may seem like it is merely you. But when you identify that feeling by the Word of God, you discover that it is not you. It is God operating in you. Yet neither can you say that it is not you, because the desire is *your* desire. Thus, we can say that it is a mingled desire issuing from the divine life operating within our human life. The apostle Paul expressed this principle in the verse above. He admits that he labored, yet in reflecting on his own statement, he has to equally say, "yet not I, but the grace of God which was with me." Taking the initiative means cooperating with God's operation. Cooperate with the desire, and He will transform you.

185

Repentance is a gift

"When they heard these things they became silent; and they glorified God, saying, Then God has also granted to the Gentiles repentance to life." ACTS 11:18

Repentance is a gift. You do not work it up. Repentance is given to us (Ezek. 36:25-31). The fact that I could weep and repent and confess — that is a gift of God. It is not of us. The whole thing is Him, from beginning to end. You draw near to God and He will draw near to you. Then you see your dirty hands, and you see your heart — your motivation and how you manipulate people. You see the duplicity in your heart. You see how thoroughly corrupt you are. And all the time you see that, you say, "Lord, I still love You." And when you are saying this, He is diffusing His life into your heart. He is changing you. He says, "I will take the heart of stone out of your flesh" (Ezek. 36:26). It is as though He is saying, "You cannot do it. I will take it away. I will give you a new heart. I will give you a heart of flesh. And you will walk in My statutes. You will do it, because I am going to do it in you."

We once met a sister who was worn out as a believer, and was ready to give up the Christian life. She was forlorn and disappointed, and did not know which way to turn. We opened to Ezekiel 36. She sat there, her face sad because she realized the condition of her heart, but had no way to handle it. Then we looked at these words: "I will give you a new heart and put a new spirit within you; I will take away the stony heart out of your flesh . . ." Her eyes filled with tears. God was going to do it! She had never seen this before, that He would actually take away the stony heart. She began to weep for joy to see that it was God's work — God was going to do it all.

"For He made Him who knew no sin to be sin for us, that we might become the righteousness of God in Him." 2 CORINTHIANS 5:21

Notice the phrase "in Him." This means that our becoming the righteousness of God is in a sphere — in Him. To be in Him is to be in an organic union with Him. By virtue of this organic union, we have become (Gk. aorist tense) the righteousness of God. In this verse we can see our new, organic "I," joined to the Person of Christ. He is now our person, our righteousness, our standing, our foundation, our supply, our reactions, our thought-life, our feelings, our choices. Christ is *our* life!

I can participate constantly in all that belongs to this One because I am in an organic union with Him. I am joined to Him. And there is a great fact in this union — He was made sin once and for all on the cross for us. Second Corinthians 5:21 reveals that He did not know sin, but that He was made sin on our behalf. So the total sin problem, including my sinful acts in the plural and indwelling sin in the singular, was borne by Him on the cross. He bore the penalty and the judgment for it once and for all. Sin and sins all fell on Him (Isa. 53:4-6). Now, for every man, the cross of Christ and the blood of Christ solve the entire realm of the sin problem. He bore the sin, He was made sin, and consequently He has all the sin.

The fact that He was made sin (aorist tense) is part of the double transfer in 2 Corinthians 5:21. Our sin was transferred to Him, and He took the judicial judgment for it and paid the price for it with condemnation, judgment, and death. He received the sentence for sin. It was paid for, once and for all. He has the sin, that we might become the righteousness of God *in union with* Him. Now in this new "I," in union with Him, we have become the righteousness of God.

"I do not set aside the grace of God; for if righteousness comes through the law, then Christ died in vain." GALATIANS 2:21

Christ being made sin and we becoming the righteousness of God in Him is a showpiece to the universe of God's righteousness in reconciling us to Himself. We are like a trophy case. He is displaying to the universe how He has taken us fallen, ungodly sinners, and how He has righteously handled us by placing all our sin on His Son. He bore all our iniquities (Isa. 53:11). The Father was satisfied with the death of His Son and what He did on the cross. Isaiah 53:11 says, "He [the Father] shall see the travail of His soul, and be satisfied. By His knowledge My righteous Servant shall justify many, for He shall bear their iniquities." Being justified means that righteousness was transferred to us. Righteousness does not come by the law; otherwise Christ died in vain (Gal. 2:21).

The cross did two things that will forever change our relationship with God and our relationship with ourselves: sin was transferred to Jesus (He has the sin); righteousness was transferred to us (we have the righteousness). The cross is made null and void if there is one person on this earth that can somehow make it on his own. If that could happen with even one person, then Jesus did not need to die on the cross. But Calvary sends out one clear message to all mankind: righteousness is not by the law; it is imputed to us by the righteousness of God demonstrated on the cross, where He took our sin and we became His righteousness. Calvary reveals a double transfer. In our experience this transfer means "He has the sin and I have the righteousness." Hallelujah! This is now the truth and reality in our spirit — He has the sin and I have the righteousness.

"For if by the one man's offense death reigned through the one, much more those who receive abundance of grace and of the gift of righteousness will reign in life through the One, Jesus Christ."
ROMANS 5:17

Sin is a devious thing in us that Paul personifies in Romans chapter 7. Sin takes on all the characteristics of a person: it is crouching and seizing an opportunity to attack (7:8); it can deceive (7:11); it dwells (7:17); it can kill (7:11). This is the way sin is described in Romans 7. It is to this realm of sin that subjective condemnation comes. Whenever we identify with the realm of sin, whenever we own it and say, "Yes, that is right, I am feeling this way," then the law of God immediately comes in. When the law is allowed to come in and speak to the reaction of sin in our flesh, at that moment we die with a torrent of condemnation. But now that the organic union has been established in our spirit, when the enemy comes and sin shows up and knocks on our door, we have to declare, "He has the sin and I have the righteousness!" He has the sin! He bore it! He took it! He paid for it! I do not have it anymore! I have the righteousness! The righteousness that I have is the righteousness that flows directly from Calvary, where Christ's blood was spilt and shed for me. So in this organic union there is a glorious experiential reality that we can confess again and again. He was made sin on our behalf that we might become the righteousness of God in Him — in union with Him, in fellowship with Him.

Whenever the enemy comes to accuse us, we need to say, "Satan, the moment you touch sin in my flesh, you touch what God condemned at the cross. You are touching what Jesus has borne away. So you must talk to Him, not me. My Jesus has my sin and I have His righteousness." Oh, brothers and sisters, we have to see that we have a new, organic "I." In this organic "I," our spirit is life because of righteousness. And we must be clear about whose righteousness this is. It is not mine, it is His. It is that imputed righteousness given as a gift. It is the kind that is given not on the basis of works, but on the basis of grace. You do not work for this kind of righteousness. It is the kind that you receive and rejoice in (Rom. 5:17).

The church and daily life   July 6th

"But put on the Lord Jesus Christ, and make no provision for the flesh, to fulfill its lusts." ROMANS 13:14

To be a member who is enjoying the Body life with all the other members is dependent on our daily life of following the Lord. The lesson in Romans 13 is that our daily life will affect the kind of church life we have. If we tell lies, cheat on our taxes, and are disrespectful and unruly toward authority, we could never know the church life in an organic way. To live in a fleshly way in any area of our life will cause us to be an insubordinate person who has no regard for spiritual authority and relationships in the Body.

We are not living one way at work and another way in the meetings of the church. No. When we throw off the works of darkness and put on the Lord Jesus Christ, making no provision for the flesh, this ushers us into an unfeigned church life that is full of Christ. Our daily living of Christ is a common factor between us all that prepares us for the building up in the church. Then, when we come to the practical church life, our capacity to receive the saints and keep the organic reality of the kingdom in our relationships is directly related to how much we have experienced Christ in our attitude toward people at work, in paying our taxes, and in dealing with fleshly habits (Rom. 14). How we have interacted with Christ in our daily life determines how we will interact with Him in the Body life. This is the significance of Romans 13 — that we would experience Christ in all the areas of our daily life. Our experiences of Christ are carried directly over into our thoughts, views, and concepts in the church life.

Vision affects morals   July 7th

"By faith he forsook Egypt, not fearing the wrath of the king; for he endured as seeing Him who is invisible." Hebrews 11:27

This verse clearly reveals that Moses was under a controlling vision. It was that vision and sight that enabled him to break the hold that the world had upon him. Oftentimes we struggle with sin, the world, the flesh, and the devil. We become depressed over ourselves. We read books on how to be delivered and how to overcome. The answers we seek, or the ones presented to us by various ministries, are many times like band-aids that only give superficial help. What we really need is one big healing dose of vision that will infuse us with power to experience the Lord in our lives. We need to have our eyes opened to see *why* God made us, and *what* our purpose is on the earth!

Paul applied this principle of vision to the Corinthians in dealing with their fornication. In 1 Corinthians 6:19 he says, "Or do you not know that your body is the temple of the Holy Spirit who is in you, whom you have from God, and you are not your own?" In other words, he is saying, "Don't you know? Don't you have vision concerning yourself? Haven't you seen who you really are? Instead of wasting your life in fornication, consider the revelation God gives concerning your body — Your body is the temple of the Holy Spirit."

Paul's way of handling this problem was not merely to apply a band-aid to it or to condemn the behavior in itself. He wanted to bring the believers up to a higher level of living. Rather than superficially dealing with the problem, he wanted them to have vision about their bodies. He knew that vision would not only cause them to break the chains of an immoral life, but it would lift them to a new plateau of Christian life. Vision makes a difference in how we relate to sin, the flesh, and the world. In effect, vision controls us.

The ability of vision   July 8th

"But recall the former days in which, after you were illuminated, you endured a great struggle with sufferings." HEBREWS 10:32

In 1989 there was an earthquake in the San Francisco area during a World Series baseball game. The 75,000 people in the stadium felt the shaking of the earthquake. This had an immediate effect upon their excited feelings about the game. The earthquake had the ability to automatically cause the fans and many of the baseball players to lose their sense of value for a baseball game. Seemingly, nothing could subdue the excitement of a World Series game; but the earthquake had the ability to do it. It had the effect of causing baseball not to seem so important after all. That is what vision does. It has an automatic ability to quickly sort out what is important in our lives in contrast to the fleeting and passing lusts of the world. Vision brings with it an infused ability that directs and controls our daily life and carries us through all our trials and problems.

We may be struggling in our Christian life, going through many cycles of victory and defeat. We are trying to live a crucified life, trying to overcome a besetting sin, trying to get deliverance from the power of lust that defeats us again and again. We endeavor, but to no avail. What is the problem? Why this endless string of defeats? It is because we are lacking a dimension in our lives that God intended every believer to have. That dimension is vision. We need vision!

Vision gives us the ability to drop so many things, and it brings victory where there was no victory. Our problems are often due to having no vision. We do not have revelation. Nothing has attracted us. Nothing has caused us to drop things. It seems that nothing has the ability to effectively win our hearts and produce absolute consecration. However, when you see something that attracts you, that thing or object has an ability and a power in it to control and direct you. Vision in the Christian life will bring us through the hard times. It will bring us through disappointments and all kinds of difficulties. It has an ability.

Failure   July 9th

"And you shall remember that the LORD your God led you all the way these forty years in the wilderness, to humble you and test you, to know what was in your heart, whether you would keep His commandments or not." DEUTERONOMY 8:2

To know the self is part of knowing the Lord. If we do not know the self, we cannot adequately know the Lord. And when we adequately know the Lord, we know ourself — we know that we are untrustworthy and that there is nothing good in us. So experientially, the more we get to know the Lord, the more we know ourself in God's light (Psa. 36:9).

The Lord humbled the children of Israel and tested them. Their being humbled came about through many testings and failures. It was not that the Lord needed to learn more about them, or get to know them; but they needed to get to know themselves. It was the same with Peter in the Gospels. Obviously, he was a person full of self-confidence, because he had so many opinions. So the Lord allowed him to fail the most.

We may express our opinion, living it out toward our husband or wife, or toward the brothers and sisters. We are so strong. We feel that we are so right. We are convinced that the other person is wrong and we are right. But then in some area of our personal life, we sin. We live in the flesh. We fail. But we may not connect our opinion with our failure. Yet this failure is intended to cause us to open ourself to the Lord and to tell Him, "Lord, I do not know anything. I cannot do anything. I just open to you, Lord, to cast down not only the sin, but all of my opinion." Through dealing with failures in this way, we are brought more and more to the place of having no confidence in ourself but in the Lord Himself.

Love in His loving

"And because you are sons, God has sent forth the Spirit of His Son into your hearts, crying out, Abba, Father!" GALATIANS 4:6

The love of God is now in the Holy Spirit. It is concentrated there. This love is being dispensed into us, poured out in us, through the Holy Spirit. So when we speak about the love-life of the bride, we are not speaking about natural energy that tries to work up a love for God. We are talking about relaxing and resting in a poured-out love that already exists in our spirits and hearts. All we have to do is give voice to it. Just give voice to it a little bit. Echo it. Praise in His praising! Sing in His singing! Love in His loving!

To have the Spirit of the Son in our hearts *crying out*, "Abba, Father" seems somewhat objective. It seems that we need to put a stethoscope up to our heart and listen for an "Abba, Father." But when Romans 8:15 says, "You have received a spirit of sonship in which we cry out, Abba! Father!" (NASV), it becomes subjective in our experience. Who is crying "Abba, Father"? The Son in our hearts or we in our spirits? By putting Galatians 4:6 together with Romans 8:15, we can see that there is one crying and also one loving. He cries in our crying, He loves in our loving. In our crying, it is Him. In our loving, it is Him. It is Him crying, loving, worshipping,

194

and saying "Abba." By this we see that there is one love, and this one marvelous love poured out in our hearts is what we are giving voice to.

"The what" July 11th

"Likewise the Spirit also helps in our weaknesses. For we do not know the what we should pray for as we ought, but the Spirit Himself makes intercession for us with groanings which cannot be uttered." ROMANS 8:26

God has unique designs with every one of us — to so arrange our environment and circumstances that we would be brought on to conformity to the image of His Son (Rom. 8:29). Thus, there is the intercession of the Spirit with groanings which cannot be uttered. Due to our weakness, we do not know how to pray as we ought. Verse 26 says, "Likewise the Spirit also helps in our weaknesses. For we do not know *what . . .*" In the original Greek, the definite article "the" is before the word "what." Thus it would read "We do not know *the what* we should pray for as we ought."

Now, what is *the what?* According to the context of this passage, *the what* refers to the specific things that are divinely arranged to take place in our environment. Whatever these things turn out to be, they are working together for good — to cause us to be more conformed to the image of God's Son. They may include what we would consider negative. They may be specific things and situations that are contrary to what we would choose or prefer. Hebrews 12 tells us that these environmental things are our discipline under the Lord's hand. The discipline may come in the form of a physical problem. It may be a family problem. It may be a job problem. It may be some pressure in your marriage relationship. It may be pressure in other relationships. The Lord knows exactly what every one of us needs.

"That the God of our Lord Jesus Christ, the Father of glory, may give to you a spirit of wisdom and revelation in the full knowledge of Him." EPHESIANS 1:17

To have a spirit of wisdom and revelation requires the full knowledge of God. This means that we may know God, yet not fully know Him. Paul's prayer for the believers is that they would have a fuller knowledge of God — knowing His desires, knowing His intentions, knowing what His plan is.

You may know me, but you may know me only in part. If you fully know me, then you will know my deepest desires and intentions. This is like the relationship between a husband and wife. After getting married they begin to fully know each other. In a proper marriage you fully know each other, and then you please each other based upon what you fully know. To fully know each other is to fellowship with each other at the deepest level and to open up to know each other's heart, desires, longings, and aspirations. It is then that you fully know, or have full knowledge.

Paul's prayer for the believers was that they would have a spirit of wisdom and revelation in the full knowledge of God — that they would *fully know Him.* As a believer, it is not enough to be satisfied merely with knowing that you are saved and going to heaven. That is good, but there is something deeper, higher, and richer that the Lord desires. Paul would have us enter into what God's heart's desire is in this universe. Why did He save us? Even, why did He create us originally? What was God's purpose before sin entered into the picture?

The Lord wants us to fully know Him in a way that touches His desire and purpose. How do we know the Lord? In what way do we know the Lord? Do we know Him according to full knowledge? This full knowledge is related to vision and revelation. It is not something we devise. It is not something we figure out or make up.

196

Rather, the full knowledge of God is something that comes out of eternity past. According to His good pleasure, He unveils it and makes it known through the apostles' New Testament ministry.

The major things on God's heart   July 13th

"Having predestined us to sonship by Jesus Christ to Himself, according to the good pleasure of His will."
EPHESIANS 1:5

According to its deepest meaning in the New Testament, vision is an opening of our eyes to see the major things on God's heart. The vision that can direct and control our lives, the vision that restrains us, is the vision that opens our eyes to see the unique will and purpose in God's heart. It is the vision of the good pleasure of His will spoken of in Ephesians 1:5. It is the vision of God's eternal purpose in Ephesians 3:10-11. And it is the vision of the main burden of the apostle Paul's ministry, which he defines as "the mystery of Christ" in Ephesians 3:2-7.

When we have vision in this sense, the scales are taken off our eyes to see directly into God's heart the way Paul saw, the way John saw, and the way Peter saw. The apostles lived under a heavenly vision. They had revelation. They had the full knowledge of God. Their ministry brought enlightenment to people. To have vision means to enter into the identical revelation of the apostles' New Testament ministry.

If you and I were believers in the early church under Paul's ministry, one of his main burdens for us would have been that we would enter into the same controlling, heavenly vision that governed his own life. To the Ephesians who were already saved and filled with the Holy Spirit, he said, [15] "Therefore I also, after I heard of your faith in the Lord Jesus and your love for all the saints, [16] do not cease to give thanks for you, making mention of you in my prayers: [17] that

197

the God of our Lord Jesus Christ, the Father of glory, may give to you a spirit of wisdom and revelation in the full knowledge of Him, [18] the eyes of your heart being enlightened; that you may know . . ." (Eph. 1:15-18). In other words, when Paul found seeking Christians, he bowed his knees and prayed for vision and revelation in their lives. He prayed that their eyes would be opened to know something deeper and fuller: "the eyes of your heart being enlightened; that you may know [1] what is the hope of *His calling*, [2] what are the riches of the glory of *His inheritance* in the saints, and [3] what is the exceeding greatness of *His power* toward us who believe" (vv. 18-19). It is this kind of vision that governs God Himself, that governs the universe He created, and that should govern us as His children.

I know why   **July 14th**

"According to the eternal purpose which He accomplished in Christ Jesus our Lord." EPHESIANS 3:11

S tep by step, Paul moves forward to define the eternal purpose of God. First, he mentions the mystery hidden in God; second, he links it with the purpose of creation; and finally, he specifically tells what the purpose is: [10] "To the intent that now the manifold wisdom of God might be made known *through the church* to the principalities and powers in the heavenly places, [11] according to the eternal purpose which He accomplished in Christ Jesus our Lord" (Eph. 3:10-11).

The vision Paul opens up consists of God's eternal purpose, which He executed in His Son and which is now being worked out in and through the church. This purpose revolves around the church. The church, as the Body of Christ exhibiting and displaying God's manifold wisdom, is the governing vision that Paul and the apostles were under. Concerning the church, Paul could testify, "I was not disobedient to the heavenly vision" (Acts 26:19). To have this governing vision means that my Christian life is not wasted. I am not

198

aimlessly going on. I know why I am saved. I know why I am filled with the Spirit and growing in the Lord. I am saved and growing in the Lord for the purpose of being in the church, which displays the unsearchable riches of Christ and manifests the wisdom of God. The meaning of life centers in living the kind of church life that expresses God to the universe. This is the major thing on God's heart. This is the heavenly vision that directed and controlled Paul, and that he sought to open up to others.

If God would light up neon signs in the universe to declare what is the major thing on His heart, those signs would tell us that His Son is producing and building His church for the display of His manifold wisdom. Thus, my life should be under this kind of vision that sees the major things on God's heart. This is what vision means in the New Testament. It is something more than a charismatic experience. It is more than my own personal experience of the Lord's leading and guiding. It is more than the Lord showing me something new in my life. As wonderful as these things are, the highest vision and revelation for every believer is to see what is on God's heart and to know that our lives are counting on this earth for that. Our daily life is intended by God to be the testimony of Jesus — the builded church. This is the major thing on His heart.

Life-consciousness   July 15th

"When Christ who is our life appears, then you also will appear with Him in glory." COLOSSIANS 3:4

To understand the Lord's voice as a life-voice, we must understand the main characteristic of the Lord's life in us. This characteristic is revealed in Romans 8:10 which says, "And if Christ is in you, the body is dead because of sin; but the spirit is life because of righteousness" (ASV, cf. Col. 3:4). First, Christ, who is our life, is not in us merely in a general way, but He is in us in a specific way.

Indeed, He is dwelling and living in our spirit. It is our human spirit that has become the residence of the Lord's life. Second, with the Lord's life in us, there is the corresponding consciousness that belongs to that life. Every kind of life has a life-consciousness. This is true about the nature of animal life and human life, as well as the divine life. Every life has its own kind of consciousness. We may say that the consciousness is the inherent voice of the life. The consciousness of life is the intrinsic speaking of that life.

Consciousness means having an awareness of something, a recognition or perception of something. It means to come to know something experientially. Any particular kind of life brings with it its own kind of awareness. For example, in a cat's life we can observe cat-consciousness. Cat life simply brings with it a consciousness and an awareness that is unique to that life. Kittens especially have a vivid imagination. The kind of life they have gives them the kind of consciousness that causes them to flit and dart around as though something was attacking them. This consciousness is due to their cat life. We observe this consciousness in any kind of animal, whether it be a dog, a bird, or a fish. Its particular kind of life gives it a corresponding consciousness that, in turn, expresses itself in some kind of animal behavior. The principle is very clear — with every kind of life, there is a consciousness that goes with that life.

A fresh consciousness   July 16th

"For I consider that the sufferings of this present time are not worthy to be compared with the glory which shall be revealed in us."
ROMANS 8:18

You may be in the throes of a situation where you find yourself perplexed, confused, and depressed. You do not know what is going on in your life. You are not clear about what the Lord is doing.

You find yourself in the grip of anxiety. At that specific juncture, you need your vision renewed. You need a fresh realization that you are a child of God, an heir of God, and a joint heir of Christ. The Spirit needs to redraw on the screen of your heart that your destiny is to suffer with Christ and be glorified together with Him. You need a *present* life-consciousness that you are on the pathway of the cross, which leads all the way to the throne, to sit with Him on the throne (Rev. 3:21). For this realization to be your experience, you need to stimulate your spirit.

You do not need to live feeling that everything is wrong and that all hope has vanished. You simply need to exercise your spirit to cry "Abba, Father!" When you do, a fresh consciousness will begin to arise in you. A fresh realization of your destiny as a child of God will begin to take hold of you. Fresh vision will emerge, and you will be able to sort out things from God's viewpoint. This is the meaning of Romans 8:13-19. To stimulate our spirit is to usher ourselves into inwardly applying the cross. This is the genuine leading of the Spirit mentioned in Romans 8:14. It is being led by the Spirit to put to death the practices of our body.

God's will for God   July 17th

"And do not be conformed to this world, but be transformed by the renewing of your mind, that you may prove what is that good and well pleasing and perfect will of God." ROMANS 12:2

Knowing God's will is sometimes a difficult thing for us as believers. We all want to find God's will for our life. But often the motivation in seeking God's will is self-centered. It is God's will for *me*, with the emphasis upon *me*. Of course, God has a will and purpose for each of us, but many times we may have no idea that God's will is *for God!* It is not just His will for me. It is His will for Himself.

Vision gives us the ability to prove what is not only the "good"

201

but also the "well pleasing and perfect will of God." Romans 12:2 indicates that in order to prove the perfect will of God, we need the transformation that comes from the renewing of our mind. Transformation and mind-renewing are related to vision. The vision of the major things on God's heart automatically imparts the ability to prove the will of God.

Without vision, we will be trying to figure out what God's will is. Finding God's will for *our* life becomes a major pursuit. We look for some indication of His leading. We look for impressions. We are expecting that perhaps God will speak to us in a dream. We often are eagerly waiting for an open door. This is not to say that the Lord does not use various means to reveal His will to us, but many times we are seeking for something that has nothing to do with God's own will for Himself. We are without the overall vision of the mystery of His will, which is Christ and the church — the governing vision of the universe. Let me illustrate. When I join the Army, I am under the direction of *the big will* of the Army. My decisions and *my little will* about where I live, how I spend my time, and when I am going on vacation are all within the scope of *the big will. The big will* is really the will that controls and directs my life. My *little will* moves within the sphere of *the big will.*

We all must know that there *is* a *big will* for every believer. *That big will is Christ and the church!* That *is* God's revealed will for you and for me. My little will — who I am going to marry, where I am going to school, where I am going to live — is to be discerned within the sphere of God's big revealed will. And this revealed will of God is identical to the heavenly vision that Paul obeyed. Thus, like Paul, we can prove and know the perfect will of God. It is vision that gives us the ability to prove it!

Jesus, my Repairman July 18th

"You shall raise up the foundations of many generations; and you shall be called the Repairer of the Breach, the Restorer of Streets to Dwell In." ISAIAH 58:12

Draw near to God. Draw near, not after you adjust yourself, but before you even try. Because the blood has been shed, we can enter into God — the real Savior. He is the real Repairer. He is the real Healer. He is the One who cleans up our heart. He is the real Cleaner-upper. He is the real Restorer. He does all this, and He does it while we are in contact with Him.

Being oriented to Christ in my experience means that I am in contact with Him — no longer living to myself but to Him. My point of reference is no longer me. My point of reference is Christ. For example, if I am broken down, and I need some repair, then I need to go to the Repairman. Jesus is my Repairman. I do not know how to fix anything. I am just simple to come to Jesus. This is what I appreciate about some saints. They have their weaknesses, but amazingly, even in their frailty, weaknesses, and feelings of failure, they still have that boldness to just keep coming to God. Sometimes we may wonder how a saint could be testifying in a meeting so boldly when they are feeling so weak. But this is the right way — "Just as I am, without one plea . . . Fightings within and fears without, O Lamb of God, I come, I come." Just like that. And He does the work in us.

"Sins" and "sin" July 19th

"For what the law could not do in that it was weak through the flesh, God did by sending His own Son in the likeness of sinful flesh, on account of sin: He condemned sin in the flesh." ROMANS 8:3

When 2 Corinthians 5:21 declares that Christ was made sin, this includes the sin spoken of in Romans 8:3 — sin in the flesh. When Christ died, He died for this thing called *sin*. Sin is a living, moving thing resident in our flesh. "Sin" is different from "sins" that we have committed. Sin dwelling in our flesh is that thing that feels "wrong" in us — that thing that wants to think on its own, that wants to be depressed, that wants to get angry, that wants to lust, that wants to live with its drives and compulsions. Sin moves, it reacts, it gets hurt.

Sin in us is something that involuntarily happens by virtue of our being in the flesh. For example, you do not choose to wake up depressed. Before you even decide how you want to be, you are already depressed. That means sin in the flesh is a living kind of feeling that we coexist with and that is present alongside our organic union with Christ. It shows up in different ways. Sin in the flesh is the greatest factor in a believer's life for receiving all kinds of condemnation, accusation, and categorization from the devil. Because of the ugly manifestations of sin in the flesh — things that surface and show up in our thoughts and our emotions — there is a tug-of-war inside of us. Paul briefly describes this conflict in Galatians 5:17. While something for God is operating in us, simultaneously something else is operating that wants to sin. Sin plans to sin. It has already planned to do its next thing.

Spiritually insistent   July 20th

"For you died, and your life is hidden with Christ in God. When Christ who is our life appears, then you also will appear with Him in glory." COLOSSIANS 3:3-4

The emphasis here is on your life hidden with Christ. It is *your* life! You are in an organic union with Christ. You are joined to Him. The issue of this joining is *your* life. It is subjective. Since it is your life, you can initiate Him or you can let Him just be there.

Because of the union, the organic "I," you and I can exercise our spirit to take the initiative to let Christ be Christ in us and through us. Or we can remain passive in the realm of the flesh, wasting more hours under the law, and getting reminded once again that we cannot make it on our own. We need to cultivate an intimacy from our inner being to learn how to live off of Him, how to bring everything to Him, and how to be spiritually insistent. We need to learn how to be bold. Tell Him, "Jesus, You have to live, or it is not going to happen. It has to be You, Lord!" We can be this bold because the arrangement in our union is that *we* are joined to *His life*, and it is *His life* that we participate in.

When Colossians 3:4 tells us that Christ is *our* life, it means He is our person. As our person, He is our righteousness. Experientially this means that He is how you feel about yourself. On the level of our feelings and consciousness, Christ being our righteousness means that I can own His state and condition as my very own. I no longer have to identify with *my* state and *my* condition. Is He condemned? His state is out of the reach of condemnation. If Christ could be condemned then I could. But if Christ cannot be condemned, then I cannot (Rom. 8:1). No wonder Paul says, "Who shall bring a charge against God's elect?" (Rom. 8:33). He does not investigate whether the charge is legitimate, whether you feel that you deserve the charge, or whether there are some facts behind this case. He boldly says, "Who shall bring a charge against God's elect? It is God who justifies. Who is he who condemns?" (vv. 33-34). Paul does not refer to anything related to the actual state of the person. There is no examining of preexisting conditions, no introspection. He simply says, "It is Christ who died, and furthermore is also risen, who is even at the right hand of God" (v. 34). Thus, Paul is saying, "If you lay a charge against me, then my Father will turn you to His Son who loved me and gave Himself for me" (cf. Gal. 2:20).

"I have been crucified with Christ; it is no longer I who live, but Christ lives in me; and the life which I now live in the flesh I live in faith, the faith of the Son of God, who loved me and gave Himself for me." GALATIANS 2:20

Like Paul, we can say "Christ lives in me." Christ is not floating in the air. He lives in *me*. He is *in* me! Then Paul says, "and the life which *I* now live." He had just finished saying "It is no longer I." This tells us that there are two "I's" Paul is speaking of here. There is an old "I," and there is a new "I." The old "I" is the independent "I" of the flesh seeking to have an independent relationship with God and striving to make it with God on its own. This old "I" has been crucified with Christ. The new "I" is an organic "I." It is my regenerated spirit joined to the Lord in a life union.

Paul describes the "I" that lives after regeneration: "The life which *I* now live in the flesh *I* live in faith . . ." We are still living in the flesh. We have the surroundings of the flesh. We can still feel the rumblings of the flesh. We can feel it showing up, knocking at our door, trying to categorize, to accuse, to be depressed — trying to do what it does. So the life that I am now living in the flesh, how do I live it? I live in the sphere of faith, "the faith *of* the Son of God, who loved me and gave Himself for me." That means I am living off of His life infusing me with faith as I behold Him. I live gazing at Him. I live looking away from everything to this lovely Person who loves me, who gave Himself for me. He did it all for me. And as I am looking and beholding, my beholding of Him infuses faith right into me — the faith of the Son of God. So my living in faith is not my work or doing. No! Faith is the response *in me* to His work and doing. Faith is the gift of God served to me freely on the platter of a message I hear about Christ. I see Him openly portrayed before my eyes, crucified! When I see His work, faith is in my heart and in my mouth.

One love in three directions   July 22nd

"Now hope does not disappoint, because the love of God has been poured out in our hearts by the Holy Spirit who was given to us." ROMANS 5:5

W e need to see the nature of God's unconditional love, because this love is the very essence of His relationship to us. And this love should be the very essence of our relationship to Him. It should also be the essence of our relationship to one another. God's love first comes to us and causes us to love Him; and in loving Him, we love one another. These three dimensions are the dimensions of the love of God—His love toward us, our love toward Him, and our love toward one another.

The nature of our love toward the Lord and toward one another should not be any different from His love toward us. The love that reaches us and is poured out into our hearts by God is the same love that returns back to Him in worship, praise, enjoyment, and intimate fellowship. It is also the same love that flows out from us to one another. It is altogether one love flowing in three directions — God's unconditional love coming from God to us, and then going back from us to God, and then horizontally going out to one another. This is one kind of love, not three different loves. There is not one kind of love that God has for us, then another kind of love that we have toward God, and then a third kind of love that we have toward one another. No, the *agape* love is one love; it is one essence. It has one nature, and that nature flows in all directions.

Relationships in God's love   July 23rd

"Where can I go from Your Spirit? Or where can I flee from Your presence? If I ascend into heaven, You are there; if I make my bed in hell, behold, You are there." PSALM 139:7-8

The nature, or essence, of God's love includes His choice and His plan. Because He chose us, He set His love upon us. This is beyond our comprehension. We have become the objects of His love and can only say with David, "Where can I flee from Your presence?" We cannot get away from God's love. It will find us out. It is the greatest hound that you will ever meet up with. Just as the police dogs sniff out hidden things, God's love will sniff us out. Regardless of where we are, even if we are buried under sin and condemnation, the love of God will come and find us there, because we are the objects of that love.

Brothers and sisters, this is the love of God toward us. And this is the same love we bear toward one another. This is the love in the church. We are not together because we each decided to join a group. We have assembled together with others of His chosen ones. We are with others who have a destiny over their life to be conformed to the image of God's Son. Who are we to receive or reject a member of the Body of Christ based on our little rules? If a person has been born again, he is loved by the Lord. He is God's choice, and he is also one over whom God's plan is being worked out. Thus, our part is only to acknowledge what God has done and receive him whom Christ has received. We are to "receive one another, just as Christ also received us, to the glory of God" (Rom. 15:7).

The love that chose me, predestined me, and reconciled me is the same love in our relationships with one another. So our relationships with one another have their source in eternity. It is not accidental that we are together. We are related to one another and we know one another as brothers and sisters. Our relatedness is based upon God's choice and His plan in eternity. Now, in time, we are with one another, regardless of our condition, our background, our race — whatever. All those things mean nothing. God's love has been set over all of us; and now that love has been poured out in our heart, so we can simply let it flow toward one another.

Praying in the Holy Spirit   July 24th

*"But you, beloved, building yourselves up on your most holy
faith, praying in the Holy Spirit, keep yourselves in the love of God,
looking for the mercy of our Lord Jesus Christ unto eternal life."*
JUDE 20-21

God's love is made up of the Spirit's transmission. The Spirit
transmits all that is in this love — God's choice and His plan,
Christ's redemption, resurrection, ascension, and intercession. Now
we can have the reality of this love in our experience. We can have
"the good" of it by the Holy Spirit. The participial phrase "praying
in the Holy Spirit" modifies "keep yourselves in the love of God."
So the way we keep ourselves in the love of God is by praying in the
Holy Spirit. When we pray in the Holy Spirit, we enter the realm of
the poured-out love of God. This is how we keep our hearts in the
unconditional love of God.

It is so easy for a day to go by — you go to work and come home.
Maybe you have been burdened down with all the cares of life and
have had no prayer and fellowship with the Lord. You feel
somewhat beaten down. And you feel like God does not love or care
about you that much. You do not have the present enjoyment of His
love in your sensation. But Jude tells us, "Keep yourselves in the love
of God." Take some initiative now. Do not go away from the love,
but keep yourself in it. He tells you how — "praying in the Holy
Spirit." It is not praying just from your mind, but praying in the Holy
Spirit. That means you use your spirit to pray, fellowship, talk, call
out, cry out, and sing. This activates your spirit and brings you into
the realm of the Holy Spirit. Sometimes there is a breaking-through
period, but the principle is that we can keep ourselves in the love of
God. This is God's unconditional love toward us through the Spirit's
transmission.

As we see the composition of God's love, we discover that it is
not just a shallow, superficial feeling in God. This love is eternal.

This love can never be defeated or frustrated, because it met the devil, it met sin, it met every obstacle, and it overcame. It overcame through death, through resurrection, and through ascension. And now this love is transmitted into us by the Holy Spirit.

One in the wounds of Jesus   July 25th

"But now in Christ Jesus you who once were far off have been made near by the blood of Christ." EPHESIANS 2:13

As believers we all receive the benefits of the transactions that took place on the cross. On the cross there was a double transfer. Christ became sin so that we might become the righteousness of God in Him (2 Cor. 5:21). Sin was transferred to Christ, and righteousness was transferred to us. On the cross this glorious double transfer took place. Now we can shout, "He has the sin, and I have the righteousness!" When sin shows up in our flesh in the form of negative reactions, and the devil comes to accuse us, we can say, "Sorry, Satan. My Christ has the sin, and I have the righteousness." This double transfer accomplished on the cross is now made real to us in our union with Christ in our spirit. All of us can enjoy this double transfer. No wonder Paul speaks of being near in the blood of Christ. Brothers and sisters, we are one in the wounds of Jesus! We are near to God, and we are near to one another. This is all because of the righteousness of God, which is a major factor between us. We are linked together in God's righteousness.

Not only in Romans but also in 1 Corinthians, Paul brings in righteousness as the factor for the saints to be linked together. In 1 Corinthians 1:29-31 he says, [29] "That no flesh should glory in His presence. [30] But of Him you are in Christ Jesus, who became for us wisdom from God — that is, righteousness and sanctification and redemption — [31] that, as it is written, He who glories, let him glory in the Lord." In these verses, the common factor between us is Christ as our righteousness. This is the factor of our boasting and glorying. We are boasting in the Lord. This kind of common boasting links us together.

It is of God that we are all in Christ Jesus. God's wisdom was to put us all in Christ. Now, Christ is our righteousness, sanctification, and redemption. Every Christian has this boast. Our boast is nothing but Christ and Him crucified (1 Cor. 2:2; Gal. 6:14). When Paul wrote to the Corinthians, he was dealing with a church problem of division. But the way he handled this problem was not by dealing with the issue of the church. He did not discuss how to organize the church, how to set up the church in an outward way, or even how to properly stand on the ground of the church. Paul did not touch those kinds of matters. Rather, he turned the saints to Christ: "Is Christ divided? Was Paul crucified for you? Or were you baptized into the name of Paul?" (1 Cor. 1:13). It is "Christ the power of God" and Christ "the wisdom of God" (1 Cor. 1:24). It is as if Paul was shouting, "Saints, come back to Christ!" His burden was to reconnect the divided saints by a major factor in God's New Testament economy — Christ our righteousness.

Vision discerns us   July 26th

"For the word of God is living and powerful, and sharper than any two-edged sword, piercing even to the division of soul and spirit, and of joints and marrow, and is a discerner of the thoughts and intents of the heart." HEBREWS 4:12

The dividing of soul and spirit does not come by our subjective introspection. None of us by ourselves have the ability to divide our soul and spirit. Indeed, God never appointed us to do that. But the word of God that brings to us the governing vision of the entire Bible can divide what is of our soul from what is of our spirit. This kind of word that defines the vision of God's purpose, with a call to

211

enter into it, does the dividing work. We can talk for many years about the soul and spirit being divided and not get very far in our experience. But once we come under the vision and heavenly revelation of God's word about His eternal purpose, that word has the effect of making us clear concerning what is from the soul-life and what is from the spirit. The word as vision has the ability to divide soul and spirit, making everything spiritually clear to us.

The word of God as vision also has discerning ability. It discerns the thoughts and intents of our heart. Our heart, with its thoughts and intentions, surely needs to be discerned if we are to live on this earth fulfilling God's heart's desire and goal. If our heart is living for its own goal, and we are presented with the vision of God's goal of building the church, we will not want to hear about it because it threatens our own private goal. This is an indication that the vision has discerned us. If we have to make a choice either to live for our goal or to live for God's goal, we are in a situation in which our thoughts and intents are exposed to the light of the vision.

Some of us may remember when we were children and were doing something in a sneaky way. The moment our mother called from the kitchen and asked us what we were doing, her call not only confronted us, but it immediately discerned our bad intents and actions. That is exactly what vision does. It has the ability to divide our soul and spirit as well as to discern the thoughts and intents of our heart. It has the ability to shine on everything in our lives.

Sink yourself into Christ   **July 27th**

"And He is before all things, and in Him all things consist."
COLOSSIANS 1:17

The last part of this verse can also be translated "all things are held together in Him." This is very deep because it tells us that the Lord Himself is the cohesive factor that causes us to be held together. Whenever we are experiencing Christ with one another, there is such a sense of being glued together. Our cohesion is Christ.

What is the church? The church is Christ. How is the church Christ? The church is Christ when the members, in their daily living, in their relationships with one another, allow Him to have first place. You are not qualified to talk back to your husband. You are not qualified to say those words to your wife. Simply walk in spirit. Experience Christ with your husband or your wife. You are not even qualified to deal with your failures. You are not qualified to deal with your sinking feelings of condemnation. Instead, sink yourself into Christ. Call "Jesus." Paul said, "O wretched man that I am!" (Rom. 7:24). He was at the bottom. He was in the pit. He had failed over and over again. What he wanted to do he did not do, and what he hated he did. He was a wretched man. Finally he asked, "Who will deliver me?" Then he replied, "I thank God — through Jesus Christ." It was *through* Jesus Christ. He was the means by which Paul handled his own wretchedness. This shows us that the church is not a group of perfect people. Rather, it is a group of failures who handle Christ. We are not condoning sin or failure, but we can handle our failures and condition through Christ. When we experience Christ in this way, the church is full of the cohesion of Christ, full of the glue that holds us together.

Handle Christ   July 28th

"And He is the head of the body, the church, who is the beginning, the firstborn from the dead, that in all things He may have the preeminence." COLOSSIANS 1:18

Cohesiveness means that there is something sticky. We stick together. There is a fellowship, there is a knitting, there is a bonding. The bonding is not because we agree mentally on certain things. It is because the Christ within us automatically coheres and bonds us together. We *feel* that fellowship, that joy, that oneness. We are not detached units by ourselves. We are not divided or separated. There is a sense of togetherness. There is a sense of flow. What is this? It is Christ! It is not just a good feeling. It is Christ who is the cohesive factor holding everything together.

As we experience Christ and know Him, He Himself becomes the holding factor. Notice how Paul continues from "in Him all things consist" to "He is the head of the body, the church, who is the beginning, the firstborn from the dead, that in all things He may have the preeminence" (Col. 1:17-18). Verse 18 shows us the practical way that we can enjoy the experience of this cohesiveness. It is by all of us allowing Christ to have the first place in all things, to be everything to us, and to be the center of our being, so that our relationship with one another is Him. He is before everything. He has the priority. I do not handle my flesh. I do not handle my reactions. I do not handle my resentment. I do not handle my hurt. I do not handle my problems. I do not handle my self. I am not qualified. I simply handle Christ. I handle Him first. I give Him first place. I am not qualified to be my savior. He is my Savior. He is my life. He is my relationship with my self. He is my relationship with the Father. He is my relationship with sin. He is my relationship with the flesh. He is my relationship with the world. He is my relationship with the devil. He is my relationship with the law. He is my relationship with all the saints. Christ is my life.

Intimacy and compatibility   July 29th

"As the Father loved Me, I also have loved you; abide in My love. If you keep My commandments, you will abide in My love, just as I have kept My Father's commandments and abide in His love."
JOHN 15:9-10

To understand what it means to live a life of compatibility with the Lord, we need to consider the example of the Lord's human living. What we see in the Lord's relationship with the Father is that His compatibility with the Father came out of His intimacy with the Father. John 1:18 reveals that the only begotten Son is "into the bosom of the Father." This shows His intimate fellowship with the Father. John 15:9-10 indicates that He was abiding in the Father's love. It was out of this kind of love-intimacy that He lived a life of complete compatibility with the Father's life and will.

The Lord's example reveals the principle by which we can live day by day being compatible with His voice. It is simple. Compatibility with the divine life comes by cultivating a life of intimacy. We all recognize that this is true in the marriage life. How is a wife compatible with her husband? How does she live to please her husband? The compatibility of a wife with her husband is dependent upon her intimacy with her husband. Her intimacy with her husband creates and nurtures the desire to please him.

The Holy Spirit's terms in the New Testament for compatibility are "pleasing" and "well pleasing." John 8:28-29 says, [28] "Then Jesus said to them, When you lift up the Son of Man, then you will know that I am He, and that I do nothing of Myself; but as My Father taught Me, I speak these things. [29] And He who sent Me is with Me. The Father has not left Me alone, for I always do those things that *please* Him." In other words, the reason for His compatibility with the Father was that He heard the Father's voice because of His life of intimacy with the Father. He was sensitive to what the Father *taught* Him, not only because the Father was with Him all the time, but also because He was always abiding in the Father's love. This was the reason there was such a constant supply coming from the Lord. He lived in the Father and was always doing that which was compatible with the Father.

*"The Lord G*OD *has given Me the tongue of the learned, that I should know how to speak a word in season to him who is weary. He awakens Me morning by morning, He awakens My ear to hear as the learned. The Lord G*OD *has opened My ear; and I was not rebellious, nor did I turn away."* ISAIAH 50:4-5

According to this Old Testament prophecy about the Lord's life, the Father woke Him morning by morning and opened His ear to hear His voice. Then in the Gospels we observe the way He lived His life from morning to night — where He went, those He saw, those He prayed for, those He related to — how He went about His daily life. He always did the things that pleased the Father. His intimacy with the Father was the factor that supplied the ability to live a compatible life with the Father.

By observing the Lord's life of intimacy and compatibility with the Father in the Gospels, we discover the nature of the life that is now dwelling in us. It is a life that thrives on intimacy with the Father (Gal. 4:6; Rom. 8:15). It is a life that always desires to prove, by testing, what is well pleasing to the Lord (Rom. 12:2; Eph. 5:10). It is a life that knows compatibility with the Father's life-voice in all the details of daily life (Eph. 4:20-21). Now this life is living in us.

May the Lord grant to us multiplied grace in our spirit, so that the love of God, the grace of Christ, and the fellowship of the Holy Spirit would be our daily portion (2 Cor. 13:14). As we inwardly merge with the intimacy in the Triune God, we will not only abide in His love, but we will develop a finer and more delicate sensitivity to the consciousness of life within us. It is by the love of God and the grace of Christ flowing in the fellowship of the Holy Spirit that we can be a person that is compatible with the Lord's voice. Amen!

The law of our being

"For the law of the Spirit of life in Christ Jesus has made me free from the law of sin and death." ROMANS 8:2

We need to be renewed in our minds about a part of us — our spirit. This part of our being is *the law* of our being. It is something working and operating constantly. When my spirit is regenerated, the Lord's life is immediately imparted into me. My spirit is filled with Christ as the life-giving Spirit. He resides in me as such a One. Our spirit is the part of us that is joined to the Lord, who is the Spirit. The two spirits have become one. So we do not wait for an inspiration or some kind of feeling to prompt us to pray, to sing, to speak, or to call on the Lord. Just as my body has been born, and all my faculties are mine, and I learn to use my faculties, so my spirit has been born and my spirit is mine. With my spirit, I can take the initiative to pray and open myself up to the Lord. By contacting the Lord with my spirit, I can turn my mind. Whenever I use my spirit, I merge with the *law* of the Spirit of life.

Let me illustrate what it means for us to relate to a law. The airline industry is not based on an intermittent phenomenon that happens with airplanes. Flying an airplane is not an unpredictable occurrence. It is not that one time an airplane "happens" to make it up in the air, but the next time it does not, and then the next time *maybe* it will. No, it does not work that way. There is a law of aerodynamics. In the same way, in whatever you are passing through, if you use your spirit — that part in you that is regular and reliable — then you are in the right realm to be freed. The law of the Spirit of life is the realm that freed us from the law of sin and death. "Freed" in Greek is in the past tense — it has already happened. We have already been freed. Now we simply enter into the good of the freedom. We merge with the freedom.

August

Stop yourself for a moment

"And suddenly a voice came from heaven, saying, This is My beloved Son, in whom I delight." MATTHEW 3:17

S pending time with the Lord will supply us, deliver us, save us, and transform us. We do not need human effort, religion, or outward improvement of behavior. We do not need to adjust ourselves with our natural energy. We just need time to be with the Lord and allow ourselves to abide in His love. The Lord described our participation in the love-life of the Triune God in John 17:26 by saying to the Father, "And I have declared to them Your name, and will declare it, that the love with which You loved Me may be in them, and I in them." This means exactly what it says. The very same love that Jesus enjoyed from the Father is in us, not imitated by us or worked up by us. We experience the Triune God's love-life dwelling in us by allowing this love-life to pass through our being from our spirit (Rom. 8:15) into our heart (Gal. 4:6). In light of this, who would be so foolish as to neglect spending time with the Lord enjoying this flow of liquid love!

Who can fathom the intensity of the Father's love and delight in His beloved Son? Step out of yourself for a moment. Do not consider your condition. Stop your struggle for victory. Cease from all your preoccupations. Just stop and consider one thing — the Father's love to the Son! The Father declared from the heavens at Jesus' baptism, "This is My beloved Son, in whom I delight." The Son is the Father's delight! Not you! Not me! Not our condition! But the Son! The flow of the Father's love is all channeled to the Son. Now listen to John 17:26 once more: "That the love with which You have loved Me *may be in them, and I in them*." What you and I need is not to find out how to solve our problems, but rather to place ourselves before the Lord and simply give Him some time for His love-life to pass through us. The flow of the divine love is conveyed to us by the Spirit (John 7:37-39) and not only solves our problems, but brings us everything we need. The love-life of the Triune God Himself is our portion and enjoyment. We just need to spend time cultivating it.

One unique relationship August 2nd

"All things have been delivered to Me by My Father, and no one knows the Son except the Father. Nor does anyone know the Father except the Son, and he to whom the Son wills to reveal Him."
MATTHEW 11:27

We do not have a separate relationship with God apart from the Father and Son's own relationship. God is not establishing new relationships with others. He has established one relationship, and that is with His Son. Then He gives that relationship away as a gift. This is the meaning of the gift of eternal life in the New Testament. Eternal life is receiving the Son of God into us and participating in His relationship with the Father. John 17:3 says, "And this is eternal life, *that they may know You, the only true God, and Jesus Christ whom You have sent."* Also, 1 John 5:20 says, "And we know that the Son of God has come and has given us an understanding, *that we may know Him* who is true; and *we are in Him who is true, in His Son Jesus Christ. This is the true God and eternal life."*

When we receive eternal life, we receive the Father and Son's very own relationship. Now Christ Himself is my relationship with the Father. You and I do not have a different relationship with God from the one Christ has with the Father. This is why, after the Lord revealed the one unique relationship in the universe between Himself and the Father, He immediately said, "Come to Me, all you who labor and are heavy laden, and I will give you rest" (Matt. 11:27-28).

This means that there is no longer any need to labor and struggle in our souls, trying to establish our own relationship with God (Rom. 10:3-4). We only need to come to Jesus and learn from Him. When we do, we become one with Him and discover that *our* relationship with the Father is actually *His* relationship. We are merging with His relationship with the Father, and this brings rest to our souls.

How I am alive to God   August 3rd

"Likewise you also, reckon yourselves to be dead indeed to sin, but alive to God in Christ Jesus our Lord." ROMANS 6:11

To speak of Christ as our relationship with sin does not sound so positive, yet the New Testament reveals that Christ's relationship with sin has become our relationship. *Christ* is our relationship with sin. God dealt with sin in Christ. Then He put us in Christ, so that now our relationship with sin is to be found in Christ. Romans 6:8-11 clearly shows us *how* Christ is our relationship with sin: [8] "Now if we died with Christ, we believe that we shall also live with Him, [9] knowing that Christ, having been raised from the dead, dies no more. Death no longer has dominion over Him. [10] For the death that He died, He died to sin once for all; but the life that He lives, He lives to God. [11] Likewise you also, reckon yourselves to be dead indeed to sin, but alive to God in Christ Jesus our Lord." On the positive side, we are alive to God in Christ Jesus; on the negative side, we are dead to sin. Since Christ died to sin once for all, His death to sin has now become my relationship to sin. There is no way to have a victorious relationship toward sin apart from Christ's relationship to it. Sin is a powerful force dwelling in our flesh (Rom. 7:14-24). To attempt in ourselves to overcome this indwelling sin is to end up in the same condition as the apostle Paul's at the end of Romans chapter 7 — defeated and wretched.

In His crucifixion, Christ died to sin once for all. Now in

resurrection He lives to God in another realm. In the same way, we died to sin in His death (Rom. 6:6), and now in Him we also live to God in another realm. Our history, our life, and our existence are all bound up with Him. This is a most astounding fact. I can declare with boldness by the Word of God that I am alive and living to God in Christ Jesus. This truth renews my mind regarding *how* I am alive to God! This is truth that sets us free!

What molds your thinking? August 4th

"My little children, for whom I labor in birth again until Christ is formed in you." GALATIANS 4:19

The verse above tells us that Christ was no longer formed in the hearts of the Galatian believers. What was formed in them was Moses and the law. When something is formed in you, your mind goes to that. Your thoughts go to that. It is like a mold in there, and you think and reason according to that mold. In their relationship with God, the Galatians were oriented to laws and rules. That is what was formed in them. That is what had molded their thinking. That was their point of reference.

When your thinking is molded by the law, the law is like a mirror looking right back at you — at your law-breaking flesh, your failing self, your unfinished, untransformed, unconformed state. You see all the blemishes, and it is terrifying. That is what happens when you are related to the law, because you are related to God's goal as *a demand* that *we* must attain instead of *a result* of interacting with Christ. The final goal of conformation to Christ takes care of itself when our spirit and our heart simply stay engaged with loving Christ. "God *sent forth* the Spirit of His Son into our hearts." God wants our hearts to be occupied with Him! This does not mean that we are "finished products." But this is *how* you become a finished product. This is the way — by handling everything with Christ.

222

Liquid love

"I in them, and You in Me; that they may be made perfect in one, and that the world may know that You have sent Me, and have loved them as You have loved Me." JOHN 17:23

When the Lord says, "You in Me," He is referring to the Father in Him. The Father loves Him, and He is "into the bosom of the Father" (John 1:18). This speaks of the mutual love between the Father and the Son. The first part of the above verse says, "I in them," which means the Son is in us. Of course, when He is in us, that brings the Father into us, because the Son comes with the Father. He comes with Their love relationship. He comes with this wonderful liquid love flowing between the Father and the Son, and the Son and the Father. Now the Lord is in us. He is in us moving with that love. In John 15:9 He says, "As the Father loved Me, I also have loved you; abide in My love." Let that love move in you. That means let the divine life flow. When the life flows, the love flows. When you release life, love comes with that life.

"I in them" means "I am moving in them, I am loving in them." It is a love relationship. The Lord wants to establish in us a relationship with Him and the Father that casts out all fear. He wants us to be comfortable with Him. He wants us to know the security of His love. As the Father has loved the Son, the Son loves us. He wants us to know that love. He wants our whole relationship to be in that love. He wants us to know that even when we are failing, we are loved by Him. He died for us. He wants us to know the security of coming to Him after a horrible defeat and saying, "Jesus, forgive me." He wants us to know in the security of that love that the blood is cleansing us from all sin.

223

Proper understanding

"And they said to one another, Did not our heart burn within us while He talked with us on the road, and while He opened the Scriptures to us?" LUKE 24:32

All proper human understanding has Christ as the focus and centrality (Col. 1:16-17); otherwise, the word "understanding" is only a borrowed term. According to God's creation and His Word, the only genuine, proper understanding is to understand everything in Christ, from Christ, through Christ, and unto Christ. Without this, you have no understanding. You do not understand your life. You do not understand anything properly. Unless you see Christ, you only have the husk of an understanding. He is the kernel of all understanding. From God's point of view, to understand means to enter into His thoughts about everything — about creation and His purpose. So for us as human beings, the proper understanding is to see Christ as all and in all. That is understanding. This comes from having our minds renewed.

There is only one way to study the Scriptures, and that is to come to the Scriptures to see Christ. If you come to the Scriptures to study the Bible, to simply get Bible knowledge, you do not see and you do not understand the Scriptures. You may have Bible knowledge, but what links everything together? In Luke 24:27 the Lord opened the Word from Genesis through Malachi, clearly showing the disciples the things concerning Himself — that He was the focus of all the Scriptures. After the disciples' eyes were opened, they said to one another, "Did not our heart burn within us while He talked with us on the road, and while He opened the Scriptures to us?" A burning heart comes when we can take the Bible and talk about Christ and apply Christ. It is the understanding of the Bible with Christ as the focus that causes our heart to burn.

A focused ministry

"Where there is neither Greek nor Jew, circumcised nor uncircumcised, barbarian, Scythian, slave nor free, but Christ is all and in all." COLOSSIANS 3:11

Paul's ministry was focused on Christ and the church. This focus came right out of the heart of God. It was hidden there. Paul makes this clear in Ephesians 3:9: "And to make all people see what is the administration of the mystery, which from the beginning of the ages has been hidden in God who created all things through Jesus Christ." God had something hidden in Himself that He did not make known for a long time. This may be considered as God's suppressed desire for the universe (Rom. 16:25-26). This desire is wholly focused in Christ. Paul understood this focus, and thus his ministry never deviated from making known the unsearchable riches of Christ through the church (Eph. 3:8-11).

When we see the focus of Christ in this universe according to the Lord's use of Scripture and the apostles' ministry, it is quite clear that the church is just Christ! What else could the church be? If "Christ is all and in all," then the church, even logically, must be Christ. Understanding the church as Christ is very simple when we see that Christ is the centrality of the church, the content of the church, the reality of the church, and the expression of the church.

When we understand the church as Christ, this understanding issues in a focused daily life with many experiences of Christ. This is the meaning of Paul's word in Colossians 2:2 — that the full assurance of understanding is *unto* an experiential knowledge of Christ. To experientially know Christ is to know Him increasingly as our relationship with everything.

"God is faithful, by whom you were called into the fellowship of His Son, Jesus Christ our Lord." 1 CORINTHIANS 1:9

Paul told the Corinthians that they had been called into the fellowship, the participation, of God's Son, Jesus Christ. God had called them to participate in Christ. How do we participate in Christ? It is by calling His name, "Jesus." When we say "Jesus," we participate in Jesus. His name is the practical handle for us to participate in Him. And when we participate in Him, we must realize that we are participating in all the phases of His existence. The Lord Jesus passed through incarnation, human life, death, burial, resurrection, and ascension. Today all these phases are in the Spirit, who has been poured out like a flowing river for us to drink. When we call "Lord Jesus," we drink the Spirit (1 Cor. 12:3, 13-14). As we drink the Spirit, we are participating in the phases of His existence — in His incarnation, His human life, His death, His burial, His resurrection, and His ascension. We participate in His life and become living members of Him.

We also participate in the Lord Jesus by eating Him (John 6:48-63). And when we eat Jesus, we eat His humanity, the glorified humanity made available as living bread. The manhood that He lived out was not lost 2,000 years ago. That manhood has now been put into the Spirit to be a constant supply of bread for us to eat (1 Cor. 15:45). Now we can eat the thinking of Jesus and the reactions of Jesus and the choices of Jesus. We can eat His mind, His emotion, and His will. It flows in the Spirit. We all need another disposition to live our human life. We need the divine disposition. How do we obtain such a disposition? It is by feeding on Jesus in the Word, by calling on His name, and by drinking of the Spirit.

"How can I give you up, Ephraim? How can I hand you over, Israel? How can I make you like Admah? How can I set you like Zeboiim? My heart churns within Me; My sympathy is stirred."
HOSEA 11:8

Here we see the intrinsic revelation of God's love. His very being is expressed in His speaking: "How can I give you up, Ephraim?" This is like God speaking to you. Maybe you feel like you have been joined to idols. You have spoiled God's discipline in your life. You have resisted Him. You feel like a cake unturned. You have even taken the devil's categorizing that you are just a spoiled piece of humanity, that you have sinned yourself to ruin. Maybe all of this is how you feel. But over and above your feeling is God's revelation of His love to you. And He is saying, "How can I give you up?" In other words, God's love goes beyond Ephraim's being joined to idols, being a cake unturned, rejecting the Word of God, and being full of lies and deceit.

When the Lord says, "My heart churns within Me; My sympathy is stirred," God's love is revealed as something intrinsic to His very being. You cannot take it out of Him. This is His churning love. On the one hand, Ephraim deserves every kind of judgment for his absolute, willful rebellion against God. His awful record merits his being cast off completely. Yet, when God's judgment comes to the foreground, mercy prevails and love overcomes Him. Far more than the consideration of any kind of judgment, love and mercy prevail. "My heart churns within Me" means that there is a turning in God Himself. This turning is also exemplified in Genesis 18:16-32 when Abraham prayed for Sodom: "Suppose there were fifty righteous within the city? . . . Suppose there should be forty righteous found there? . . . Suppose ten righteous should be found there? . . ." Abraham appealed to the Lord in this way when He was about to destroy Sodom. Abraham's prayer could actually turn God and remind Him of His mercy and His love; and that is what prevailed — His churning heart of love.

The atmosphere of freedom   August 10th

"It was for freedom that Christ set us free; therefore keep standing firm and do not be subject again to a yoke of slavery." GALATIANS 5:1 (NASV)

One of the chief things used by Satan to nullify Christ is an atmosphere of legality. This kind of atmosphere can subtly creep into the church. It was one of the primary problems that invaded the church life in the New Testament. The Gospels are filled with accounts of the scribes and Pharisees nullifying the Word of God by their tradition and detailed legalities (Mark 7:6-9). The book of Acts does not cover up the fact that the church in Jerusalem was filled with believers who were zealous for keeping the law (Acts 21:20). Many of the Epistles were written due to the battle with Judaizers, who were going about to spy out the believers' freedom in Christ (Gal. 2:4).

From the New Testament days until now, Christ is nullified when the church loses the atmosphere of freedom. Paul says that it is for the express purpose of an atmosphere of freedom that Christ died on the cross to set us free. Freedom is the state or atmosphere that believers are to live in. Indeed, Paul exhorts the saints to "keep standing firm" in this blood-bought freedom.

Nullifying Christ   August 11th

"Indeed I, Paul, say to you that if you become circumcised, Christ will profit you nothing." GALATIANS 5:2

For Christ to no longer "profit" us means that we nullify Christ. By speaking in this way, Paul brings out the serious consequences of losing the atmosphere of freedom. When saints are being *compelled* to conform to a spoken or unspoken standard or practice, this constitutes the loss of freedom (Gal. 2:3; 6:12). The saints had lost that precious freedom that preserves an atmosphere in which the love of God can freely flow from God to man, from man to God, and from man to man. To preserve the flow of the love of God in all its sweetness, we must preserve the atmosphere in which it can happen. This means that in the church life there must always be an atmosphere of freedom in which the love of God is able to flow among us. Love cannot flow where there is no freedom. When love does not flow, Christ has been nullified (cf. Gal. 5:2, 4 with verse 6). Where there is law, where there is obligation, where there is a legal mind-set, it not only chokes the flow of love, it makes it impossible for love to happen. For example, if I tell my wife, "I am your husband, I am your head; therefore you *must* love me," the more I talk to her in this way, the more I make it impossible for her to love, even if she wanted to. How could she *freely* give love when I am demanding it from her? Love needs the atmosphere of freedom in order to exist. If freedom is not the atmosphere in our relationships, Christ and love are nullified. To love God and to love one another requires the atmosphere of freedom.

Nothingness escorts us to Christ   August 12th

"For I say to you, that unless your righteousness exceeds the righteousness of the scribes and Pharisees, you will by no means enter the kingdom of heaven." MATTHEW 5:20

When the Lord speaks of having a surpassing righteousness for entering into the kingdom, He is applying a finer measurement with a much higher demand than the law. The standard of the law could be compared to measuring in "inches," but the Lord's word in Matthew 5—7 could be compared to measuring in "picas," which are a fraction of an inch. This means the measurement is much finer and more detailed. The Lord measures our emotions, our attitudes, our reactions, our exaggerations, our comments about others — He measures it all! He measures our heart, He measures what we think, He measures the fantasies in our mind, He measures how we look at others, He measures lust, He measures anxiety. He measures how we react in situations that touch our selfishness and personal convenience — going two miles instead of one, or giving our outward coat as well as our inner garment. Nothing escapes being measured.

If we were discouraged by the law of Moses, we are even more discouraged by Matthew 5—7. Indeed, in Matthew 5:48 the Lord reaches the point of saying, "Therefore you shall be perfect, just as your Father in heaven is perfect." Perfection in this verse is the demand to love exactly as the Father loves. It is not merely putting up with our enemies, but praying for them and blessing them. Such a measuring of our love finds us all short, but at the same time it escorts us to Christ as our life and life-supply. When we are escorted to Christ, we become *partakers* of His love. This is why the Lord begins Matthew 5—7 with "Blessed are the poor in spirit, for theirs is the kingdom of heaven" (Matt. 5:3). When we are poor in spirit, we realize that in ourselves we do not have the divine love toward our enemies. We realize that we are nothing and can do nothing. The Lord's high standard is intended to cause disappointment over ourselves so that we would be drawn away from our own nothingness to the energy and strength of Another life. It is this sense of nothingness that escorts us to Christ.

Disguised escorts August 13th

"For we do not want you to be ignorant, brethren, of our trouble which came to us in Asia: that we were burdened beyond measure, above strength, so that we despaired even of life." 2 CORINTHIANS 1:8

Being confronted and measured by the divine demands is always for the purpose of escorting us to Christ. God uses not only the law and the Sermon on the Mount to measure us, but He also uses our environment. Our environment makes demands upon us that cause us to sense our frailty and weakness. How we meet our environments, face them, and interact with them is used by God to escort us to Christ. Environments include your husband, your wife, your children, your money, your job — all persons, matters, and things in your daily life that affect you. In fact, according to the biblical understanding, environment is simply *that which affects us.* A stormy relationship can affect us, money problems can affect us, taking a thought about a past mistake can affect us. Whatever may affect us — this is environment. Environment is like the law making a demand upon us that is beyond our capacity to handle. Just as the law escorts us to Christ, God intends that our environmental trials would also escort us to Christ. This means that we accept the "all things" of Romans 8:28 as being under God's sovereignty. Categorically, all things are working together for good, because under the mighty hand of God they escort us to Christ.

Environment, which is measured out by God, is always pushing us a little bit too far. We have environments that we cannot cope with in ourselves. We get discouraged. We get depressed. We turn inward upon ourselves and sigh, "How can I go on?" or "I can't make it." Oh, brothers and sisters, that is right! That is exactly right! God intends that our environments would push us beyond our limits. This experience of being pushed beyond what we are able to do becomes our escort to Christ. This was Paul's experience in 2 Corinthians 1:8-

10: [8] "For we do not want you to be ignorant, brethren, of our trouble which came to us in Asia: that we were burdened beyond measure, above strength, so that we despaired even of life. [9] Yes, we had the sentence of death in ourselves, that we should not trust in ourselves but in God who raises the dead, [10] who delivered us from so great a death, and does deliver us; in whom we trust that He will still deliver us." Here Paul allowed his "despair of life" to escort him to the God who raises the dead, knowing that He would deliver him. Thus, again and again, every kind of demand in our environment is actually a divine escort in disguise to lead us to Christ.

Beyond our capacity   August 14th

"And you shall remember that the Lord your God led you all the way these forty years in the wilderness, to humble you and test you, to know what was in your heart, whether you would keep His commandments or not. So He humbled you, allowed you to hunger, and fed you with manna which you did not know nor did your fathers know, that He might make you know that man shall not live by bread alone; but man lives by every word that proceeds out of the mouth of the Lord." DEUTERONOMY 8:2-3

When the Lord said, "to humble you and test you," He meant "to measure you." When He said, "to know what was in your heart," He meant that in their hearts, the children of Israel would discover murmuring and rebellion manifesting itself. They would find themselves coming short of God's standard. In other words, all their negative reactions to their environment were allowed by God to escort them to live by every word that proceeds out of the mouth of God.

The fact that the Lord allowed them to hunger and then fed them with manna signifies that they were pushed beyond their capacity in order that they would be escorted to eat divine food. Not to "live by bread alone" meant not to live by the natural life, but by every word that proceeds out of the mouth of the Lord. In the wilderness, God was seeking to escort them to Himself, to learn to live by Him as their source and supply. In the same way, God humbles us through environments that we cannot cope with. It is at those junctures that we need to quickly recognize our escort! The feelings of not being able to cope *are* the escort. Our escorts leading us to Christ come in the form of frustration, desperate feelings, and failure. We need to recognize these escorts and allow them to guide us to live by manna, by Christ as our bread!

A life-voice   August 15th

"My sheep hear My voice, and I know them, and they follow Me. And I give them eternal life." JOHN 10:27-28

Christ as the life-giving Spirit now dwells in our regenerated human spirit, making our spirit life. Our spirit is life because Christ, the life-giver, lives there. This helps us to realize the location of the life-consciousness within us. It is in our spirit! Thus, not only is our spirit life, but our spirit is also the source from which every kind of life-consciousness flows into our being (cf. John 7:37-39; 10:10).

We need to make the connection between experiencing the Lord's *life* and hearing the Lord's *voice*. This connection is presented by the Lord Himself in John 10:10 and 16 as well as John 10:27-28: [10] "I have come that they may have *life,* and that they may have it more abundantly.... [16] And other sheep I have which are not of this fold; them also I must bring, and they will hear My *voice;* and there will be one flock and one shepherd.... [27] My sheep hear My *voice,* and I know them, and they follow Me. [28] And I give them eternal *life,* and they shall never perish; neither shall anyone snatch them out of My hand." By these verses we can see *the way* the Lord's voice is experienced by us. It is by the Lord's life that we experience His voice. It is a life-voice!

"How that by revelation He made known to me the mystery (as I wrote before in a few words, by which, when you read, you may perceive my understanding in the mystery of Christ)."
EPHESIANS 3:3-4

We need to be enlarged and expanded in our understanding concerning the mystery of Christ, the church. Paul wants us to perceive his understanding in this mystery. A mystery in the Bible is not something we cannot know. It is simply something we cannot know by our natural thought. It cannot be known apart from divine revelation in our spirit. That is why the church in the Bible is not in the category of our thought. The church is in the category of God's thought. No one can create the church, no one can explain the church or understand the church. The church is one hundred percent in the realm of mystery. This means that no one knows the church until God reveals it (Matt. 16:16-18).

The church is not in the realm of man's choice — my choice, your choice, his choice, their choice. It is simply not in that realm. This is just like salvation. Salvation is not in the realm of our choice. For example, there is no salvation in Buddha, there is no salvation in Confucius, and there is no salvation in the New Age movement. We know that salvation is not a matter of our choice. There is only one name under heaven given among men whereby we must be saved (Acts 4:12). This means that concerning salvation, it is altogether a matter of God's choice. And the church is no different. It is also in the realm of God's choice. The choice has been made. We simply see it.

234

Winds of teaching versus Christ   August 17th

"That we should no longer be children, tossed to and fro and carried about with every wind of doctrine, by the trickery of men, in the cunning craftiness by which they lie in wait to deceive."
EPHESIANS 4:14

When we do not have the proper focus of Christ, we are always subject to distracting and even heretical things. These distractions are very unsettling to our souls. Acts 15:24 says, "Since we have heard that some who went out from us have troubled you with words, *unsettling your souls,* saying, You must be circumcised and keep the law — to whom we gave no such commandment." Legalistic teachings and tones are not focused on Christ and are always unsettling to our souls. Paul calls these teachings winds of doctrine. Only being rooted and grounded in Christ Himself can save us from these kinds of things.

We need to have the same value system that the Triune God has in this universe — Christ. It is Christ that must be our emphasis and our atmosphere. If something else comes in and replaces Christ, regardless of how good it may be, it is a wind of doctrine. It may be a good teaching from the Bible, it may be a particular practice, it may be a gift of the Spirit, it may be an emphasis upon a gifted person. Whatever it may be, it will have the effect of unsettling our soul. Anything that brings us down to a level lower than Christ is not the church. The church's emphasis and focus is always Christ.

With the full assurance of understanding that Christ is all and in all, we are solid, just like a rock. Nothing can change or influence us. We are not left to blow in the wind, wondering what direction we should take. Our course is set and our way is clear because we are under revelation. It is not a matter of speculation, negotiation, or experimentation. Christ and the church is a matter of revelation. Revelation motivates us! Revelation is our leading! Revelation is

235

our mandate! Once we see the revelation of the church as Christ, that very revelation becomes a mandate to practice the church life on this earth (Eph. 1:9-10). We have no choice. Indeed, the revelation is referred to by Paul as "the command of the eternal God" (Rom. 16:25-26). The command is made known for the obedience of faith. This is the ultimate issue of understanding the church as Christ — that we rise up to gather together to experience a rich Christ for the church life.

"This Rock" August 18th

"And I also say to you that you are Peter, and upon this rock I will build My church, and the gates of Hades shall not prevail against it." MATTHEW 16:18

What constitutes the full meaning of "this rock"? It is the saints making a confession of Christ Himself as everything out from the realm of revelation. This revelation/declaration of Christ is the factor for the church to be Christ in reality. Such a declaration of Christ as "this rock" proceeds from our spirit of revelation, which sees Him as everything. It is unique, simple, and available for all of us to utter — "You are the Christ, the Son of the living God." When we declare this in our daily life we are saying, "You are the qualified One! You are my all in all! You are the One who has the relationship with the Father! You are the One who has the relationship with the saints. You are the One who has a relationship with the law, the flesh, the self, the devil, condemnation, and sin. Lord, You are the Christ, the appointed One to be my relationship with all things."

In the presence of this kind of revelation and declaration, the Lord seized the opportunity to say to Peter, "Upon this rock, I will build My church." In other words, in that brief declaration — "You are the Christ, the Son of the living God" — Peter had summarized every forthcoming truth in the entire New Testament about the all-sufficiency of the indwelling Christ. Thus, to confess "You are the Christ" means "You are revealed in me. You are everything to me. You are living Your life in me. You are my relationship with all things." To declare "You are the Christ" is saying "I am no longer living to myself. I am no longer my point of reference. Lord, You are! You are! You are!" This becomes our constant confession in our daily lives, and this is the rock upon which the church is built.

"You are the Son of the living God"   August 19th

"And Simon Peter answered and said, You are the Christ, the Son of the living God." MATTHEW 16:16

With this confession we drop our self as the source of our living. We drop *our* decision, *our* choice, *our* view, *our* way, and we take Christ as our all in all. Then the Lord has the "rock" upon which to build the church. When we are persons constituted with this revelation and confession in our daily living, we bring in the reality of "this rock" upon which the Lord will build His church — the church that the gates of Hades will not prevail against (Matt. 16:18). The word "prevail" implies a struggle. Nevertheless, even with the struggle, the gates of Hades will not be strong enough to overpower the building of the church. Why? Because in your weakness and in your frailty you do not refer your *self* to yourself anymore! But with your mouth you declare, "Jesus, You are the Christ!" With your thoughts, with your feelings, with your reactions, with your considerations, you inwardly experience this One by saying, "You are the Son of the living God!" That is saying, "Lord, You know how to live. I do not know how to live. I am just a branch in You as the Vine. Without You I can do nothing!" That is the significance of saying, "You are the Christ, the Son of the living God!" And this kind of declaration coming from this kind of revelation is the rock upon which Christ builds His church in reality.

237

To say "You are the Christ, the Son of the living God" is not a mere doctrinal confession. It is saying, "You are the Christ loving and forgiving the saints." It is saying, "You are the Christ that died to sin and the flesh." It is saying, "You are the Christ where there is no condemnation." I am not a condemned person anymore because I am not qualified to take any condemnation! God did not leave me in myself. He put me in Christ Jesus! Now there is no condemnation to those in Christ Jesus! He is the Son of the living God, so He is my relationship with the Father! I am in His love. I am in His joy. I am not imitating His love. I am not imitating His joy. I have the actual joy of Jesus in me! It is revelation that causes me to make these declarations about Christ, and it is "upon *this* rock" that the Lord builds His church.

Withdraw for fresh supply   August 20th

"Then the report went around concerning Him all the more; and great multitudes came together to hear, and to be healed by Him of their infirmities. So He Himself often was withdrawing into the wilderness and was praying." LUKE 5:15-16

A marked feature of how the Lord spent time with the Father was that He practiced withdrawing into the wilderness to pray. The Lord not only rose up early in the morning to be with the Father, but also on many occasions during the day and night He withdrew from the crowds privately to pray. Luke 5:16-17 says, "So He Himself often *was* withdrawing into the wilderness and *was* praying.... And the power of the Lord *was* present to heal them." The repetition of the Greek imperfect tense (continuous action in past time), translated as "was," clearly shows that the Lord's power to heal was in direct proportion to the time He was spending withdrawing to pray. A paraphrase might help to grasp the sense of this passage: "He Himself was continuously withdrawing in the wilderness and was

238

continuously praying, . . . and as a result, the power of the Lord was continuously with Him to heal."

The Lord's practice of withdrawing reveals how much He was actually dependent upon continuous supply to meet His present needs. Even the Lord Jesus Himself needed fresh supply, fresh infusion, and fresh energy imparted into His humanity in order to live a life expressing God. The way He received these fresh supplies was by His practice of withdrawing to spend time with the Father in prayer. By this we can see that the Lord did not live trusting in His divinity to carry Him through His human existence. In His humanity, He needed to withdraw to spend time with the Father for His daily life. If He as the very Son of God depended upon this time, how much more do we need to practice withdrawing in order to be continuously supplied by the divine life!

The blood is active   August 21st

"Now may the God of peace who brought up our Lord Jesus from the dead, that great Shepherd of the sheep, in the blood of the eternal covenant, make you complete in every good work to do His will, working in you what is well pleasing in His sight through Jesus Christ, to whom be glory forever and ever. Amen." HEBREWS 13:20-21

That the God of peace brought up from the dead the Lord Jesus "in the blood of the eternal covenant" means that the power of resurrection was in the blood. Then Paul immediately applies this resurrection power to us: ". . . make you complete in every good work to do His will, working in you what is well pleasing in His sight."

When the Lord was in the tomb, that was a death situation. There was no feeling, there was no sensation. There was a cessation of any kind of feeling. It was blank because death was there in the tomb. Yet the blood was working all the time. The blood never ceased. And it was the power of the blood that raised Him from the dead. It was the blood of the eternal covenant. That means the effectiveness of the blood is operating in us and over us when we do not feel a thing. Be sure that when you are the lowest and when you have no emotion, the eternal blood is there. The blood of the eternal covenant is there doing in us what is well pleasing in God's sight. Our relationship with God is steady and constant. He is operating in our environment, moving a few things around to bring us to Himself directly. All the while, the blood is there. The blood is active. Its effectiveness stands sure without interruption.

Does God love Christ?   August 22nd

"And I have declared to them Your name, and will declare it, that the love with which You loved Me may be in them, and I in them."
JOHN 17:26

Here in John 17 the Lord prayed that the love with which the Father loved Him would be in us! The same love that is between the Father and the Son is now *in us*. How is it in us? The Lord said, "I in them." When He gets into us then the same love is flowing in us. When we sing or pray a little, just exercising our spirit, we discover that there is liquid love flowing there. That liquid love is the Father and the Son loving one another right within our spirit. When we sing and pray, we are merging into Their love. We are taking the on-ramp into the freeway-flow of the Father and the Son. They are loving one another and enjoying one another, and we have an on-ramp in our spirit to merge into Their love. Hallelujah, there is only one love in this universe. It is the love that is flowing between the Father and the Son. There is not another love that God has toward us. There is only one love. It is the love of the Father for the Son. And that love has been poured out in our hearts through the Holy Spirit (Rom. 5:5).

Brothers and sisters, we are in Christ. We are included in this beloved One. You ask, Does God love me? Actually, you need to change your question to, Does God love Christ? You are in Christ. If you are in Christ, you cannot help but be loved because we know that God loves Christ. You are in the object of the Father's love. Regardless of our condition, we are eternally the objects of divine love and divine grace.

Do not dispute with the Father   August 23rd

"And suddenly a voice came from heaven, saying, This is My beloved Son, in whom I am well pleased." MATTHEW 3:17

Experiencing the centrality of Christ in our lives is essential for Him to be the reality of the church. Practically, His centrality is worked out when we give Him the first place in all things. This means that we do not initiate things in our lives. Our mind, emotion, and will are not the initiators in our living. We do not think on our own, feel on our own, decide on our own, choose on our own, go on our own, stay on our own. In everything He has the first place! We are not qualified to initiate anything. We are not qualified to speak; neither are we qualified to issue a rebuke! In everything He must have the first place! This is how His centrality is worked out.

Christ becomes the centrality of all things in our lives when we actually give Him the first place. To give Him first place is to stand on the same ground that the Father stands on. It is the Father who recognizes Christ as the centrality of all things. Do not dispute with the Father. Do not dare to think differently from the Father. The Father has already made the decision about who the centrality is in this universe. The Father made Christ to be everything by making Him the firstborn of all creation (Col. 1:15). The Father has caused the fullness of the Godhead to dwell in Christ bodily (Col. 1:19). When the Father said, "This is My beloved Son, in whom I am well pleased," He put His stamp of approval entirely upon His Son. He wants His Son to be the source of all things. Do not reason and dispute in your small, feeble thinking that you are going to have the first place in your life or in the church. No! Christ has the first place. We must let Him be our relationship with everything by calling on His name and submitting to His inner authority. As we let Him transmit Himself into us, He infuses us with His life and virtues. In this way, He is the centrality and He has the first place.

The Father's point of view   August 24th

"All things came into being through Him; and apart from Him not one thing came into being that has come into being." JOHN 1:3 (NASV)

Do we see how the Father feels about His Son? The Father would not handle the universe apart from Christ. This indicates how deeply the Father feels about His Son. When Peter said, "You are the Christ, the Son of the living God," the Lord responded, "Flesh and blood has not revealed this to you, but My Father who is in heaven." In other words, Peter received the revelation of how the Father feels about the Son. He is the Christ, the Son of the living God! Get out of your well. Get out of your problems. Get out of your own thinking, and come over to the Father's side. Come on over, and let us stand and look from the Father's point of view. Let us look and see how He feels about His Son. If you would just say from your spirit, "You are the Christ, the Son of the living God," God's Spirit will witness with your spirit. You will be taking the Father's testimony, the Father's viewpoint, about His Son. The Father's value of His Son is so high that He would not handle creation apart from His Son. Just consider this statement: "And apart from Him not one thing came into being which has come into being." Not one thing! The Father did not do one thing apart from Christ! Should we be any different from the Father? The Father handles everything with Christ.

"And he said, Please, show me Your glory. Then He said, I will make all My goodness pass before you, and I will proclaim the name of the LORD before you. I will be gracious to whom I will be gracious, and I will have compassion on whom I will have compassion." EXODUS 33:18-19

When Moses said to the Lord, "Show me Your glory," the Lord's reply was simply, "I will make all My goodness pass before you, and I will proclaim the name of the Lord before you." The Lord further responded to Moses by saying, "So it shall be, while My glory passes by, that I will put you in the cleft of the rock, and will cover you with My hand while I pass by" (v. 22). Following this speaking, Moses presented himself to the Lord to see His glory: 5 "Then the Lord descended in the cloud and stood with him there, and proclaimed the name of the Lord. 6 And the Lord passed before him and proclaimed, The LORD, the LORD God, merciful and gracious, longsuffering, and abounding in goodness and truth, 7 keeping mercy for thousands, forgiving iniquity and transgression and sin" (Exo. 34:5-7).

The Lord's answer to Moses' request, "Show me Your glory," consisted of a wonderful heavenly scenery passing before him. Four times in these verses the Lord emphasized the matter of Moses seeing something pass before him: "I will make all My goodness *pass* before you," "My glory *passes* by," "I *pass* by," and "the Lord *passed* before him and proclaimed." From this we can see that to behold the Lord's glory means to see the scenery of His Person and His work pass before us. It was beholding this scenery that transformed Moses so that "the skin of his face shone" (Exo. 34:30).

For Moses to behold the scenery of God's glory passing by, the Lord told him that He would put him in the cleft of the rock and cover him with His hand (Exo. 33:22). In typology this signifies being hidden in the crucified Christ, who died for us on the cross and shed

His precious blood so that we can approach God directly and behold His glory. Thus, because of the blood, because of Christ's finished work, because of that once-and-for-all sacrifice, because He entered into the Holiest of All and made a way for us to be there and live there, now we can fully enjoy the glory of the Lord by letting this redemptive scenery pass before our spiritual eyes. Only the blood of Jesus ushers us into the glory. Growth does not get us into the glory. Being a believer for twenty-five or fifty years does not merit our getting into the glory. Only one thing qualifies us to enjoy the glory of the Lord — the precious blood of the Lamb. That is all. Just the blood. We can declare, "I am forgiven, I am washed, I am cleansed, and now I am qualified to behold the Lord face-to-face." Paul describes this privilege as our having "the knowledge of the glory of God in the face of Christ" (2 Cor. 4:6).

Beholding   August 26th

"But we all, with unveiled face, beholding as in a mirror the glory of the Lord, are being transformed into the same image from glory to glory, just as by the Spirit of the Lord." 2 CORINTHIANS 3:18

When Moses was on the mountain with God, he was not doing anything. He was not analyzing his own situation. He was not looking at himself. He was simply there watching the scenery, watching everything pass by him. Moses was just there and God passed by proclaiming His name, His goodness, His mercy, and His forgiveness. It was after seeing all of this that Moses came down from the mountain shining.

In 2 Corinthians 3:18 Paul says, "But we all, with unveiled face, beholding . . . the glory of the Lord." To behold this glory we need to exercise ourselves to let the glory of Christ's Person and work pass before us. Paul practiced this in his preaching of the gospel. Thus, he could write to the Galatians about how the Lord Jesus had been openly portrayed crucified before their eyes (Gal. 3:1). By such a gospel scenery they came under "the hearing of faith" and received the Spirit (Gal. 3:2). In other words, they received the Spirit by letting the crucified Christ pass before them by means of hearing the gospel. They beheld His Person and work and were infused with the Holy Spirit.

There are many other verses in the New Testament that talk about beholding the Lord, such as beholding the glory as of the only begotten from the Father in John 1:14, seeing Jesus in Hebrews 2:9, seeing the ascended Son of Man in John 6:62, beholding His glory in John 17:24, and looking away unto Jesus in Hebrews 12:2. These kinds of verses stress the importance in our daily life of allowing the Lord's entire redemptive process to pass before us, including His incarnation, human living, crucifixion, resurrection, ascension, and enthronement. We also need to behold all that His wonderful Person is, with all His attributes. What transforms us is seeing His mercy, His kindness, His goodness, His righteousness, His holiness, and His worthiness. All that Jesus is and all that He has passed through in His redemptive process needs to become our daily scenery. To be transformed, we just need to spend time with the Lord and let this scenery pass before us. Every day, even every hour, we can behold the glory of the Lord.

Love transmitted   August 27th

"Now hope does not disappoint, because the love of God has been poured out in our hearts by the Holy Spirit who was given to us." ROMANS 5:5

The flow of love between the Father and the Son is the same love that is being transmitted to us! It is wonderful to know that in this universe there is only one love. We do not have any love for God. We might think we have love for God, but in ourselves, none of us have any love for God (Rom. 3:10-11). Every bit of love in us toward God is God. Perhaps you feel you do not have that much love for the Lord. You find your heart loving the things of the world. But let me tell you, if there is even a little bit of love within you, a little bit of desire for the Lord, that *is* the Lord. Take that little bit of love, baby it, nourish it, and let it grow. Just tell the Lord, "Thank You for this little bit of love. It is You, Lord. The love in me for You, even if it is so small, is You. It is God."

There is one love, and that one love has been poured out in our heart. That is why we do not work up love. We cannot be loving in ourselves. We need to get into another kingdom, another realm, where the divine love is flowing. We need to be born again. When we are born again, we see the kingdom and we enter into the kingdom. We enter into the realm of the divine love. Our spirit becomes joined to the Lord, so that we are joined to the transmission of divine love between the Father and the Son. So right inside of you is the love of God (John 17:26). It is in you.

To experience this transmission of divine love, just get on your knees and start thanking Him for *everything* in your life. Thank Him for every problem. Thank Him for every impossibility. Thank Him that all things are working together for good to those who love God (Rom. 8:28). Just start loving Him and thanking Him. After a short time, the tears will come down, and you will begin to merge with the divine life and love that is within your being. That life is so thankful to the Father. That life knows how to suffer. It knows how to pass through difficulties. That is why the Bible talks about entering into the fellowship of His sufferings (Phil. 3:10). It is not gritting our teeth and hoping for a better day. It is participating in the satisfaction and the contentment of His life (Phil. 4:11-13). Nothing outwardly changes, but inwardly you are joyful in God. God is enough. You say "Thank You" to the Lord, and there is a wonderful transmission of life and love.

"Therefore you shall be perfect, just as your Father in heaven is perfect." MATTHEW 5:48

The love of God moves us, preserves us, keeps us, and reaches us wherever we are. And this very love is the love we have toward one another in the church. This unconditional love of God is the love with which we love each other. This is what makes the perfect church. All the members, with all their imperfections, are in a fellowship with one another in the love of God. The perfect church is the church that has the love of God flowing in all the imperfect members toward all the other imperfect members.

In Matthew 5:48 when the Lord said, "You shall be perfect, just as your Father in heaven is perfect," He was not speaking of a moral kind of perfection — having a completely righteous and rectified life without any problems, faults, or sins. Of course, we are not condoning sin; but here the Lord was not referring to a sinless life. When we think of "perfect," we think of living a perfect life of absolute holiness according to God's standard. But here the context of being perfect is Matthew 5:44: "But I say to you, love your enemies, bless those who curse you, do good to those who hate you, and pray for those who spitefully use you and persecute you." This means love the unlovable. Love the ones who are irritating to you. Love your enemies. Then He says, "Therefore you shall be perfect, just as your Father in heaven is perfect." This means that the Father's love is perfect toward all sinful men. That is the meaning of perfection. Also, in Colossians 3:14 Paul tells the believers, "Put on love, which is the bond of perfection," or "the bond of perfectness." Thus, there can be a perfect church.

Perfection in my response August 29th

"Jesus said to him, I do not say to you, up to seven times, but up to seventy times seven." MATTHEW 18:22

W hat is the perfect church? It is a forgiving church. It is a longsuffering church. It is an enduring, patient, caring church that is receiving all the failing, sinful, ungodly people who have Christ in them. There is forgiveness up to seventy times seven. And there is love and there is mercy. There is this kind of relationship that you do not find in any other place. In other places, when someone treats me unfairly or I am offended, I leave and go somewhere else. But that does not accomplish the Lord's desire to perfect the church in the realm of God's unconditional love. This is the meaning of His prayer in John 17:23, "that they may be made perfect into one." Being perfected into one is simply this: the love of God being perfected in us toward one another. This does not mean the perfection of your condition. It means the perfection in my response to your condition — how I receive you, love you, pray for you, and have mercy toward you. It is how I receive you and make you the object of God's love, no matter what condition you are in.

The church is filled with the love of God — the love He has toward us, the love we have toward Him, and the love we have toward one another. How marvelous that this is the love in the church. The love-life in the church is the unconditional love of God coming to us. We know what He has done for us. We know how He has received us. Now that same love is demonstrated toward one another.

The brothers as Christ August 30th

"But when you thus sin against the brethren, and wound their weak conscience, you sin against Christ." 1 CORINTHIANS 8:12

I f this realization were really in our consciousness — that to sin against a brother is to sin against Christ — how differently we would treat one another. Brothers and sisters, we are members of Christ. So we need to keep the precious oneness of the Spirit between us. God is between us. We are not making up or manufacturing a oneness. We are sharing in the oneness of the Father, Son, and Spirit. Their oneness is in us! We do not have another kind of oneness.

Brothers, there is a oneness of the Spirit. We can keep the oneness of the Spirit because God is between us as the bond of peace. The way you keep the oneness of the Spirit is to keep checking the monitor of peace. Is there peace? In taking the steps that you are taking, is there peace? Do not interfere with the peace. The peace between us is so sweet. The kingdom of God is righteousness, peace, and joy in the Holy Spirit (Rom. 14:17). Where there are no other factors but Christ between us, no legalities being imposed on us, there is peace! It is called the peace of Christ. That peace is not just a good feeling between us. That peace is a Person! He made peace. He Himself is that peace (Eph. 2:14). And keeping peace is keeping Christ between one another (Col. 3:15). That is what the church is. The church is Christ dispensing His peace between us. This is the sense in which we understand that the church is Christ.

Satisfy the inner demand   August 31st

"I have heard the murmurings of the children of Israel. Speak to them, saying, At twilight you shall eat meat, and in the morning you shall be filled with bread. And you shall know that I am the Lord your God." Exodus 16:12

The children of Israel experienced a special capacity to collect and enjoy manna early in the morning before the sun became hot (Exo. 16:21). In the same way, there is a special capacity to experience and know the Lord, who is the true manna, early in the morning. I cannot fully explain or tell you why, but according to my experience there is a capacity to hear His voice and receive His impressions early in the morning. I have found that there is a special portion of the enjoyment of the Lord in the early morning that is different from any other time.

This life is a life of feeding upon the Word. This life is a life that gets up early to be with the Father. It is a life that practices withdrawing. This is the life that dwells within us. So we need to pay attention to the Lord's speaking to us about our schedules, our daily living, and our priorities. We will never be a satisfied person unless we satisfy the inner demand of Christ, who is "our life," to spend time enjoying God. We need to spend time for this love-life and relationship between the Father and the Son to be cultivated within our hearts until we are a reproduction of Christ. The Spirit of His Son is in our hearts crying, "Abba, Father," loving the Father. It is in this triune flow of love that we spend time with Him and enjoy Him. Do not mourn over yourself. Do not waste time taking condemnation and looking at your condition. Enjoy the Person in whom the Father delights. Just say, "O Father, You delight in Your Son! Look at His blood! Look at His righteousness! Look at His worthiness! Look at what He has attained and accomplished! Father, You cannot turn away the presence of Your Son. Nothing can separate me from Your love which is in Christ Jesus my Lord" (Rom. 8:39). We just need to leave our preoccupation with ourself and enjoy this Person.

September

A life of withdrawing

"You also helping together in prayer for us, that thanks may be given by many persons on our behalf for the gift granted to us through many." 2 CORINTHIANS 1:11

We must realize that all of the pressures we face in our environments are continuous calls to us to spend more time with the Lord. Even our fleshly disposition with its negative reactions, lusts, and moods is another call and a sign that we need to withdraw and pray. The apostle Paul also faced many difficult situations, such as the one he describes in 2 Corinthians 1:8: "For we do not want you to be ignorant, brethren, of our trouble which came to us in Asia: that we were burdened beyond measure, above strength, so that we despaired even of life." Here, not only did Paul face a desperate environment, but he also had to handle his reactions of despair to the environment. Yet in verse 11 he could testify that God would deliver him by means of prayer. We must see that the practice of withdrawing to pray and spend time with the Lord should increasingly become a normal part of our Christian life.

The Greek word translated withdraw *(hupochoreo)* in Luke 5:16 is a compound word made up of two prepositions, one meaning *under* and the other meaning *apart*. The combination of these two words indicates that He withdrew into privacy. He separated Himself "apart" in privacy to be with the Father. If we desire to cultivate our love-life with the Lord, we will surely discover the Lord Himself moving in us, prodding us to withdraw from all the empty talk and looseness in our living in order to spend more time with Him. To practice withdrawing we need a vision, and this simply means having before us a vision of the kind of life the Lord

Jesus lived on this earth spending time with the Father. He was continuously withdrawing to cultivate and nourish His life with the Father. This is how He expressed God. And this is the life that is now within us. It is a life of withdrawing.

The law given to the flesh   September 2nd

"So then, those who are in the flesh cannot please God." ROMANS 8:8

This verse clearly reveals that the flesh cannot please God. One day God gave the law. The law was given specifically to the flesh. The law was not given to the spirit. Why then did God give the law when He knew the flesh was fallen and could not keep it? God gave the law as a child-conductor, or escort, to lead us to Christ (Gal. 3:24). How does the law lead us to Christ? The good flesh in man wants to keep the law in order to be a proper person. But even though it has a good intention, it is independent from God. It is seeking to keep the law on its own. Of course, it fails. And when it fails, it wants to pick itself up again. It wants to try again to measure up to the standard of the law. The flesh likes the law. It really wants to keep it. But it can only come up with repeated failure in its relationship with the law. Thus, the law was given to the good flesh in order to tire it out, discourage it, depress it, and defeat it. It was given to convince us that there is no hope in the realm of the flesh. The very giving up of the flesh in discouragement is what God uses to lead us to Christ.

The flesh as a source is without life and life-supply. The spirit as a source is life, because Christ Himself lives there (Rom. 8:10). The law was never given to the spirit, because the law could not give life. It could only state facts and leave you to yourself. Whenever we are under the demand of the law, feeling driven and compelled to try to attain to something, we are totally in the realm of the flesh.

252

The law was given to our flesh to wear us out, to convince us that we need Another life. We need another source. We need to go to another person — "*Who* will deliver me from this body of death?" (Rom. 7:24). God's way of deliverance out of the flesh-law syndrome is to graft us into Another life. He joins us to Christ in spirit so that we are one with Him to share and participate in all that He is and does. This joining to be one spirit with Him produces our new "I." This is an organic "I" in which one being shares the life of another. This "I" is in resurrection with the One who has lived the life we need to live. And this "I" is now resident within our spirit transmitting that life to us. Now our part is to merge with and participate in Him.

Revelation and consecration   September 3rd

"For this reason we also, since the day we heard it, do not cease to pray for you, and to ask that you may be filled with the full knowledge of His will in all wisdom and spiritual understanding; that you may have a walk worthy of the Lord, fully pleasing Him."
COLOSSIANS 1:9-10

Paul is praying that the vision of the major things on God's heart would be opened to the believers. Once we see those things, our life will begin to change to please the Lord. This is because the vision or scene before our spiritual eyes changes us. The change in us is not because we are so victorious in ourselves, but because of the transforming effect the vision has on us. For example, when the vision is a reality within us, it makes a difference whether we carry a grudge or a bad feeling toward a brother or sister. Thus, our inward life is radically changed and regulated by what we see.

The manifestation of the radical change in our life is our personal consecration. Because consecration is our response to revelation and vision, the higher our revelation, the greater and deeper will be our consecration. The lower our revelation, the less will be our consecration. Why are so many believers distracted? They attend church meetings on Sunday, but practically speaking there is not much reality in their daily life. Why? No vision. No revelation. No ministry from Paul's, Peter's, or John's revelation. Brothers and sisters, we need to be in the identical revelation of the apostles. We need to see what they saw. We do not create something new. Rather, in our spirit we see the same things they saw. This is revelation.

Called into one unique fellowship   September 4th

"Jesus said to him, I am the way, the truth, and the life. No one comes to the Father except through Me." JOHN 14:6

Based upon redemption, God can now give away His relationship with His Son. Galatians 4:4-6 says, [4] "But when the fullness of the time had come, God sent forth His Son, born of a woman, born under the law, [5] *to redeem* those who were under the law, *that we might receive the sonship.* [6] And *because you are sons, God has sent forth the Spirit of His Son into your hearts, crying out, Abba, Father!"* To receive the sonship is to receive the rights, privileges, and relationships of the Son of God. Our God took His relationship with His Son and put it right into our hearts! We do not have a separate fellowship with the Father. We have been called *into* the one unique fellowship of His Son, Jesus Christ our Lord (1 Cor. 1:9). "Truly our fellowship is with the Father and with His Son Jesus Christ" (1 John 1:3).

This relationship and fellowship means that we are not standing in our own righteousness, but in Christ's alone (1 Cor. 1:30). Neither are we dependent on our condition or status as the basis of our relationship with God. We are not trusting in anything related to ourselves (Phil. 3:7-9). We are nothing and have nothing. When we wake up in the morning, we do not need to inspect *our* relationship with God; rather we say, "Lord Jesus, how are You doing today? How is Your relationship with the Father?" Never again do we need to doubt our relationship with God since our relationship with God is Christ (Rom. 8:38-39).

The uniqueness of the Lord's relationship with the Father is emphasized in John 14:6: "Jesus said to him, I am the way, the truth, and the life. No one comes [is coming – present tense] to the Father except through Me." When He said, "no one," it means categorically *no one* (Rom. 3:10-12). No one is coming to the Father except through Him. When He said, "I am the way, the truth, and the life," He was, in effect, saying, "I am your constant relationship with the Father." How could we ever sink to puny, morbid introspection again? This kind of inner activity is useless! It is wasted time and energy. Our relationship with the Father is Jesus Christ our Lord. He does not change. Every morning we can wake up and open ourselves to God with a released spirit, knowing that our joy, our love, our relationship with the Father, is absolutely wonderful. What a Christ we have!

Let the defeats escort

September 5th

"Let us therefore come boldly to the throne of grace, that we may obtain mercy and find grace to help in time of need." HEBREWS 4:16

The law is beyond our capacity. The Lord's words in Matthew 5—7 are beyond our capacity. Our environments also push us beyond our capacity. All these things are absolutely God's favor to us, because He is not leaving us to ourselves. He exhausts us. He allows us to be defeated and feel discouraged. But the problem is this — we do not see discouragement as an escort to Christ! May the Lord open our eyes to see what is happening to us in the midst of our reactions, that we might seize our discouragement and let it escort us to Christ.

Have you had any escorts lately? There is great hope in our escorts. They turn defeat into hope. The most defeated can use their very defeat as an escort to Christ. Whatever the Lord may expose in our lives — our reasoning mind, our divided heart, our motives — causes us to feel undone, naked, and defeated before Him. We need to realize at that time that the Lord is simply escorting us to Himself. Paul says in Hebrews 4:13, "And there is no creature hidden from His sight, but all things are naked and open to the eyes of Him to whom we must give account." Following this verse, in which we are exposed to the core of our being, Paul says in Hebrews 4:16, "Let us therefore come boldly to the throne of grace, that we may obtain mercy and find grace to help in time of need." This speaks of being escorted to Christ *at the very time* of being naked and laid bare. Thus, all the demands and all the defeats are our personal escorts to Christ.

The demand of the law, the demand of Matthew 5—7, and the demands of our environment are all arranged by God to lead us out of our own limited capacity and ability. God's intention is to bring us into Another life. He wants us to touch the life that now dwells in our spirit. Touch the life that has already made it into glory! Touch the life who is the victory!

The inner drawing   September 6th

"No one can come to Me unless the Father who sent Me draws him; and I will raise him up at the last day." JOHN 6:44

Hearing and understanding the Lord's voice is a vital and integral part of our daily Christian life. We are actually participating in Christ's own experience described in Isaiah 50:4-5: [4] "The Lord GOD has given Me the tongue of the learned, that I should know how to speak a word in season to him who is weary. *He awakens Me morning by morning, He awakens My ear to hear as the learned. [5] The Lord GOD has opened My ear; and I was not rebellious, nor did I turn away."* The Lord Himself needed to have His ear awakened morning by morning in order to live an obedient life in His

256

humanity. The Lord lives His life in us today in the same way that He lived His life on the earth. Indeed, His human life is being reproduced in us by the Spirit. Thus, we should become more familiar with this aspect of His life so that we can hear and understand His voice in us.

The Lord's voice in us is described in John's Gospel as an inner drawing. In John 6:37 the Lord says, "All that the Father gives Me will come to Me, and the one who comes to Me I will by no means cast out." And again in verses 44-45 He says, [44] "No one can come to Me unless the Father who sent Me *draws him*; and I will raise him up at the last day. [45] It is written in the prophets, And they shall all be taught by God. Therefore everyone who has heard and learned from the Father comes to Me." Thus, to hear God and be taught by God is, in essence, to experience an inward drawing toward the Lord Jesus. That is, this inward speaking is experienced as an attraction toward Christ. This inner drawing indicates His direct speaking to us.

Christ formed in us   September 7th

"My little children, for whom I labor in birth again until Christ is formed in you." GALATIANS 4:19

There are two ways that this verse has been understood. One way is that Christ is formed in us progressively; the other is that Christ is formed in us instantly. Christ being formed in us in a progressive way has been illustrated with a hand and a glove. A glove is shaped according to a hand. Now, I start slipping my hand into the glove in a progressive way. First, I put my index finger into the glove, then my thumb, and then all my other fingers, one by one. Eventually my whole hand is formed into the glove. This illustration has been applied to our experiencing the Lord gradually over a long period of time until Christ is formed in us. Experiencing the Lord progressively in our daily living is a reality that we enjoy. Such an experience is scriptural, yet it should not be applied to this portion of the Word. The question then is, What did Paul mean when he spoke of laboring again for the believers until Christ was formed in them?

The second way to understand Christ being formed in us is that it happens in an instant. Christ comes into us and immediately is formed in our heart as our point of reference, our relationship with everything. This is a constant inward state that every child of God can live in from the day of his new birth until he reaches full maturity. So Christ formed in us does not refer to our arriving at a final stage of maturity in the growth of life. If this was the case — if Christ being formed in us referred to one, long growth process — then Paul would not be laboring for it to happen once again. And surely Paul is not expecting the believers to be born again a second time. There is no such teaching in the New Testament. They were already born again. But something had happened in their experience to remove them from Christ (Gal. 1:6). He was not formed in their hearts as their point of reference for them to grow in the Lord in a proper way.

Our continuous point of reference   September 8th

"My little children, for whom I labor in birth again until Christ is formed in you." GALATIANS 4:19

To understand the exact sense of this verse, it is important to see its context. The Galatian believers had fallen into a state of legality. The words "again" and "until" tell us something. At one point in the believers' experience, Christ had already been formed in them. Then they lost Christ as the One who was everything in their hearts. Now Paul is travailing *again until* Christ is formed in them. This substantiates the truth that Christ being formed in them was not a process; otherwise, they would be waiting indefinitely for this to take place and would not need Paul's "again" prayer. Christ "formed" is Christ restored instantly in our hearts as our center, our focus, our point of reference for relating to all things. Paul was travailing again until this would happen in the believers.

To know the meaning of Galatians 4:19, it is also important to understand the significance of the verb "formed" as it was used by Paul. In elementary school, we all learned that verbs are action words. In our English language, verbs emphasize the time in which the action takes place, whether past, present, or future. Thus, in English *the time of the action* is what is important. However, in the Greek language, the emphasis with the verb is on *the kind of action* taking place, rather than *the time of the action*. The action takes place either in an instantaneous way or in a progressive way. Instantaneous action is called *punctiliar*, and progressive action is called *linear*.

For Christ to be formed in us means that He is instantly poured out into our hearts, so that He becomes our relationship with everything from that moment on. He is now our continuous point of reference. He is the source from which we live. He is the way we handle everything in our lives. He is the way we relate to ourselves. He is the One in whom we constantly abide. He is the Christian life living His life in us. In short, He is our life. Christ formed in us means that He is formed within our hearts as our all in all!

Inner supply   September 9th

"For the law was given through Moses, but grace and reality came through Jesus Christ." JOHN 1:17

The Lord's voice under the new covenant comes as an inner infusion and supply. Galatians 3:21 says, "Is the law then against the promises of God? Certainly not! *For if there had been a law given which could have given life,* truly righteousness would have been by the law." God's voice under the old covenant was correct and proper in itself, but as an outward law it could not give life. It could not infuse and supply life. It could only tell you what to do. No doubt, the law given by Moses accurately defined our condition, but it could not supply life to carry it out. Grace and reality coming through Jesus Christ is different from an outward law being handed to us. Grace and reality is the Lord Himself in person coming to us to infuse His very life into our being.

The law was *given* but grace *came*. There is a big difference. For example, I can communicate with you in two ways. I can send you a letter, or I can come in person to communicate with you. The law given by Moses is like receiving a communication by letter. But grace and reality coming through Jesus Christ is receiving a communication from Christ Himself. When He comes in person, we receive direct infusion and supply. This supply is the new covenant way God speaks to us. His speaking to us is His simultaneous supply into us. Jesus said in John 6:63, "It is the Spirit who gives life; the flesh profits nothing. *The words that I speak to you are spirit, and they are life.*" The very words themselves *are* spirit and life. Thus, His speaking means infusion and inner supply.

God-taught **September 10th**

"But concerning brotherly love you have no need that I should write to you, for you yourselves are taught by God to love one another." 1 THESSALONIANS 4:9

The Lord's speaking is not merely an intermittent or sporadic speaking, but a constant supply of life in our being. For example, we may experience an inner infusion of love toward our relatives to pray for their salvation. The love we feel for them is God's way of speaking to us about them. God did not come and outwardly tell us to love our relatives and pray for them. He does not do it that way. Rather, He wells up within us with compassion and burden. The compassion and burden *are* the Lord's voice, because His voice comes with the infusion and supply of what He wants us to do. As we learn to read the feelings within our heart, we are learning to hear the Lord's voice.

Often, His voice comes like a little seed planted within our hearts in the form of a thought or burden. If we would pay more attention to those burdens and fan them by prayer, we would discover the voice of God in our daily life in an increasing way. However, if we consider His speaking as merely an objective, outward voice, we may miss the hundreds of times God desires to subjectively and inwardly fulfill something within us. Paul refers to this inward teaching in 1 Thessalonians 4:9 when he says that we are taught by God to love one another. The phrase "taught by God" in Greek is a compound word meaning God-taught *(theodidaktos / θεοδίδακτος)*. In other words, we are intuitively God-taught to love one another. This inward God-kind of teaching comes from a present and continuous supply of the Holy Spirit (1 Thess. 4:8).

Comprehending the Scriptures   **September 11th**

"In the beginning was the Word, and the Word was with God, and the Word was God." JOHN 1:1

Comprehension is a vehicle of the Lord's voice. Because of this, it is important to know what it means to "comprehend" in the biblical sense. The Greek word for comprehend is a compound word that means "putting things together in a way that causes you to grasp or understand something." For example, the disciples did not understand the Scriptures until the Lord opened their mind to comprehend them (Luke 24:27-32). It was when He opened up the Old Testament, book by book, and unveiled *Himself as its focus* that they were able to comprehend the Scriptures. At that point, they could put everything together. They understood and comprehended the central meaning of the Scriptures.

To be able to put everything together and properly comprehend the Scriptures, we need to know that the focus of God's speaking is Christ (Heb. 1:1-2). Christ is the Word, the *logos,* God's unique utterance embodied in one Person (John 1:1). When we see Christ as all in all, then we truly begin to comprehend the Scriptures. Furthermore, with this comprehension we are able to know the Lord's speaking. Our comprehension of the proper focus of the Scriptures becomes the factor of the Lord's speaking, and this speaking automatically gives us discernment concerning all other voices and speakings which are not the Lord's.

In Ephesians 3:2-11 the apostle Paul unveils that God's speaking comes through the proper comprehension of His eternal purpose. In verses 3-4 he says, [3] "How that by revelation He made known to me the mystery (as I wrote before in a few words, [4] by which, when you read, you may understand my knowledge in the mystery of Christ)." Paul had a comprehension of the mystery of Christ, which is the central focus of God's heart's desire. This was one of the main reasons that he had so much of the Lord's speaking. God's desire, as Paul unfolds it in Ephesians 3, is centered in Christ being expressed through the church to display God's manifold wisdom to the universe. In verse 11 this is called "the eternal purpose," or "the purpose of the ages." Comprehending or understanding this purpose constitutes the main subject of all the Lord's speaking.

Comprehension is His speaking   September 12th

"Having made known to us the mystery of His will, according to His good pleasure which He purposed in Himself, that unto an administration of the fullness of the times He might head up all things in Christ." EPHESIANS 1:9-10

E very Christian who enters into the apostles' comprehension of Scripture will never be void of God's speaking. The comprehension of God's purpose is itself a mandate. It is the Lord's voice to carry out His purpose on this earth today. The above verses are a testimony of Paul's own comprehension of God's purpose. God's full salvation came to Paul "in all wisdom and prudence" (v. 8). This simply meant that God had made known to him the mystery of His will. He was able to comprehend God's eternal purpose. Yet his comprehension was "unto" something, which is explained in verse 10 as the heading up of all things in Christ. To Paul, his comprehension of God's purpose was not for mere doctrinal knowledge. It was the Lord's voice to him for a practical working out of His administration to head up all things in Christ.

If today we comprehend something of God's eternal purpose with the church — if indeed the Holy Spirit has enlightened us by the written Word of God to be able to put it all together — then that in itself is the Lord's voice speaking to us to take steps for a practical working out of the church life on this earth. Our comprehension of God's plan in His Word *is* His speaking to us today.

God's intrinsic love   September 13th

"As the Father loved Me, I also have loved you; abide in My love." JOHN 15:9

We are not just hoping that God will feel a certain way. He intrinsically feels a certain way toward us. And His intrinsic feeling of love is eternally flowing because of the finality of the cross. Because of the finality of what happened on our behalf at Calvary with the shedding of the Lord's blood, the Father has once and for all received us fallen, sinful people. God so intrinsically loved the world that He gave His only begotten Son (John 3:16). And He demonstrated that love: "while we were yet sinners, Christ died for us" (Rom. 5:8).

Because of Christ, God betrothed us to Himself "in righteousness and justice" (Hosea 2:19). He entered into a love relationship in righteousness, making Christ our imputed, legal righteousness, and taking us out of our own standing. Now we are clothed with Christ Himself as our righteousness. So our love relationship with the Lord is based upon Him being our righteousness. God has betrothed us in justice. He judged our sins once and for all. On the cross, all our sins — past, present, and future — were laid on Christ. The sin question has been answered conclusively at Calvary. This is all tied in to God's unconditional love. This is how I am related to Him. My relationship is characterized by that love based upon blood — based upon righteousness and justice.

God betrothed us not only in righteousness and in justice, but also "in lovingkindness and mercy" (Hosea 2:19). Now God's intrinsic feeling toward us can only be love because of Jesus, because of blood. Our whole relationship with Him is characterized by this — "God loves me." Just stay in His love. Do not leave it. Abide there. Remain there.

The church — not an afterthought   September 14th

"To the intent that now the manifold wisdom of God might be made known through the church to the principalities and powers in the heavenly places." EPHESIANS 3:10

In this verse Paul reveals that the manifold wisdom of God is to be made known through the church. Then immediately, so that we will not put the church on a low level or think lightly of it, Paul adds a qualifying phrase, "according to the eternal purpose which He *made* in Christ Jesus our Lord" (v. 11). "Made" comes from the Greek verb *poieo* (ποιέω) and can also be translated "produced." This shows that the church is not an afterthought of God's, but rather it is the chief priority of His heart. The church was produced in the sphere of Christ Jesus our Lord according to the eternal purpose. Thus, the church is not an expedience to God, to accommodate some problem in the universe. The church is the good pleasure of His will. It is what He prefers above all else. It is what He has cherished and kept hidden in His heart from ages past.

The administration of the mystery is the church meeting on this earth according to what was conceived in eternity past and produced on the cross — nothing more and nothing less. The church cannot be man's innovation or man's creation. The church is the place where God's manifold wisdom is displayed. Ephesians 3:10 says that God's manifold wisdom to the principalities and powers in the heavenly places is made known *through the church.* In other words, the church as the *ekklesia* (ἐκκλησία) — the called out ones, the assembled, gathered saints — is God's administrative unit on this earth and in this universe.

It is an awesome thing in the universe that the church is on this earth. Because of this, God's administration has a way to be worked out. Not only do we enjoy the riches of Christ, but we are gathered as the church where this administration is displayed and opened up.

Being driven out of yourself   September 15th

"And He said to me, My grace is sufficient for you, for My strength is made perfect in weakness. Therefore most gladly I will rather boast in my infirmities, that the power of Christ may tabernacle upon me." 2 CORINTHIANS 12:9

Paul had a thorn in the flesh. It was a chronic problem that caused him to feel weak. He asked the Lord three times to remove it, but the Lord did not remove it. The Lord answered him instead with His grace and His strength. When Paul realized that God was using an environment to put a demand upon his flesh that was beyond his natural strength, he completely changed his attitude toward his thorn in the flesh. He said, "Most gladly I will rather boast in my infirmities, that the power of Christ may tabernacle upon me.

Therefore I take pleasure in infirmities, in reproaches, in needs, in persecutions, in distresses, for Christ's sake. For when I am weak, then I am strong." In other words, Paul was saying, "When I am weak, I allow my weakness to escort me to Christ! It is in my weakness that He tabernacles over me and I draw from Him. Instead of my weakness becoming a frustration to my experience of the Lord, it has become a path to lead me to the One who supplies me continuously with His grace."

Paul learned this through his experience of the demands in his environment. So none of us should allow any environments to embitter us. Instead they should sweeten us, because they bring us so much God. In all the demands, God is teaching us one lesson — "I do not want you to live by your own life anymore. I am simply driving you out of yourself into Myself so that I can be your all in all!" Brothers and sisters, there are hundreds of hallelujahs within us as we appreciate the fact that all the demands in our lives are one escort after another, lined up, to lead us continuously to the all-sufficient Christ!

Aspects of God's will   September 16th

"Therefore do not be unwise, but understand what the will of the Lord is." EPHESIANS 5:17

It is important to distinguish between two aspects of God's will. First, there is the aspect of God's will related to personal matters in our lives. Paul expressed this aspect in Romans 1:10 when he said, "making request if, by some means, now at last I may find a way in *the will of God* to come to you." On this occasion Paul was referring to the will of God concerning his travel plans. This aspect of God's will is not always immediately understood by us; however, it is made known under the Lord's specific leading in our lives.

The second aspect of God's will is actually the main and primary one. It has to do with the revealed will of God that we can understand, or comprehend. It is this aspect of the will of the Lord that Paul refers to in Ephesians 5:17. Understanding this will can cause our daily life to be accurate and in harmony with His goal and purpose. We can have this will of God so fixed in our being that it becomes the controlling factor of our life.

It was by this principle of the revealed will of God that Noah, Abraham, and Moses lived. They all understood what the will of God was. God's will was an ark in Noah's day. God's will in Abraham's day was the good land and the city whose Architect and Maker is God. Abraham was controlled by this vision. God's will in Moses' day was the tabernacle. This revealed will caused him to forsake Egypt and suffer affliction with the people of God, rather than to enjoy the pleasures of sin for a season. Moses had revelation, and this was the factor that controlled him. He was motivated by the vision of God's will for His dwelling place, the tabernacle. In the same way, as believers today, we need to know what God's revealed will is. Knowing and understanding the one unique will of the Lord will not only give meaning to our lives, but it will also bring the dimension of God's eternal purpose into our daily life.

The cross to our members   September 17th

"Therefore put to death your members which are on the earth: fornication, uncleanness, passion, evil desire, and covetousness, which is idolatry." COLOSSIANS 3:5

The world is filled with all the things that stimulate the flesh — the television, the radio, the music, the lyrics. Even the atmosphere in many worldly places is designed by the devil to ruin humanity for God's purpose. It causes humanity to become lower and lower in uncleanness, looseness, fornication, in all the moral filth that is filling the earth today. So I say strongly that we need to exercise our spirit to be strict with everything immoral; otherwise there is no way to grow in our Christian life. Some may think that this kind of fellowship is only for the unmarried. But this is as much for the married as for the unmarried. The flesh does not cease at marriage. Lust does not stop, evil passion does not stop. It may continue in married life. This is why Paul said, "That each of you should know how to possess his own vessel in sanctification and honor, not in the passion of lust, like the Gentiles who do not know God" (1 Thess. 4:4-5). Possessing your own vessel can refer to possessing your own body, or it can also be understood as possessing your spouse. Even in a legitimate marriage relationship, Paul exhorted that the believers were to be sanctified.

We were not called to uncleanness, but we were called in holiness and honor (v. 7). This means we need to be specific to apply the cross to our members. Our members here are not spoken of as being our eyes, ears, or mind. Paul actually refers to our members as fornication and uncleanness. That is how constituted the flesh is with sin. So we must put to death. We must kill. Do not entertain. Do not think. Do not let anything start. Immediately interrupt it with your spirit. Allow your spirit to come out and put it to death. "Lord, I am in Your economy. I am not here being wasted in filth, wasted with my eyes, wasted with my mind, wasted in my flesh, giving my body to uncleanness. I am not here for that. My body is to be sanctified. It is to be holy. It is Yours, and one day it is to be conformed to Your glorious body." In this way, we inwardly apply the cross to our members.

Our state of perfection   September 18th

"I in them, and You in Me; that they may be made perfect in one, and that the world may know that You have sent Me, and have loved them as You have loved Me." JOHN 17:23

In our relationships with one another, we are handling a state of perfection. You might ask, "What do you mean? We are not perfect. We have a long way to go." However, we must see from the divine point of view that we are in a state of perfection. In John 17:21 the Lord Jesus prayed for the believers: "That they all may be one, as You, Father, are in Me, and I in You." His prayer is that we would be brought into Their oneness, Their love. There is only one love in this universe. It is not a matter of your love or my love. Even as Christians, we ourselves have no love. No, there is only one love. It is the love of the Triune God that has been deposited right within us. We just need to recognize it. The love of God is in me for you. The love of God is in you for me. We have been brought into the Triune God, and Their relationship has been brought into us.

In verses 22-23 the Lord continues to pray, [22] "And the glory which You gave Me I have given them, that they may be one just as We are one: [23] I in them, and You in Me; that they may be perfected into one." The word "perfected" could unsettle us. It seems as though we must labor and struggle to arrive at a state of perfected oneness. But actually this is not the case at all. "That they may be perfected" is in the perfect tense in Greek. Thus, it could literally be translated "that they may be brought into a state of perfection." Kenneth Wuest's translation of the New Testament captures the full meaning of the perfect tense: [23] "I in them and You in Me, in order that they, *having been brought to the state of completeness with respect to oneness, may persist in that state of completeness,* to the end that the world might be understanding." We have been brought into a state of perfection, or completeness. The oneness that we have been brought into is the perfect oneness between the Father and the Son. When the Lord says, "I in them, and You in Me," this is the state of perfection. We have been brought into Them to participate in this perfect state of oneness.

269

"Just as He chose us in Him before the foundation of the world, that we should be holy and without blame before Him in love, having predestined us to sonship through Jesus Christ to Himself, according to the good pleasure of His will." EPHESIANS 1:4-5

According to Ephesians 1:4, before there was an earth — before creation, before the foundation of the world — God had a will originating from His good pleasure. The very fact that this verse uses the word "foundation" indicates that God had a design and plan to execute His will. When God created the universe, He laid a foundation because He wanted to build something. His desire was to build a habitation for Himself, together with His Firstborn Son and all of us as the many brothers conformed to His Son's image (Rom. 8:29; Heb. 2:10-11).

The Father's will is a revealed will, a tangible and understandable will. It is defined as sonship. This sonship begins when you and I merge with the Son of God by receiving Him and becoming one spirit with Him. Then this process of sonship continues as we enjoy the unsearchable riches of Christ in our daily life. By this enjoyment He saturates our being from center to circumference to make us persons who express a living like the apostle Paul's — "For to me, to live is Christ" and "Christ is all and in all" (Phil. 1:21; Col. 3:11).

The controlling will of the whole Bible is that we would be transformed and conformed to the image of God's Son (Rom. 8:29). From Genesis to Revelation we see that this one unique will was not only behind the creation of the universe, but it is also controlling the whole universe at this moment in time (Rev. 4:11).

Compatible with His life   **September 20th**

"And let the peace of Christ arbitrate in your hearts, to which also you were called in one body; and be thankful." COLOSSIANS 3:15

Hearing the Lord and being one with His speaking is the same as being compatible with His life. Indeed, following the Lord in our daily life is a matter of always remaining compatible with His life. As regenerated believers we have Another life in us that has another feeling and another consciousness. As we experience His life, we discover different kinds of responses within us that are according to His life. These responses tell us how to remain compatible.

If we do not remain compatible with the Lord's life in any area of our living, we will sense an inward awkwardness and lack. If I do not let the peace of Christ make the decision in my heart when I am tempted to engage in argumentative talk, at that moment I am not compatible with the feeling or registration of the Lord's life within me. As a result of not remaining compatible, we feel the effects within ourselves. We may sense that we are at odds with the Lord. Even *we* do not feel quite normal in our demeanor or inward posture.

Life and peace   September 21st

"For the mind of the flesh is death; but the mind of the Spirit is life and peace." ROMANS 8:6 (ASV)

The Lord is not speaking to us with a loudspeaker out of the heavens. Rather, He manifests His voice to us by the feeling or registration of His life. The Lord feels a certain way within us, producing either the sense of "life and peace," which tells us that we are compatible with His life, or a sense of "death," which tells us that something in our talking, our attitude, or our behavior does not match the nature of His life. In our experience, the mind of the flesh is the consciousness of death, and the mind of the Spirit is the consciousness of life and peace. Of course, the more we drink of the Lord as the Spirit day by day, the richer and deeper will be our fellowship with Him, and the richer and deeper will be our sensitivity to the consciousness of His life. This means we will be His sheep that are compatible with His life-voice (John 10:27).

Being compatible with the Lord's voice and life simply means being agreeable with Him on His terms. It means always being harmonious with His registrations of life and peace within us in our daily life. It is by living compatibly with Him that we grow in life, spontaneously being changed and transformed into His image. So not only do we enjoy Him in a general way, but as we enjoy Him we grow rich in the consciousness of that life. We learn to specifically recognize His inner approval or disapproval in our walk. In other words, we seek to make that life happy and satisfied all day long. Whenever that life is not happy and satisfied, we quickly care for it to make it happy again.

Loving God   September 22nd

"And we know that all things work together for good to those who love God, to those who are the called according to His purpose." ROMANS 8:28

Loving God is an exercise of our spirit. It is contacting Him. This causes our spirit to rise and be filled up with Christ. We may pray, "Lord, I have come to the end of my resources. I cannot live through this. I cannot meet this. I cannot face this. But, Lord, I sink myself into You once again. I open to You and take You as my life and supply. Lord, I am not complaining. I am not living with a feeling of being treated unfairly or getting a bad break in life. There is no such thing in my thought, because all things are avenues to lead me to experience more of the riches of Christ." By touching Him in this way, He saturates our being with Himself.

The riches of Christ include His sufferings and His crucifying life. Romans 8:36 says, "For Your sake we are killed all day long; we are accounted as sheep for the slaughter." Of course, none of us naturally want to be slaughtered. But verse 37 says, "Yet in all these things we are more than conquerors through Him who loved us." Though we may be brought low, by His life we are raised up again with Jesus. We rise with more of Christ wrought into our being. We come up with more renewal of our mind. Experiencing Christ is our unique goal. This is what everything is for. So ultimately all things are working together for good. Loving God turns our "all things" into the good — conformity to the image of God's Son.

The Lamb disposition   September 23rd

"And I said to him, Sir, you know. So he said to me, These are the ones who come out of the great tribulation, and washed their robes and made them white in the blood of the Lamb." REVELATION 7:14

The blood of the Lamb! The source of the blood is His Person. The nature of His Person is that of a Lamb. The Lamb nature, or disposition, includes the meekness, the innocence, and the submission of the Lamb. Isaiah 53:7 says, "He was led as a lamb to the slaughter, and as a sheep before its shearers is silent, so he opened not his mouth." He did not open His mouth. This reveals the absolute submission of the Lamb nature. The blood of the Lamb is the blood of this soul-life that was totally submitted to the Father. This is the disposition of His soul. He made no choices on His own. He lived only by the Father's life, ruled inwardly by the Father: "The Father works and I work. I only do what My Father does."

The innocent Lamb, who laid down His life, eventually becomes the chief figure in the book of Revelation to fight all the battles and to bring in God's administration. It should be that the one who represents God and rules for God is the one who inwardly is like the Lamb in disposition, submitted to the Father. All the problems we pass through are tests on us, to bring forth the Lamb's disposition. Everything is a test. The oppositions, the hurts, the misun-

273

derstandings, the tearing down — these are all testings on us. Eventually you can react, you can write others off, you can be bitter, you can be hurt, or you can merge with the Lamb disposition and tell Him, "Lord, You have not made one mistake. There is not one thing that is not included in the all things working together for good." You submit to be delivered from all the touchiness of the self-life and its reactions.

Called to love sinners   September 24th

"That you, being rooted and grounded in love, may be able to comprehend with all the saints what is the width and length and depth and height." EPHESIANS 3:17-18

God uses the high demand of the church life to escort us to a richer and deeper Christ. This demand comes with the revelation of the church that is according to the New Testament apostles. Once we see the church by revelation, we see how short we are in our ability to live such a life. The most basic point related to the demand of the church life is to love as Christ loves. The church life requires loving one another, not only *with* Christ's love, but *in* His love — loving as Christ loves, loving all the saints for the building up of His one unique Body. This requires the divine love, the kind of love that is beyond our capacity, the kind of love that we do not have in ourselves.

The kind of church life described in the New Testament requires a higher and deeper love than we have in our natural life. We are called to love sinners. We are called to love those who are unfinished, who are still in the process of being transformed. We are called to love weak, and oftentimes failing, saints. Divine love is Calvary love — the love demonstrated on the cross. It is love that flows out to despicable kinds of people — ugly people, hateful people, dirty people, rebellious people, deceived people. The love of God in Christ is all-embracing and full of forbearance and longsuffering.

To have the church life that is unveiled in the pages of the New Testament demands this divine love. It is a church life that is beyond the reach of our natural man. In ourselves we do not have the capacity to love one another the way Christ loves us. But that is okay. When we are overwhelmed with the demand of the church life, we are put more and more into contact with Another life that can supply us with divine love. The demand escorts us to Christ.

We cannot introspect ourselves   September 25th

"The heart is deceitful above all things, and desperately wicked; who can know it?" JEREMIAH 17:9

B ecause our heart is deceitful, we cannot know or diagnose it ourselves. We are not qualified to introspect and analyze our heart. We cannot deal with our own heart by ourselves. The Lord knows our heart, and He will give us a new heart (Ezek. 36:26). So the best thing to do is just draw near to God. Draw near to God and He will draw near to you. And when He draws near, then He knows what is in us. He knows how to talk with us. He knows where to point His finger: "That is sin in your life. Confess it. Drop it." He knows how to diagnose your heart. While you are fellowshipping with the Lord, you are under the Spirit's activity. He tells you, "Look at your heart. You have another goal. Your goal is your bank account. Your goal is your ambition. Your goal is not single." As we are under this kind of activity, it is the divine life, the divine Lord, giving us a new heart, taking away the stony heart: "*I* will take away the stony heart out of your flesh. Let Me have the privilege of doing it. Do not handle yourself. Do not try to fix yourself." Draw near to God, and He will draw near to you.

In that enjoyment of drawing near — while you are enjoying Him, while you are fellowshipping with Him — He talks with you.

He points things out for some cleansing, for some rebuking, for some adjustment, to make us more single so that we have a good heart. All the rocks are going out, all the weeds are going out, and all that hard ground is being plowed up just by our drawing near to God.

Demand and supply   September 26th

"For the grace of God that brings salvation has appeared to all men, teaching us that, denying ungodliness and worldly lusts, we should live soberly, righteously, and godly in the present age." Titus 2:11-12

To properly understand the Christian life, we need to apprehend a divine principle that governs God's relationship with man: whenever there is demand from God, there is always supply waiting to meet that demand. We just need to be escorted to the source of the supply. Whether it is the demand of the law, the Sermon on the Mount, our environmental dealings, the church life, or the kingdom — all are to lead us to Christ to interact and fellowship with Him, that we might partake of His victorious life. May this word govern us the rest of our lives, so that we would realize again and again that our weaknesses are our escorts out of ourselves into Another life. When our flesh reacts to the Lord's measurement, instead of staying in the reaction, or fueling the reaction, we need to allow the reaction to bring us to Christ in a specific way. Various kinds of reactions — discouragements, defeats, and temptations — are all our escorts to experience more of Christ.

Yes, your flesh is lustful. Your lustful feelings affect you in a negative way. But walk in the Spirit and you will turn those feelings into paths to Christ. None of us can change our flesh (John 3:6). It is irreparable and unchangeable. However, while we are still in these mortal bodies as redeemed children of God, God uses the flesh to lead us to Christ over and over again! Therefore, when we allow our greatest weakness to escort us to Christ, it will become the factor of our greatest supply of life.

All our problems are solved   September 27th

"For what the law could not do in that it was weak through the flesh, God did by sending His own Son in the likeness of sinful flesh, on account of sin: He condemned sin in the flesh." ROMANS 8:3

Whether or not we understand all that is in the law of the Spirit, when we touch this law we get all that is in God. So it is a great matter to be a person oriented to the Spirit, to be according to the Spirit. It is not a small thing to wake up in the morning and find your orientation to yourself by contacting the Lord — by fellowshipping with Him, opening to Him, interacting with Him, surrendering afresh to Him, that His life could be lived out. This means stopping yourself and taking every problem — whether at the start of it, in the middle of it, or near the end of it — wherever you find yourself, and bringing yourself to the Spirit. It is in the realm of the law of the Spirit that everything has been accomplished and all our problems are solved.

It is a marvelous thing to interact with the realm of the Spirit. This realm is not just a feeling, not just our emotion. We are interacting with the Father's sending of the Son and with the Person of the Son and His full accomplishment. This includes everything that is incorporated into Him. Christ has become a life-giving Spirit to give us His kind of life. He is giving us His own incarnated life, His human life, His crucified life, His resurrected life, and His ascended life. This is the kind of life He is giving. This is the only kind of life He gives. He does not give any other kind of life. Thus, the life we experience in Him will be conformable to His human living, crucifixion, resurrection, and ascension.

277

Dealing with a justified person September 28th

"But if we walk in the light as He is in the light, we have fellowship with one another, and the blood of Jesus Christ His Son cleanses us from all sin." 1 JOHN 1:7

God can deal only with a justified person. He will not touch your raw, natural life apart from His justification. He dare not, because there is nothing to work with. You and I first have to know our fixed position in Christ. He is our absolute righteousness and standing before God. In Him we are beyond the reach of condemnation. We have to stand in Christ, our righteousness. When you and I have this as our point of reference, then God can afford to begin to deal with us. He can dismantle our pride and our motives, and expose the hidden things in our heart. And we can afford to let the light shine on us and to let the Spirit operate in us to show us how utterly bankrupt we really are. When the light shines, we see that we are far worse than we knew. It is so bad. We realize it is a bottomless pit. Nevertheless, it is wonderful that the light shines. Now, "Walk in the light as He is in the light." This means walk in the total light of the gospel that reveals God's righteousness. We can walk in that light because "the blood of Jesus Christ His Son cleanses us from all sin." So just confess your sins. Just admit you are wretched, you are no good. Admit it, because you are admitting it as a justified person! You are not admitting it as a cowering person in yourself. This is why God can deal with you in Romans 7 and 8. He has laid a solid foundation of justification in Romans 3—5.

"And when he brings out his own sheep, he goes before them; and the sheep follow him, for they know his voice." JOHN 10:4

From John 10 we see that the Lord's voice in our experience is like an inner knowing. Verses 4-5 say, ⁴ "And when he brings out his own sheep, he goes before them; and the sheep follow him, for *they know his voice.* ⁵ Yet they will by no means follow a stranger, but will flee from him, *for they do not know the voice of strangers.*" Also, in verse 14 the Lord says, "I am the good shepherd; and *I know My sheep, and am known by My own.*" This inner knowing of the Lord's voice is similar to experiencing an inner drawing. We are moved and touched from within. There is a deep inner consciousness and conviction. This means that the Lord's voice is written into our very consciousness. For example, when we received Christ into us, it was because we were convinced by this inner knowing that we should receive Him. *Outwardly,* we may have *heard* a preacher sharing the gospel, or we may have *read* a tract explaining to our mind the way of salvation. But *inwardly* we *knew* that receiving Christ was the right thing to do. This inner knowing to follow the Lord as our Shepherd is simply His voice speaking in our consciousness.

Another example of this inner knowing is given in Romans 8:16: "The Spirit Himself bears witness with our spirit that we are children of God." The Spirit witnessing with our spirit is an inner knowing and consciousness. This is His way of speaking to us in the most intimate and personal manner. Instead of hearing an outward voice, something apart from us, we have an inner consciousness of His abiding presence. This is how we know and understand the Lord's voice.

"My Father, who has given them to Me, is greater than all; and no one is able to snatch them out of My Father's hand." JOHN 10:29

Our inner knowing of the Lord's voice has a long history. It goes back to eternity past and stretches forward to eternity future. In John 10:3 the Lord says, "The sheep hear his voice; and he calls his own sheep *by name* and leads them out." We must see that the reason He can call His own sheep by name is because in eternity past we were given by the Father to the Son *by name.* He knows us by name. In fact, we were all personal gifts given by the Father to the Son. In John 10:27-29 the Lord says, ²⁷ "My sheep hear My voice, and *I know them*, and they follow Me. ²⁸ And I give them eternal life, and they shall never perish; neither shall anyone snatch them out of My hand. ²⁹ *My Father, who has given them to Me,* is greater than all; and no one is able to snatch them out of My Father's hand." These verses, together with Hebrews 13:20-21 that tells us about the Lord being the great Shepherd of the sheep in the blood of an eternal covenant, show us something of the substance of our inner knowing of the Lord. Namely, that our inner knowing of His voice *today,* in time, is our response to the Father and the Son's *eternal* knowing of us. So we can confidently say that we know Him because He first knew us (cf. Gal. 4:9).

The Son willingly took us by name, and in the eternal covenant He agreed to shepherd us all the way — out of eternity past, through time with all the problems of sin, the flesh, the world, and the devil, and into eternity future. Overcoming all obstacles, He will bring us through, fully conformed to His image.

October

The prayer of God

"Now it came to pass in those days that He went out to the mountain to pray, and continued all night in prayer to God."
LUKE 6:12

One of the most striking examples in the Gospels showing *how* the Lord Jesus spent time with the Father is the record of His spending a whole night in prayer. The phrase "in prayer to God" may be translated more literally "in the prayer *of* God." Although most versions of the Bible translate the phrase as an objective genitive — "in prayer *to* God," it is equally proper to translate it as a subjective genitive — "in the prayer *of* God." This simply means that in the prayer, God is not only the object to pray to, "*to* God," but He is also the source of the prayer itself, "*of* God."

In his *Commentary on the Gospel of Luke*, Frederick L. Godet brings out the more literal translation of Luke 6:12: "The term προσευχῇ τοῦ θεοῦ, literally, *prayer of God*, is also a unique expression in the New Testament. It does not denote any special request, but a state of rapt contemplation of God's presence, a prayer arising out of the most profound communion with Him." Such a unique description of the Lord's all-night vigil in prayer discloses something of what took place during His prolonged and concentrated time with the Father. "The prayer of God" indicates that in and as a result of His "profound communion" with the Father, the Lord merged with the burden and prayer of God. He so allowed the Father to pass through Him during His communion and fellowship with Him that He became perfectly one with God. He merged with God. This meant God could pass through Him unhindered. He was emptied of self and completely open to the flow of prayer coming directly from God.

281

"And he showed me a pure river of water of life, clear as crystal, proceeding out of the throne of God and of the Lamb."
REVELATION 22:1

In spending time with the Lord, in order to merge with the prayer of God, we need to learn to allow God Himself to pass through us. This is fundamental in our fellowship with the Lord. It implies an opening of our entire being to God for Him to flow and pass through us. In the Bible, God is described as a flow. So the nature of our fellowship with Him must be like a flow of "living water" (John 4:10). The Triune God is a flow. Jesus declared in John 7:38-39, [38] "He who believes into Me, as the Scripture has said, out of his innermost being will flow rivers of living water. [39] But this He spoke concerning the Spirit, whom those believing in Him would receive." These verses make it clear that to know God is to know Him as a flow.

When we spend time with the Lord, our one need is simply to allow ourselves to be a channel for the Triune God to pass through us. What a vision of prayer! Spending time with the Lord is a release of our spirit whereby we consciously merge with God and allow Him to pass through us. God is a flow. He wants to flow Himself out into our hearts. It is this flow that the apostle Paul describes in Galatians 4:6: "And because you are sons, God has sent forth the Spirit of His Son into your hearts, crying out, Abba, Father!" Experiencing the reality of this flow is directly related to our merging with it by the active exercise of our spirit. The sister verse to Galatians 4:6 is Romans 8:15, which shows us the need to cooperate with this flow by opening our mouth to contact God: "For you have not received a spirit of slavery leading to fear again, but you have received a spirit of sonship in which *we cry out,* Abba! Father!" (NASV). It is in this cry that God bears witness by flowing in us. The Spirit Himself bears witness with our crying spirit (Rom. 8:16).

Push Him out October 3rd

"Always bearing about in the body the putting to death of the Lord Jesus, that the life of Jesus also may be manifested in our body. For we who live are always delivered unto death for Jesus' sake, that the life of Jesus also may be manifested in our mortal flesh."
2 CORINTHIANS 4:10-11

To inwardly apply the cross, we need to coordinate our spirit with our environment. In these verses we have both *the inward cross* and *the outward cross*. "Always bearing about in the body the putting to death of the Lord Jesus" speaks of the inward cross. Then this inward cross is coordinated with the outward cross by the word "for": "For we who live are always delivered unto death for Jesus' sake, that the life of Jesus also may be manifested in our mortal flesh." The inward cross and the outward cross operating together is the "death working in us" that produces "life in you" (v. 12).

In verse 11 we are handed over, or delivered, unto death. We may be handed over into weakness, into a trial, into insults, into misunderstanding — into being crossed out. We are handed over again and again to all kinds of outward environments. Just as the Lord Jesus was handed over to the smiters, to those who rejected Him, to all the environment that was sovereignly laid out for Him, we also are always being handed over. So do not be surprised. This is our lot because we have a destiny and a goal — to follow the pathway of the cross, to enjoy resurrection life, and to be conformed to His image.

We are always being handed over to death *"for* Jesus' sake." In Greek, the preposition used here can be literally translated *because of*. Thus, it would read, "For we who live are always delivered unto death because of Jesus." He is the cause of all this! He is in our spirit, and God's desire is to push Him out into our soul — to manifest Him, to display Him, to make Him known. Jesus is not happy being confined to our spirit. He wants to spread out into our whole being.

And because many times we do not take the initiative to pursue Him, we get handed over to a death situation — to a trying environment or to a disappointment. We are just handed over. This is because God is so desirous that Jesus be manifested in our mortal flesh.

Administrating a collapsed universe October 4th

"Having made known to us the mystery of His will, according to His good pleasure which He purposed in Himself, unto an administration of the fullness of the times that He might head up all things in Christ, both which are in heaven and which are on earth — in Him." EPHESIANS 1:9-10

The phrase "having made known" is *unto* something. That is, the mystery of God's will was made known to Paul for the purpose of an administration of the fullness of the times to head up all things in Christ. This means that in Paul's vision the universe is under God's administration; and God's administration is centered in Christ and the church, His Body.

This universe is in a state of collapse because of Satan, sin, the flesh, and the world, which have sought to disorient and damage God's creation. Evil spirits and demons are also included with the satanic things ruining and spoiling man and corrupting the earth. God made the universe with man in His image for Himself, but Satan came in to damage the man that God created.

However, the Lord became a man and came to this earth, not only to redeem us personally, but also to secure a footing in this universe to head it up and administrate it with Himself as Lord. When we say, "Jesus is Lord!" we are saying that He is Lord over all as a God-Man on the throne of the universe. He is the God-Man who glorified humanity in His own Person by living a perfect sinless life. Then He was glorified in His body. First Timothy 2:5 declares, "For there is one God and one Mediator between God and men, *the Man*

Christ Jesus." This means that when He came out of the grave, He was a resurrected Man. He was God, but He was equally man; and He will remain a God-Man for eternity. He will never lose His manhood. He assumed it. He put it on, never to put it off. He took humanity to the throne and was seated there, and God made Him Lord and Christ in this universe.

Through His death, resurrection, and ascension, Jesus triumphed over principalities and powers, rising far above all, and was seated in the heavens. The saints who were filled with the Holy Spirit on the day of Pentecost saw the ascended Christ and declared that He was Lord. He headed us up in the Body, and made us one with Him. Thus, as members of Christ we are a part of God's administration.

Steps in God's administration   October 5th

"And He is the head of the body, the church, who is the beginning, the firstborn from the dead, that in all things He may have the preeminence." COLOSSIANS 1:18

It is important to understand the steps that God takes in heading up the universe. He does have a procedure in the way that He heads it up. His first step was to make Jesus, as the God-Man, both Lord and Christ. That step has already been accomplished. His second step is now to head up His Body by heading up each individual member. So when we experience Christ in our practical daily life, we are not just becoming more spiritual for our own sake; but we are becoming more a part of the administration of the universe. When God's administration and kingdom actually comes in us as Christ's members, Satan's rule and the flesh are terminated, and God's kingdom has advanced one step further in the universe. When Jesus is Lord in me, He has become Lord in one more member of His Body. Thus, the more practical a position He obtains on this earth in and through His members, the more He becomes the Head of the Body in reality, and the more God's administration is manifested in the universe.

Sisters, have you ever considered that taking care of your children in spirit is part of God's administration in the universe? Things in our lives may seem mundane at times, and apparently unimportant. As a mother you may not regard your daily life as being important. But when you see this vision of Christ and the church, and of God's administration in this universe through the vehicle of the church, then your experience of the Lord with your children becomes something of major consequence. Loving them, caring for them, nurturing them, bringing them up in the fear and admonition of the Lord, and being exercised in your spirit to follow the Lord in your daily schedule is all part of God's administration of this universe. This is because when He heads you up, He is heading up a member of the Body of Christ; and this is part of His procedure in the heading up of the universe.

The expulsive power of a new affection October 6th

"Now hope does not disappoint, because the love of God has been poured out in our hearts by the Holy Spirit who was given to us." ROMANS 5:5

When we see Christ as all in all, He then becomes not only our relationship with all things, but He also becomes the new realm we live in. Thus, the way we experience death to sin is not by trying to be dead to it in ourselves. It is by staying in the realm of resurrection. The realm of resurrection is the realm of the Spirit and life (1 Cor. 15:45). In this realm we are automatically freed from sin. The power of sin is broken in our lives by what one servant of the Lord has called "the expulsive power of a new affection." This new affection is in the realm of the Spirit. It is the love of God poured out in my heart by the Holy Spirit that enables me to put to death the practices of my body (Rom. 5:5; 8:13).

286

Dealing with sin is not achieved in a process of trying to overcome it. Rather, it is by drawing from the life-power of Christ in the realm of resurrection. Instead of interacting with sin as though it was my responsibility to overcome it in myself, I interact with Christ, who is my relationship with sin. In *that* relationship, sin is a dead thing to me. Because I can exercise my spirit *where* I am alive to God in Christ, I come under the expulsive power of a new affection for God and the things of God (Rom. 8:5-6). It is this affection that immobilizes the force of sin in my life. In the realm of the Spirit, indwelling sin forever remains a dead thing to me, because I died and my *new me* is now hidden with Christ in God (Col. 3:3-4).

A gentle inner persuasion   October 7th

"The LORD *has appeared of old to me, saying: Yes, I have loved you with an everlasting love; therefore with lovingkindness I have drawn you."* JEREMIAH 31:3

The Greek word for draw is *helkuo* (ἑλκύω) and may be properly understood as a gentle inner persuasion. It is something in you that attracts and persuades you toward the Lord and the things of the Lord. It is the same kind of experience spoken of in the verse above. So the manner of the Lord's speaking is that gentle persuasion of love that draws our hearts to Him.

The speaking of the Lord under the new covenant is an inward drawing resulting from a divine operation in our being. The drawing *is* His speaking. Even though we are sometimes indifferent to that inner drawing, it is still there in us. We can run away from it or we can nurture it. Whatever measure of drawing to the Lord we may have, it is deserving of our thanksgiving. We should say, "Thank You, Lord, for the desire that I find in myself for You." Even a little bit of desire in us for the Lord should be considered His speaking.

His speaking manifests itself by an inward drawing. He does not normally speak with audible words, telling us what to do or not to do. Rather, He actually imparts into us the very substance and reality of His speaking. For example, if He is speaking to us about willingness in an area of our lives, He will incline and draw our hearts in that area. Philippians 2:12-13 makes this clear: 12 "Therefore, my beloved, as you have always obeyed, not as in my presence only, but now much more in my absence, work out your own salvation with fear and trembling; 13 *for it is God who works in you both to will and to do* for His good pleasure." God Himself operates within to produce the willingness and the working. This illustrates that knowing the Lord's voice is related to recognizing His drawing from within our hearts.

A transcendent Person   October 8th

"Do not think that I came to destroy the Law or the Prophets. I did not come to destroy but to fulfill." MATTHEW 5:17

The Lord Jesus came to fulfill the Law and the Prophets. In Matthew 5:18 He said that nothing was going to pass from the law until all was fulfilled. In other words, Christ Himself became the fulfillment of everything He taught in Matthew 5—7. His teaching does not come to us apart from the supply of Himself. Indeed, it is because of the reality of His indwelling life that He can make such exacting demands.

Because the Lord reveals Himself as the fulfillment of the Law and the Prophets, He is saying, "Do not be bothered by how high My word is to you. Do not be bothered when I tell you to go the second mile, to live without lust, to not have an inflated idea about yourself, to not have a negative attitude toward your brother, calling him a fool. And do not be intimidated by My telling you not to swear, but to just say yes or no. Do not be threatened when I tell you to love your enemies and pray for them, because I am the fulfillment of it all. I am the last Adam, and I have become a life-giving Spirit. My humanity is now available to you to live this life. As the Spirit, I am going to reproduce Myself in you. Just stay with Me in the realm of the Spirit. That is where I live. I live as the Spirit in your spirit. I am giving life in that realm. Just stay there. Sing there. Pray there. Call from there. Spend time there. Open to Me in your most exhausted moments, in your weakest times. I will transform you into My image. Learn how to behold Me, to take long looks at Me. Linger with Me in My presence. Abide there. Admire Me. Do not look at yourself. Just say, 'I died, Lord, and I am out of the picture.' Draw from Me! I will reproduce Myself in you in this way, as the Spirit. So do not annul any of the Law or the Prophets. Do not annul them, because to annul them is to annul Me. I am the life of Matthew 5—7. I am going to fulfill every jot and tittle in you. When you experience Me, you are going to discover that the words of Matthew 5—7 are actually Me reproducing My life in you."

Matthew 5—7 is a description of a transcendent life belonging to a transcendent Person. It is a life *above* the natural life. It transcends natural reactions. It is beyond the natural concept. It operates in us in its transcendency.

"I live in a fine way" October 9th

"You have heard that it was said to those of old, You shall not murder, and whoever murders will be in danger of the judgment. But I say to you that whoever is angry with his brother without a cause shall be in danger of the judgment. And whoever says to his brother, Raca! shall be in danger of the council. But whoever says, You fool! shall be in danger of hell fire." MATTHEW 5:21-22

The words "You shall not murder, and whoever murders will be in danger of the judgment" fit our natural mind. Our natural mind tends to think in categories and slots. It has a formed concept about our behavior according to those categories. We feel that if we do not do certain things, we are okay. So we live in this "okay" mode. We live according to general categories, which become the teachings by which we judge ourselves. But now the Lord is saying, "Formerly, you lived according to these fixed teachings, but now that you have Me, you are to live according to the feeling of life that is being reproduced in your spirit. Now that My life is being reproduced in you, you are finding that you have ambivalent feelings. Your feelings are split between *your concept* and *My life* that is rising up in you. Your concept is limited, guarded, calculating, and motivated by self-preservation. But My life is transcendent. My feelings are beyond your thought about the way to live and react to things. Your standard of judging things is far below what I am doing within you. You are satisfied with yourself because you do not kill. The category for killing has been checked off in your mind. But you are not aware that I am in you and that I am not tolerating hidden anger. You have lived by the law, but now I want to teach you to live by Me. You live in a general way. I live in a fine, detailed way."

In Matthew 5:22 the Lord says, "But I say to you that whoever is angry with his brother without a cause shall be in danger of the judgment. And whoever says to his brother, Raca! shall be in danger of the council." "Raca" means empty-headed person. It is a term that expresses contempt. By this we can see how fine the Lord's life is. He goes from anger to a form of that anger expressed toward others. Then the Lord continues by saying, "But whoever says, Moreh shall be in danger of the Gehenna of fire." From *anger* to *Raca* to *Moreh*. Moreh means fool. It is an outright statement made in a very deliberate way toward a person. Just one quick remark out of our mouth does not match the transcendency of His life in us. By saying these things, the Lord reveals that His life is transcendent in its fineness.

Life in its fineness   October 10th

"But I say to you that whoever is angry with his brother without a cause shall be in danger of the judgment. And whoever says to his brother, Raca! shall be in danger of the council. But whoever says, You fool! shall be in danger of hell fire." MATTHEW 5:22

If we are genuinely experiencing the Lord's transcendent life in us, we cannot say things that are incompatible with that life without retracing our steps in the Spirit and making it right. We cannot live in an insensitive way. We find ourselves saying, "I'm sorry. That was too much." We may apologize not just for *what* we said, but for *where* it came from. It came from the source of the self in the form of a fixed attitude that wrote someone off as a fool. When the transcendent life operates in our being, God begins touching our source about everything. Who is relating to people? You or the Lord? So life operates in us in a detailed way, checking our words by the Spirit.

This is what it means to deal with the Lord and to be dealt with by Him. It is learning to know Him as He reproduces His life in us. Matthew 5:21-22 tells us that in His transcendent life we will have dealings over our speaking, not in a general way but in a fine way, even over one extra word. Just "Raca" or "Moreh" is enough to produce an uncomfortable feeling within you. Do you know why you feel uncomfortable? It is because you are wearing the wrong clothing. You are not wearing Christ. At that moment you have not put Him on. When you put Him on, you find that He is a heart of compassion, He is longsuffering, and He is kindness. When we put on the disposition of Christ, we feel comfortable. It is like feeling comfortable with clothing that fits and matches. When we say words that do not fit and match Christ in us, we feel uncomfortable within. We realize that we are wearing the wrong words, that is, we are making Christ wear them (1 Cor. 6:15). This discomfort is the fineness of His life operating to bring us up to a higher, transcendent level, where He is. In these kinds of dealings we discover that His life is transcendent in its fineness.

In your spirit you know   **October 11th**

"For what man knows the things of a man except the spirit of the man which is in him? Even so no one knows the things of God except the Spirit of God. " 1 CORINTHIANS 2:11

Being subjective leaves us ignorant of ourself so that we do not know ourself in God's light. This is what subjectivity does. Who knows the things of man? Who knows the self? Who knows the rottenness of fallen man? Who knows that there is nothing good in himself? Who knows that this self is not to be trusted? Who knows that his opinion and reasoning are untrustworthy? Who knows himself? According to Paul's word, it is only the spirit of man that knows the things of man. This shows us that unless we are vitally joined to the most objective part of our being, our spirit, we are going to be ignorant concerning ourself. We must realize that the spirit of man is the part in man that supplies to him his objectivity. In other words, to be objective, to be divided, to know yourself, even to condemn yourself, and to not trust yourself, your opinion, or your view, is to be a person that is exercised in spirit.

When you are in the realm of the spirit, you become wise concerning your real state. You discover that there is nothing good in you, and you can admit it, confess it, and humble yourself. You can repent without strain. You can admit your fallen state. You can say, "I'm stubborn, I'm rebellious, I'm jealous, I'm bitter." You can confess your state with ease, because when you are in your spirit *you know* that in your flesh dwells no good thing. You are not trying to defend or excuse yourself. You are objective about yourself. And that objectivity makes it easy for you to always agree with God's diagnosis of the flesh (Rom. 7:14, 18).

The spirit of man is the key

"The spirit of man is the lamp of the Lord, searching all the innermost parts of his being." PROVERBS 20:27 (NASV)

When you do not exercise your spirit, you stay enmeshed with yourself. You remain a whole person, an unbroken person. You are proud, you cannot admit, you cannot confess, you cannot apologize, because there is no objective base in you. You are caught up and immersed in the feelings of pride with its stiff neck and its inability to lose its face. This self is so intact and whole that it cannot be broken through, it cannot be penetrated, it cannot be reached, because it does not know itself. It does not know its folly. Apart from our spirit, we do not know ourselves, we are ignorant of ourselves. But when we touch our spirit, we loathe ourselves. We recognize that there is nothing good in us. Through and through we are altogether flesh. We are full of sin and the flesh with its reactions, bitterness, hatred, and lust. Indeed, every gross sin is a possibility with us.

The spirit of man is the key to knowing ourselves in God's light. This is revealed not only in Proverbs 20:27, but also in 1 Corinthians 2:11: "For what man knows the things of a man except the spirit of the man which is in him?" Ezekiel 36:31 tells us what happens at the time of receiving a new spirit (cf. verse 26): *"Then* you will remember your evil ways and your deeds that were not good; and you will loathe yourselves in your own sight, for your iniquities and your abominations." In other words, from our spirit we know ourselves in God's light, we are inwardly searched, and we are able to loathe ourselves. Loathing ourselves has nothing to do with morbid introspection. It is actually a gift of grace imparting to us the ability to remain objective about our fallen state *by agreeing with God's judgment of it.*

Disassociate yourself from the devil October 13th

"Lest Satan should take advantage of us; for we are not ignorant of his thoughts." 2 CORINTHIANS 2:11

How do you disassociate yourself from the devil? You do it by identifying his activity. *"His* thoughts" in the above verse refer to Satan's thoughts in our thoughts. They are Satan's thoughts in our subjective thinking. So Paul disassociates the thoughts from himself by identifying them as Satan's thoughts. Speak to the concealed devil. This means you are going to speak to your feelings. You are going to speak to your jealousy. You are going to speak to your doubt. You are going to speak to your envy. You are going to speak to your opinion. You are going to speak to your reasoning. You are going to speak to what seems to be you! You have been enmeshed with demons, but now you have found out that an enemy has usurped your being. That is not Christ, that is not your spirit, that is not your real person, that is not really you. You discover that a hidden enemy has been occupying your thoughts and feelings.

When you start to disassociate yourself from the enemy with prayer, with the exercise of "the weapons of our warfare" that are mighty through God, you pull down the strongholds (2 Cor. 10:4). Not only does the stronghold of reasoning come down, but Satan is cast out. James 4:7 says, "Resist the devil and he will flee from you." And Revelation 12:10-11 says, [10] "The accuser of our brethren . . . has been cast down. [11] And they overcame him because of the blood of the Lamb and because of the word of their testimony, and they did not love their soul-life to the death." This means we can say, "Soul-life, I am not going to preserve you. You are the one that wants to preserve itself. You are the one that is holding back. And Satan, you are the one hiding out in my soul. You are the one that is afraid. You are the one that hides from the light. You are the one crouching as sin in the flesh. You are the one that is independent. Soul-life, you are the culprit. You are enmeshed with Satan." Declare the facts to the devil. Disassociate yourself from the enemy with a strong spirit, and demons will leave you and you will be free—free in a new source.

A church-life disposition October 14th

"That Christ may dwell in your hearts through faith; that you, being rooted and grounded in love, may be full of strength to apprehend with all the saints what is the width and length and depth and height." EPHESIANS 3:17-18

When we have a genuine experience of Christ making home in our heart, we will discover that there is a disposition to live a church life. We are strengthened into our inner man, and the result is that we are "full of strength to apprehend with all the saints ..." We receive an infused disposition. This disposition is wrought into us to live out a practical church life in which there is the need to keep the oneness of the Spirit in the bond of peace (Eph. 3:20—4:3). To meet together with all different kinds of believers at different stages of growth in the Lord goes beyond the capacity of our natural disposition. It requires a supernatural disposition. By this infused disposition we can be built up together in the knowledge-surpassing love of Christ.

If we really see by revelation the kind of church that is revealed in the book of Ephesians, we will realize that our natural disposition could never make it. We need divine enablement. It is only by Christ making home in our heart that we could be rooted and grounded in love to the extent that we have supernatural ability to apprehend the vast dimensions of Christ's love in the church.

For the Lord to gain the church as His Bride, there is the need of an infusion of the divine disposition into our disposition (Eph. 5). To live the church life together requires the divine nature and disposition. No one is naturally born "cut out" for the church life. The church life demands Another life. This is why the Lord told

Nicodemus in John 3 that in order to see the kingdom of God, as well as to enter it, it is necessary to be born again. Seeing and entering the kingdom is virtually the same as seeing and entering the church life (Rom. 14:17). The church life is altogether a matter of Another life coming into us through regeneration, and then of our being constantly infused with the disposition that is in that life.

The inner knowing   October 15th

"But the anointing which you have received from Him abides in you, and you do not need that anyone teach you; but as the same anointing teaches you concerning all things, and is true, and is not a lie, and just as it has taught you, you will abide in Him." 1 JOHN 2:27

Being compatible with the Lord's voice is described by the apostle John as being taught by the anointing. The word anointing is the verbal form of the noun, the anointed One. Anointing in Greek is *chrisma* (χρῖσμα) and simply refers to the movement and action of the anointed One, Christ *(Christos / Χριστός)*.

John says, "The same anointing teaches you." This means that the movement and action of the Lord within us has the ability to communicate to us and teach us. Thus, the way we hear the Lord's voice is by the anointing. This kind of speaking does not come in the form of plain words written on a page. Rather, it is an inner movement of the anointed One within us. The anointing abides *in* us. This anointing should not be thought of as an extraordinary gift that a few spiritual people possess. The anointing is simply the movement and inner activity of Christ Himself in all His redeemed and regenerated children.

In our daily experience the anointing teaches us by giving us an inner knowing. This teaching is by the life-movement and consciousness within us. It is a different kind of teaching from the Old Testament law of letters written on tablets of stone. The anointing is a kind of teaching that comes out of our fellowship with the Lord and our inner sensitivity to Him.

A felt presence   October 16th

"But you have an anointing from the Holy One, and you know all things." 1 JOHN 2:20

We may liken the teaching of the anointing to our being taught in the physical realm. For example, if we walk into a room in which the temperature is one hundred degrees, the presence of heat teaches us to take off our jacket. There is no need to read a sign that says, "Take off your jacket." The presence of heat automatically teaches us to take it off. It is the *presence* of something that teaches, not a teaching by audible words or outward letters of instruction. We can say that the temperature itself teaches us with the voice of a "felt presence." The anointing works in the same way within us. The anointing is the presence of a Person moving within us. Thus, whenever we are taking a certain course of action that is not compatible with the Lord, we sense a bothering or troubling within. We lose our normal inward poise of peace. For instance, you are about to complain to someone because you are right and they are wrong about something they did or did not do. But as you actually launch into your argument, the more you speak, the more there is the presence of "heat." You feel uncomfortable, you feel awkward, you lose your peace, and you yourself sense that what you are saying is not compatible with your insides.

Just as heat teaches you to take off your jacket, so the presence of the anointing teaches you to stop talking in a complaining way. The reason you are unable to keep talking is not because someone is telling you not to talk that way. You cannot talk because *you* have an inward forbidding. You are just not free and at liberty to speak that way anymore. This kind of experience is the anointing teaching you. The anointing's voice made it clear that your words were not compatible with the Lord. This kind of experience is not an occasion for taking condemning thoughts and accusations about yourself. Rather, it is an occasion for learning to be compatible with the Lord's life in your speaking and attitude.

His people's willingness   October 17th

"By this all will know that you are My disciples, if you have love for one another." JOHN 13:35

God's move throughout the Bible was always based upon one major principle, and that was the willingness of His people. Apart from the willingness embodied in His people, He would not do anything, particularly related to His corporate testimony with the tabernacle under Moses, the temple under David and Solomon, and the recovered temple under Ezra and Nehemiah. In the three sections of the Old Testament describing the tabernacle, the temple, and the recovered temple, one common thing is mentioned — the willingness of the people in serving the Lord to build His corporate testimony. The Lord's testimony always expressed itself in His people's willingness to live for God's pleasure on the earth.

We can see that the Lord embodies Himself in His people's willingness, and makes Himself known on the earth. The way He testifies to the earth is expressed in John 13:34-35: 34 "A new commandment I give to you, that you love one another; as I have loved you, that you also love one another. 35 By this all will know that you are My disciples, if you have love for one another." These verses tell us that all men are going to know. There is going to be a testimony that is visible and touchable. How will this testimony be made known? There will be groups of saints in city after city over the whole earth who have a willingness to live unto the Lord and to serve Him and to serve one another. This willingness is embodied in their relationships. It is the expression of the divine love flowing out. God makes Himself known to others by His people's willingness to live for His house. It is not "going to church." It is not attending a certain church meeting out of obligation, in a perfunctory way. It is not just token attendance, token giving, even token serving, but a welling up of Another life — a life that is consumed for the Father's house. The genuineness of the testimony of the church today on this earth is embodied in the willingness of the saints.

Christ creating willingness   October 18th

"Your people shall be volunteers in the day of Your power; in the beauties of holiness, from the womb of the morning, You have the dew of Your youth." Psalm 110:3

The *Amplified Bible* renders the above verse, "Your people will offer themselves willingly in the day of Your power, in the beauty of holiness and in holy array out of the womb of the morning; to You will spring forth Your young men who are as the dew." The first part of this verse tells us that in the day of the Lord's power, His people will offer themselves willingly. What is "the day of Your power"? It is the day of Christ as our High Priest according to the order of Melchizedek (Psa. 110:4). Our High Priest has passed through human life, crucifixion, resurrection, ascension, enthronement, and lordship, and He is now ever living to make intercession for us, to transmit the victory of His life into us.

We are the recipients of the transmission of an indestructible life that is pulsating through our being, dealing with and tearing down every blockage and hindrance in our heart, softening our hard heart. This is because the very life of God is filling our mortal bodies. All this is happening because He is interceding. He is praying it into being. The day of His power refers to His present intercession by which He is transmitting into our spirits His very life and nature. Thus, "Your people will offer themselves willingly *in the day of Your power*" means "in the day that You are on the throne, interceding and transmitting Your very life and nature into our being."

All willingness in our being, whether it is much or little, is the direct result of the intercession of our Melchizedek, who is transmitting His resurrected, ascended life into us. This transmission is delivering us from the love of this world, from the attachment to other things, from idols in our heart, from our self-centered life. It is delivering us from every realm where the enemy usurps us, in order to reduce us to the Lord Himself, to love Him, to be single for Him, and to be ones who are actually in alignment with the very thing that is on His heart — His building, His habitation. This is our Christ, who is creating the willingness within us for God's house.

The fellowship of the blood   October 19th

"The cup of blessing which we bless, is it not the fellowship of the blood of Christ? The bread which we break, is it not the fellowship of the body of Christ?" 1 CORINTHIANS 10:16

Our fellowship is the fellowship of the blood of Christ. The blood streaming forth from Him produces this fellowship and produces His Body. This is just like the blood circulating through our physical bodies. It produces the fellowship of the whole body. My right hand is having sweet fellowship with my left foot because of the circulating blood. They are unified together. My body can live and function because there is fellowship going on in my circulatory system. The blood unites every member in my physical body. Every part is related to every other part by the circulation of the blood. If you stop the circulation of my blood, there is no more fellowship between the members. There is nothing organic.

Brothers and sisters, we are participating in the fellowship of the

300

blood of Christ. When we are mutually enjoying Christ as our portion, His precious blood connects every member and unites us as the Body. This is our oneness. Our oneness is in this blood. The church is in this blood. When we throw off all our preferences, our opinions, our thoughts, our views, and come to drink the blood of Jesus together and enjoy our Christ — this one Person with all His glorious work — His blood becomes our uniting factor. It keeps us and holds us, and we become exceedingly organic. This is the fellowship of the blood of Christ.

Simultaneous action   October 20th

"This is the covenant that I will make with them after those days, says the LORD: I will put My laws upon their hearts, and upon their minds I will write them, then He adds, Their sins and their lawless deeds I will remember no more." HEBREWS 10:16-17

To God, our sin is not even in His thought. That is how powerful the blood is. How ridiculous it is to be accused, when the blood has removed all our sins from God's thought. He cannot remember them. Hebrews 10:18 says, "Now where there is forgiveness of these things, there is no longer any offering for sin" (NASV). The blood was shed once for all. So all that is necessary is to have boldness to enter into God's presence. Where is our boldness? Our boldness is in the blood of Jesus.

When the Lord was on the cross, one of the soldiers pierced His side with a spear, and out came blood and water. Simultaneously out of His side issued blood for redemption and water for life. What has the simultaneous action of the blood and the water done for us and over us? Here we are — messed up, sinful, unfinished people. As the blood is cleansing us, at the same time God is imparting His life into us. This is the new covenant. It is God's agreement that He is going to write Himself into us. He is going to operate within. He is going to change us from within. But He has to come in where all this dirt is. Where can He put Himself? It is all contaminated in us. In other words, He wants to come in and change our mind; He wants to come in and change our emotions. But how is He going to get into all those dirty parts? It seems He is restricted to one spot in us — our spirit. But the blood cleanses us for God to inhabit us and to operate on us imperfect human beings.

The bond of perfection   October 21st

"But above all these things put on love, which is the bond of perfection." COLOSSIANS 3:14

To have the bond of perfection, to have a perfect relationship, does not mean that you and I are perfect. Perfection in the Bible refers to one thing — the perfect love of God. That is perfection. Of course, we know that we are all imperfect people. We make mistakes, we offend one another, we often neglect one another unwittingly. We do things without even knowing what we have done. Sometimes we even hurt others intentionally. So how can you have a perfect church? What is a perfect church? A perfect church is simply where there are fallen sinners, who have weaknesses and failures, but who at the same time enjoy the perfect love of Calvary flowing among them. This love of God flowing is the bond of perfection.

In the church life, eventually there will be things that you are unhappy about. You will be disappointed over things that did not go the way you expected them to. Perhaps you will say, "This is not what I thought it was going to be." What you need to do at that moment is to touch the source of the perfect love of God (1 John 4:11-12, 16-17). Begin calling "Jesus." Enjoy God. There is His forgiveness, there is His kindness, there is His forbearance. When the flow of the love of God is between us, that is the building. That is Christ. We are being built up in love with one another. Paul's word in Ephesians 4:15 tells us that we should speak, or hold, the truth in love. We should not use the truth like a hammer over one another. There are imperfect situations in the church life, but there is a factor between us, and that factor is the perfect love of God.

A dependent life   October 22nd

"Therefore, to him who knows to do good and does not do it, to him it is sin." JAMES 4:17

S in in the context of James 4 means independent action. This is what sin is — independent action. From the beginning, the real source of all sin has been man acting independently of God. In this chapter, James is talking about those who say, "Today or tomorrow we will go to such and such a city, spend a year there, buy and sell, and make a profit" (v. 13). To those James says, "Instead you ought to say, If the Lord wills, we shall live and do this or that" (v. 15). "If the Lord wills" is not merely a religious saying. It means we live a dependent life about everything.

Then in verse 16 James says, "But now you boast in your arrogance. All such boasting is evil." What is this boasting, this arrogance? It is being independent in our moves, in our daily life. He continues in verse 17, "Therefore, to him who knows to do good and does not do it, to him it is sin." What is the good here? The good here is dependence upon God. I am going to the store dependent upon God. I am going to fellowship with the saints dependent upon God. To live independently is to live presumptuously and sinfully. Perhaps we have never considered sin in this way. But this is the basic definition of sin — independence from God. Every sin is traced back to our independence. So the way to be delivered from our sinning is not to act independently. How can we do this? Such a life issues from spending time with the Lord to have thorough fellowship with Him. We need to nurture and cultivate our dependent relationship with the Lord.

Not two condemnations   October 23rd

"For what the law could not do in that it was weak through the flesh, God did by sending His own Son in the likeness of sinful flesh, on account of sin: He condemned sin in the flesh." ROMANS 8:3

The content of the law of the Spirit is marvelous. The reason I am not condemned over sin in the flesh is that God already condemned it in His Son. There are not two condemnations — one laid to His charge and then another laid to mine. In Romans 8:1 there is no condemnation to those in Christ Jesus, because sin in the flesh was condemned in Him. God condemned sin in the flesh. The judgment for sin was upon Christ. It is not upon us. The debt cannot be paid twice. The debt is paid only once. Christ paid the debt. I am not going to pay it again. I am simply going to be on the receiving end and be filled with joy that the debt has been paid.

So watch how you react to paying debts in your inner life. When you are condemned, if you feel like you owe something to your good flesh, if you feel obligated to it, that is a clue that you are in the wrong realm. For many years we may have been stuck in this realm, feeling obligated, relating to our religious flesh in this way. We may not have related to ourselves in the realm of the Spirit. Notice, we are talking about realms here. There are two different realms — two different sets of feelings, two different mind-sets, two different ways of relating and interacting. Paul gives us a good description of these two realms in Romans 7 and 8. The question is not how to rid myself of condemnation, but to ask, What realm do I live in — the flesh or the Spirit?

304

"O wretched man that I am! Who will deliver me from this body of death?" ROMANS 7:24

Paul is in the realm of trying to conquer a problem in his life, the one thing that always defeats him. If it were not for this one thing, he would feel that he is okay. But this one thing makes him feel hopeless about himself. This describes Paul struggling in the wrong realm. This struggling happens especially in those who know the law, in those who have knowledge about proper and improper reactions. You may know something, but what is crucial is the source you come from with that knowledge.

In Romans 7:24 Paul cries, "O wretched man that I am!" Just look at "I am" and then look at the first word of the next phrase, "Who." You have two persons here. "Wretched man that I am" means that I have exhausted expecting anything from myself, looking to myself, working on myself. This is wonderful. Then Paul steps out of his self-effort and says, "Who will deliver me from this body of death?" He has transferred from one realm to another. His words show us his realization of the need for Another Person.

Finally, Paul says, "I thank God — through Jesus Christ our Lord!" (v. 25). Here he has absolutely shifted, not in his experience, but in his sight. Sight comes before experience. Look! Let God reveal it to you. Before you have "a track record," before you do anything, before your experience — do not even count experience — just see that God put you in Christ Jesus (1 Cor. 1:30) and say "Thank You." That is vision. That is revelation. Then what issues out of this is living in the proper realm: "I thank God through Jesus Christ."

Our normal state   **October 25th**

"These things I have written to you concerning those who try to deceive you. But the anointing which you have received from Him abides in you, and you do not need that anyone teach you; but as the same anointing teaches you concerning all things, and is true, and is not a lie, and just as it has taught you, you will abide in Him."
1 JOHN 2:26-27

Our normal living and normal state is to abide in this inner union. We may not have any high, spiritual sensations. We are just living normally. But if you had to read us and describe us, you could put one word over our being from morning to night. In the kitchen, at work, through the day, when we are tired, coming home — passing through everything — there is one word over us, and that is "peace." There is just peace. I have peace with God. I do not have any particular feeling. There is just peace here. This is normal. But if we come home and find that the house is not in order and we critically say to our spouse, "What have you been doing all day?" right away we lose something of that peace. Thank God that we lose our peace in order that we might learn to abide in Him. "Just as it has taught you" means just as the movement, the registration, has taught you. What did it teach you? It did not teach you some Bible knowledge. It taught you to abide in Him. Stay in Him. Remain in Him.

To remain in Christ is the normal state of our being. It is only when we leave our abiding that we discover something is wrong. The verses in the New Testament concerning the anointing are written in the context of some being led astray. In verse 26 when John says, "These things I have written to you concerning those who try to deceive you," he is saying, "There are some around you who are trying to deceive you. What they are saying may appeal to your thought life and may agree with some thoughts in your own mind. But there is something in you that has a repulsion toward these things, and that is the anointing, which is teaching you. What they are saying is leading you away from the normal, peaceful state of your being. It is leading you away from abiding in Him."

Inner blessedness   October 26th

"And blessed is he who is not offended in Me." MATTHEW 11:6

The *New King James Version,* as well as others, translates the phrase "in Me" as "because of Me." But the Greek preposition is *en* (ἐν) with the dative case, not the preposition *dia* (διά) with the accusative case. Thus, this phrase is better translated "in Me," as in the *American Standard Version.* So it would read, "Blessed is he who is not offended in Me," or "Blessed is he who is not offended in this union with Me, or in relationship to Me." Here the Lord is speaking specifically about John the Baptist. But the way He says it — "blessed is he" — includes all of us. It not only applies to the disciples at that time, but it also opens up a crucial principle in our own experience with the Lord.

The Lord characterizes our inward state as blessed. He is attributing the inward state of blessedness to our abiding in Him, remaining in union with Him, while He handles us, while He allows circumstantial environments over our lives, while He does what He does over us. We know that nothing is an accident in the lives of God's chosen ones. As the elect we are living under the mighty hand of God. There is a purpose in the universe over all of us. God has an ongoing goal over us year after year, month after month, day after day, even moment by moment. That goal is His Son — that we would enjoy His Son and be conformed to His Son and manifest His Son in our mortal flesh, so that we could utter the same testimony that Paul uttered, "For to me, to live is Christ" (Phil. 1:21). With this goal, with this view, the Lord says, "And blessed is he who is not offended in Me." In your union with Him, in your relationship with Him, in how He is handling you, in how He is allowing things to be the way they are with you, He adds the word "blessed." This means happy.

Answering our environment   October 27th

"At that time Jesus answered and said, I thank You, Father, Lord of heaven and earth, because You have hidden these things from the wise and prudent and have revealed them to babes."
MATTHEW 11:25

Notice the phrase "At that time." At what time? At the time everything was negative and contrary. At the time when everything was against the Lord. At the time when, naturally speaking, you would not utter a thanksgiving. When you read the word "answered," you may wonder who the Lord was talking to. In the preceding verses, He was not talking to anyone. He was going through the cities, and they were rejecting Him. They would not repent. It was at this point that Jesus answered. What was He answering? Who was He answering? He was answering His environment. He was answering what was being spoken to Him in His environment.

Brothers and sisters, we must this moment answer our environment as it is. How have you answered your environment? How have I answered my environment? "At that time, Jesus answered and said." Our environment requires answers. We cannot remain neutral. We cannot just cope with environment. There is no progress in God that way. We cannot blame environment. Not only will there be no progress, but we will go deeper into the flesh, deeper into our mind, and deeper into Satan. So we dare not answer the environment in that way.

When the Lord answered His environment, He was answering all the rejection. And what did He say? "I thank You, Father, Lord of heaven and earth, because You have hidden these things from the wise and prudent and have revealed them to babes. Even so, Father, for so it seemed good in Your sight" (Matt. 11:25-26). The Lord uttered this in His humanity, after having a disappointing environment, an environment contrary to His expectation. The Lord answered with thankfulness from His inner being saying, "Even so, Father, for so it seemed good in Your sight." So the Lord kept His blessedness.

It's official   October 28th

"For as by one man's disobedience many were made sinners, so also by one Man's obedience many will be constituted righteous."
ROMANS 5:19

To say that by one man's obedience, many were *constituted,* or *appointed,* righteous means that what happened on the cross was according to the standard of God's righteousness. We were *constituted* righteous! That means something official transpired in our relationship with God. That we are the righteousness of God in Christ is not merely a wish or a good feeling. It is a fact. It is official in God's sight (2 Cor. 5:21).

Once we had to deal with the county about the tax status of our buildings. They considered and studied our situation. Eventually, we received an official letter from them stating that we were, in fact, an exempt organization. There was no question. It became official. In the same way, when the blood of Jesus was shed on the cross in harmony with God's righteousness in the universe, we were officially constituted righteous. Our righteousness before God is not an empty imagination. It is legal and official, sealed by the blood of Christ.

The way God dealt with us and made us righteous was by putting us aside, not expecting anything from the flesh. He dealt with us in the Person of His Son. Rather than working directly on us and our problems, repairing and mending us, He dealt with our sins in His Son on the cross. He righteously solved our sin problem by accepting the sacrifice of Christ on our behalf. He then crucified our old man and terminated the source of all our problems. He put us in His Son, and put His Son into us. According to 2 Corinthians 5:21, Christ bore *our* sin, and we received *His* righteousness. What grace! We are justified with a justification that constitutes us officially righteous. This official righteousness results in life. The Son gratuitously solved our problem with God, gave us righteousness as a gift, and gave us Himself as our life (Rom. 5:10). It's official. We can rest in the legality of God's righteousness.

Faith through hearing   October 29th

"This only I want to learn from you: Did you receive the Spirit by the works of the law, or by the hearing of faith?" GALATIANS 3:2

To fully understand how God's righteousness is applied to us, we need to see that it is related to *hearing*. God's righteousness is not only His procedure on the cross, but it is our *hearing* about it. Galatians 3:2 and 5 calls this hearing "the hearing of faith." The hearing of faith consists of a hearing about the scenery of Calvary. It is *that* kind of hearing that causes faith to come into being in us. According to Ephesians 2:8, faith is a gift: "For by grace you have been saved through faith, and that not of yourselves; it is the gift of God." The way this gift is given to us is simply by hearing about the scenery of Calvary.

God wants the appropriate response to Himself. Faith is that response. The way God secures this response of faith is by imparting it into us as a gift. Furthermore, He gives the gift by putting us under a hearing which reveals God's righteousness. This is the significance of what Paul says in Romans 1:16-17: [16] "For I am not ashamed of the gospel of Christ, for it is the power of God to

310

salvation for everyone who believes, for the Jew first and also for the Greek. [17] For in it the righteousness of God is revealed out of faith into faith; as it is written, The just shall live by faith." This is a righteousness of God that, when revealed, requires faith; and at the same time, while it is being revealed in the gospel, it gives and imparts the very faith that it requires. Thus, faith *in* Jesus Christ is the faith *of* Jesus Christ (Gal. 2:16; Rom. 3:22). Faith does not originate with us. It originates with our beholding the scenery of Calvary that reveals God's righteousness. When we are in the process of *beholding* the scenery of Calvary *through hearing* (Gal. 3:1-2), we experience the faith *of* Jesus Christ. When we *respond* to what we are beholding and hearing, we experience faith *in* Jesus Christ.

Our only resolve
October 30th

"Adulterers and adulteresses! Do you not know that friendship with the world is enmity with God? Whoever therefore wants [or, resolves] to be a friend of the world makes himself an enemy of God"
JAMES 4:4

James exposes the source of our struggles. The word "wants" in this verse is very significant. It means "resolves." This same word is used by Paul in 1 Timothy 6:9-10, which sheds further light on our understanding: [9] "Those who desire [or, resolve] to be rich fall into temptation and a snare, and into many foolish and harmful lusts which drown men in destruction and perdition. [10] For the love of money is a root of all kinds of evil." The word "desire" in verse 9 is not merely an impulse to be rich. It is a resolve to be rich. It is the kind of decision one makes with a definite intention. So Paul speaks of resolving to be rich, and James speaks of resolving to be a friend of the world.

When we receive the Lord, He comes in to take over. All the rights to our life are gone. We belong to Him. We are under His

311

headship. We are under His lordship. To have any resolve other than the resolve to follow Him, to know Him, and to live by Him is to have an evil eye (Matt. 6:23). The Lord tells us that our eye should be "single" (v. 22, ASV). This means that we should have only one goal, look at only one thing, and not tolerate a divided heart. To have a single eye means to have a single heart (vv. 21-23). When the Lord spoke of having a single eye, He did not contrast it with having double vision. Rather, He used the word "evil" as the contrasting word for "single." This is because in God's thought having anything other than God Himself as our one goal is evil.

Any resolve in our life apart from the Lord Himself will lead us into trouble. There are serious consequences when we resolve to be a friend of the world or when we resolve to be rich. Even to resolve to "get rich for Jesus" is an error of the heart. We only need to have one resolve and that is, "Lord, I love You, and I am one with You. My only desire is to be under You and to follow You on the path of life" (cf. Matt. 7:14). In the New Testament, Paul uses the phrase "Jesus Christ our Lord." This confession is very significant. It means that the Lord is not someone outside of us that we are observing from afar. No! He is the One who lives and rules *in* us. When we feel inwardly restrained from doing or saying something, we need to go along with that restraint. Jesus Christ is not just our Savior. He is our Lord! Our only resolve is to say "Amen" and "Yes" to Him.

Love with which to love   October 31st

"Husbands, love your wives, just as Christ also loved the church and gave Himself for her." EPHESIANS 5:25

We love because He first loved us. Because we are in this vertical relationship, we cannot help but love. There is a necessity in us to receive and love others the way He loves us. The problem many times is that we are trying to work out a horizontal

312

relationship, when we ourselves do not know the love God has toward us. We need to enjoy that unconditional love which is based on Calvary — on the precious blood, cleansing, and forgiveness. While we were yet sinners Christ died for us, and that love is poured out in our hearts through the Holy Spirit. It is out of this love that we have love with which to love others. May the Lord show us this kind of relationship that is in the unconditional love of God. It is by our experiencing His life — by fellowshipping with Him and obeying Him — that the reality of that life will come out in perfect love which casts out all fear and brings in another kind of attitude.

If you will bring to your marriage relationship the unconditional love of God, and not your expectancies, your standards, what you hope she will be, or he will be, then you will not be disappointed. You will also avoid hurt feelings, lack of communication, and just trying to get along. None of this will come into your relationship. But if instead you have a lot of standards and expectancies and dreams, your relationship will eventually fall apart because you brought the wrong thing into it. Bring perfect love. Bring the enjoyment that you are having in fellowship with the Lord and in following Him day by day. Bring that to your relationship. And then there will be compassion, tenderheartedness, forgiveness, mercy, and enjoying God together.

November

The blood of God   November 1st

"Therefore take heed to yourselves and to all the flock, among which the Holy Spirit has made you overseers, to shepherd the church of God which He purchased with His own blood."
ACTS 20:28

Here the blood is spoken of as the blood of God. How could that be? It is very simple. Christ, in His Person, is a complete human being. He is fully human, yet fully divine. He is a man and He is God. In His one Person are two natures, the human nature and the divine nature. In this Person, Jesus Christ, God is manifest in the flesh. He is the God-Man. And the two natures, both the human and the divine, participate in each other. There is a communication of all the attributes of one nature to the other. Everything that is true of Him in His divinity is communicated to His humanity. And He has also brought humanity into God in a proper sense. Thus, we have the communication of all the attributes of both these precious natures in one Person.

The blood is the blood of Jesus Christ and the blood of God. This indicates that in His life there is a mingling of God and man. Not only is the soul-life of Jesus in His humanity our portion; but that soul-life, as it is in union with the Father's divine nature and with God Himself, is also our portion. So when we are drinking the blood and enjoying the blood, this is not only the blood of Jesus Christ, but the blood of God, because you cannot separate those two natures in His one Person. Christ is not two persons. That is a heresy. Christ is one Person, and each nature participates in the attributes of the other. This is the divine/human Jesus. In Acts 20:28 the church is identified as the church of God which He obtained, or acquired, with His own

315

blood. The blood and God are not mentioned together in any other place in the Bible except this verse related to the church. This reveals to us that the church is deeply embedded in the Father, Son, and Spirit. It is Their pleasure and Their desire. The blood of the eternal covenant is related to God and all that He is. The blood of Jesus is the blood of God. This means that when we partake of the blood, we receive all that God is.

Vision and faith   November 2nd

"For we walk by faith, not by sight." 2 CORINTHIANS 5:7

This life is a life of faith. You are living by faith. You have a spirit of faith. That is why Paul says in 2 Corinthians 4:13, "But since we have the same spirit of faith, according to what is written, 'I believed and therefore I spoke,' we also believe and therefore speak." Here Paul is quoting from Psalm 116, which speaks of taking "the cup of salvation" and calling on the name of the Lord. So the speaking in verse 13 is really a calling. Paul was calling on the name of the Lord. His exercised "spirit of faith" brought him into the realm of faith.

Vision causes us to walk by faith, not by sight. When we stimulate our spirit, we see the real situation from the view of God's economy — we are in the process of transformation, and the life of Christ is being increasingly manifested in our mortal flesh. When you exercise your spirit, you get into another realm and you begin to live by faith. Our exercised spirit brings in vision, and vision brings in faith. The more vision we have, the more faith we have.

The faith expresses itself by contacting the Lord and applying the cross: "Bearing about in the body the putting to death of the Lord Jesus, that the life of Jesus also may be manifested in our body" (2 Cor. 4:10). How much do we coordinate inwardly with the outward environment? God arranges our environments. He hands us over to the exact environments we need — those particular ones for you and for me. Then He causes those environments to be matched at the right time with the inward application of the cross. This inward application of the cross is an exercise of our spirit of faith to call on the Lord, to get refocused from what is happening at that moment to what is happening in eternity, to what is happening in God's economy. Our focus is on what is taking place in the realm of faith and eternity. Our focus is not in the realm of right and wrong, what is due us, what we deserve, or how we are being treated. We get completely out of that realm into the realm of what is happening in relationship to God's economy — how much Christ is being added to us.

The seat of our personhood   November 3rd

"For what man knows the things of a man except the spirit of the man which is in him? Even so no one knows the things of God except the Spirit of God." 1 CORINTHIANS 2:11

The seat of our personhood is our spirit. Our real "knower" is our spirit. We do not know ourself apart from our spirit. I am an empty shell without my spirit. I am a personless person without my spirit. The last Adam became a life-giving Spirit and joined Himself with my spirit. Now I can live from my spirit (Rom. 1:9). Now I find my uplifted personhood in this organic "I" (John 14:20).

Do we see this? It is marvelous to know that Christ is your person. When sin shows up, you can boldly tell it, "He has the sin and I have the righteousness." That will catapult you right into His arms to love Him, to draw from Him. He gave the law in order to exhaust us and convince us that we need to live in union with Him. He already knew the flesh was fallen, but we did not. So He came with the law and exhausted the flesh to the utmost, so that He could regenerate our spirit and get Himself into us. Romans 8:3-4 says, [3]

317

"For what the law could not do in that it was weak through the flesh, God did by sending His own Son in the likeness of sinful flesh, on account of sin: He condemned sin in the flesh, ⁴ that the righteous requirement of the law might be fulfilled in us who do not walk according to the flesh but according to the Spirit." Now we just walk according to Spirit, somewhat spiritually irresponsible. We are not obligated to what shows up in our thoughts and feelings. He paid the debt. We are not obligated to the flesh anymore (Rom. 8:12). We do not owe it anything. We do not owe it an answer. We do not owe it an excuse. We do not need to defend it. It has been judged once and for all on the cross. This is wonderful!

Life-commandments   November 4th

"For this is the love of God, that we keep His commandments. And His commandments are not burdensome. For whatever is born of God overcomes the world. And this is the victory that has overcome the world —our faith." 1 JOHN 5:3-4

John quickly turns us to life because he knows that whatever these commandments are, they are related to the supply of life within our being— "whatever is born of God." These life-commandments are the instant speakings that we have during the day— for example, "Do not look at that." or "Do not say it in that way." This is not burdensome. It is coming out of the fellowship of life. Because I am in the fellowship of this life, I experience the sensitivity of its nature. I experience the necessity of its nature, which is to love the Father and to follow Him, "to refuse the evil and choose the good" (Isa. 7:15).

The necessity of that life in me is to follow the Lord in my daily living. And when I follow Him as life, I am following His commandments, and they are not burdensome. It is not as if I am here and God is up in heaven telling me what to do, and then I am trying to do it. It is not like that. God is imparting Himself as life and supply into us, giving us an installation of divine power, with everything that pertains to "life and godliness" (2 Pet. 1:3). Then He tells us to take a step, to walk with Him. He has already installed His life into us, but there is still a step needed, a step of obedience. And when we take that step of obedience in our life, there is a deeper perfecting of the love of God in our relationships with one another. As we live in fellowship and obedience, we will be able, with an ability given to us by God Himself, to bring God's unconditional love into our relationships.

The arrangements of God's economy   November 5th

"As I urged you upon my departure for Macedonia, remain on at Ephesus, in order that you may charge certain men not to teach differently . . . rather than God's economy which is by faith."
1 TIMOTHY 1:3-4 (NASV)

God's economy refers to His plan with various arrangements. Creation was an arrangement. The choosing of the people of Israel was an arrangement. Incarnation was an arrangement. Jesus' human living was an arrangement. Crucifixion and resurrection were arrangements. Ascension and the pouring out of the Spirit were each an arrangement. And then regeneration was another arrangement. These are all part of God's economy. Now in your daily living, even the disagreeable expression on someone's face is an arrangement. Or your disappointment because of an unmet need is also an arrangement. All these arrangements in our environment are intended by God to bring us on in His economy.

We are all linked to one will, one purpose, and one economy, with many arrangements. If I see this and you see this, we can only bow down and say, "Lord, I repent for all my murmuring. I only want to do one thing in my life — to love You through all of the sovereign arrangements of Your economy."

319

All families have little problems, big problems, and even sometimes storms. Yet, through it all, when we see God's economy we have a new set of values. Our one desire is to experience Christ. We want Christ. We see that every kind of situation in our environment is for the dispensing of His life into our mind, emotion, and will. For example, the best marriage fellowship you could receive is according to God's economy. It is be counseled that your marriage is an arrangement that God has given you to experience Christ. The marriage life is one of the divinely appointed arrangements in God's economy. It is an area where conformity to the image of Christ is happening in our daily life.

What is the good?   November 6th

"For whom He foreknew, He also predestined to be conformed to the image of His Son, that He might be the firstborn among many brethren." ROMANS 8:29

As part of God's plan, we were made with a spirit, a soul, and a body (Gen. 2:7; 1 Thess. 5:23). In His economy, the arrangement is that we would be born again and He would be dispensed into our spirit to begin the process of conforming us to His image. In the Bible God's economy begins with creation and continues through the Old Testament with the called race, and into the New Testament with His Son. Then His Son is dispensed into our spirit. Now His arrangement is that our soul, with our mind, emotions, and will, would be conformed to the image of His Son. This takes place in the realm of the Spirit.

For this conformity, there is the absolute necessity of our being oriented to the Lord by walking according to spirit, by knowing that realm. For example, in the morning when I am exercising my spirit by saying, "Lord Jesus, I love You," I am linked to the whole history of God's economy. His life is being dispensed into my thoughts at the very beginning of the day. To conform me to the image of His Son, He is using not only my touch with the Spirit, but also the "all things" mentioned in Romans 8:28. All things are working together for good. What is the good? The good is my being conformed to the image of His Son. This means I must handle my problems in an altogether new way now. If I see God's economy, I am forbidden to murmur, to reason, or to complain about my spouse, my problems, my finances, my situation. I am forever forbidden if I am a person under the view of God's economy.

Terminating the self   November 7th

"Then Jesus said to His disciples, If anyone desires to come after Me, let him deny himself, and take up his cross, and follow Me." MATTHEW 16:24

To deny the self means to disassociate ourself from it, to have no connection with it, to draw the line, declaring, "That is not me anymore. That is no longer my source. That old man has been crucified. I stand crucified with Christ." Objectively draw the line in this way and deny the self. Utterly repudiate it. Have no connection with it. Do not identify with it. With the same intensity that Peter had when he would not identify with the Lord, do not identify with your self. Do not identify with its reactions of jealousy and envy. Do not identify with its thoughts. Draw the line between you and it. Disassociate yourself from it, and deny it. Do not let it live. Do not even let it suffer. Do not let it whine. Do not let it pity itself. Do not give it one moment of life. Just deny it. Terminate the self. The cross means termination. It does not mean a kind of suffering in which the self is still alive. No, we can be rid of the self, done with the self, by terminating it in the realm of the Spirit.

It is crucial that we experience dealing with the self, because it really deals a blow to the enemy. In the book of Job, the enemy is accusing, "Does Job fear God for nothing?" In other words, "Is Job pure? Is he serving the Lord from a pure heart? Or is he serving for what the self can gain from it, for what benefits the self?" Then all the dealings came in Job's life. And in those dealings the enemy was dealt with and the Lord's testimony came forth.

Taking His yoke   November 8th

"Take My yoke upon you and learn from Me, for I am gentle and lowly in heart, and you will find rest for your souls." MATTHEW 11:29

The yoke is what is laid upon two oxen. How those oxen respond to that yoke makes all the difference. They can resist the yoke, rubbing against it, trying to break away from it. Then the yoke is harsh. It is bitter. It hurts. But if the oxen simply submit to the yoke, all is well. What is the yoke? The yoke is what God has put on you. He has prepared a unique yoke for you. It may be your husband, your wife, your children, or your finances. The yoke is the will of God in our experience.

How we respond to the yoke that God puts on us will make all the difference in how much our self will get dealt with. Whether or not we take up the yoke — the calamities, the whirlwinds, the unexpected things that the Lord sends — determines whether our self gets dealt with or remains intact. To take up this yoke means to willingly accept the environment. This is crucial. In Psalm 40:8 the Lord says through David in spirit, "I delight to do Your will, O my God." This means that we do not hold any reservation toward God and what He has allowed. We do not hold the view that there is something better that could be measured out to us, or that God could work in a different way. No! No! No! A thousand times no! Your dear wife is the best that God could send you. Your husband is the best that you could have. The brothers and sisters you serve with are the best. Everything is the best that it could be.

The Lord says, "Take My yoke." It is what He has laid "upon you." Take it upon you. And after you have taken it, He says, "Learn from Me." He is saying, "Stay under it and start consulting with Me now. You are under the yoke. Do not resist it. Do not try to get out of it. Take it. Accept it absolutely, just as I took the yoke. I said, 'Thank You, Father, for the rejection. Praise You for the insults, and praise You for the lack of response. Praise You for everything against Me, Father. You are Lord of heaven and earth. Thank You. It seemed good in Your sight' " (Matt. 11:25-26). The Lord took the yoke and praised and thanked the Father for it. Now we take the yoke upon us and begin learning from Him.

Learn from Me   November 9th

"Take My yoke upon you and learn from Me, for I am meek and lowly in heart, and you will find rest for your souls." MATTHEW 11:29

To take the Lord's yoke means to inwardly stay with Him and consult with Him. Do not consult with your mind. Do not use your mind to consider or deliberate about your environment. The Lord says, "Learn from Me." So you ask, "Lord, what is in this calamity for me? Lord, what is in me that You are trying to touch by allowing this whirlwind to come?" Then stay under the yoke. Do not resist it. The Lord is saying, "Inwardly learn from Me. Touch Me. Consult with Me." Do not resort to your mind and say, "This should not have happened." Do not hope for a better day. Do not blame, but begin learning. Begin touching Him. Go inward.

"Learn from Me," He says, "for I am meek and lowly in heart." To be meek means to not resist any opposition. So the Lord is saying, "I am a Person that does not resist. If you stay in the Spirit when you are under the yoke, touching Me and learning from Me, then you will not resist. You will just stay there. You will lie there. You will simply say 'Amen.' You will say, 'Yes, Father. It seemed good to

You. It seemed pleasing to You.' This means you will learn from Me by touching Me. If you touch Me, you will find that I am not resisting. I am not fighting. Also I am lowly. That means I am not proud. I am not asserting Myself. I am not vindicating or defending Myself. I am not trying to hold up the self. I am the One who is not resisting, who is lowly in heart." This is the Lord Jesus in Matthew 11:25-29.

Life supplies death   November 10th

"When Christ, who is our life, shall be manifested, then shall you also with Him be manifested in glory. Put to death therefore your members which are upon the earth: fornication, uncleanness, passion, evil desire, and covetousness, which is idolatry."
COLOSSIANS 3:4-5 (ASV)

Apart from our experiencing the cross and denying the self, the soul-life will be preserved. The way for the self to be terminated is by denying it and taking up the cross. To deny the self is to disregard it as your source. Do not interact with it. Do not consult with it. We are not qualified to handle the self with the self. Indeed, in Christ, we are no longer obligated to it (Rom. 8:12). Instead, touch the source of the Spirit. It is the Spirit that supplies self-denying power (Gal. 5:24-25). In order to take up the cross, first discover the willingness for the cross in your spirit by crying, "Abba, Father!" (Mark 14:36, 38; Phil. 2:13). Second, learn how to merge with the inclinations of the cross that are intrinsic to the leading of the Spirit (Rom. 8:13-14). Third, obey the supplied impulse of life to interrupt the activity of the self. Do not wait for the self to be agreeable to die. Let the cross operate on it in the midst of its struggle to live.

The experience of the cross is not a long, drawn-out process. The cross in the Spirit today is already an accomplished fact and reality. It just needs to be executed by our touching the Spirit. This is why

Paul speaks in the imperative mood in Colossians 3:5: "Put to death therefore your members which are upon the earth." This is execution. The "therefore" in this verse is based upon the crucifying activity that is integral to the "Christ who is our life." That is, the nature of the *life* mentioned in verse 4 is *crucifying* life in verse 5. In other words, life supplies death — death to the self!

Self-introspection   November 11th

"Therefore, if you died with Christ from the basic principles of the world, why, as though living in the world, do you subject yourselves to regulations — Do not touch, do not taste, do not handle." COLOSSIANS 2:20-21

It is a privilege to experience the cross, because we are ushered into a divine procedure of experiencing both Christ's feelings of weakness and His actual putting to death. This experience is all Christ from beginning to end. It is marvelous to see such a provision. You never again want to be experientially outside the spirit (1 Cor. 6:17). The experience of the cross is altogether Christ as the Spirit, as it were, reenacting Himself again on the earth through us — the many sons who are being brought into glory. The way we are being brought into glory is by being led by the Spirit to know the cross operating in our lives. It is by this that we are the genuine sons of God.

There are some dangers related to this experience of the cross. One of these is self-introspection, that is, looking at the self with the self. Self-introspection is the self examining the practices of the body. It is the self trying to figure out what needs to die in me. It is the self analyzing my experience. Here we must realize a divine principle: If you are not in the Spirit, do not analyze, do not introspect about what needs to be put to death in your natural life. This kind of self-analysis only leads to something that is full of accusation and condemnation. If we are accused and condemned over this matter of the cross, it is most likely that we are just in self-introspection. We should not analyze the self by the self or with the self. The only One qualified to touch the self in any way is the Spirit. Do not dare to touch the self apart from the Spirit.

Objects of His love   November 12th

"As it is written, Jacob I have loved, but Esau I have hated."
ROMANS 9:13

This verse shows us the nature of God's unconditional love toward us. Part of what makes up that nature is His choice and His plan. It was wholly according to the good pleasure of His will that we were *chosen* in Him before the foundation of the world. This was before we were able to establish a history with God and make ourselves a little bit lovable to Him. It was before we could even set foot on the earth to demonstrate that we were a pretty good fellow, so that God would maybe look at our sincerity and say, "I like that sincerity, so I am going to make you the object of My love." Before we even had a chance to try to demonstrate any qualities that would merit God's favor, He chose us in Christ. Thus, His love in choosing us comes directly out of the good pleasure of His will. Irrespective of what was going to happen in the twentieth century — how many failures we would have, and what kind of history we would establish — irrespective of all that, He chose us in Christ before the foundation of the world and eternally made us the object of His love. His love toward us comes from eternity past and goes to eternity future, passing through time, through the devil, through demons, through failure, through sin, through the world, through guilt, through condemnation. This is God's love directed toward us out of eternity.

This love is based upon God's choice. Before Jacob was born, the word was uttered, "Jacob I have loved." Before Jacob and Esau were able to do anything good or bad, before they were out of

Rebecca's womb, God said, "Jacob I have loved, but Esau I have hated" (Rom. 9:13). Do not try to understand this. You cannot. God just says it, and in saying it He indicates that the essence of His love is altogether made up of His choice.

Sovereign love   November 13th

"But indeed, O man, who are you to reply against God? Will the thing formed say to him who formed it, Why have you made me like this?" ROMANS 9:20

God's unconditional love is a sovereign love. This sovereign love embraces the totality of our living — all our inward circumstances, such as how we feel, how we react, how we relate, as well as our outward circumstances, which are things that happen to us that cause us to react. God is wonderfully sovereign in His ways over us. He knows how our heart is prone to wander from Him. Because He knows exactly where our heart is at any given moment, He allows whatever circumstance is fitting. Thus, like Paul in Romans 9:20, we simply need to come under the sovereign love of God: "But indeed, O man, who are you to reply against God? Will the thing formed say to him who formed it, Why have you made me like this?" Who can say to the Potter, "Why have You made me like this?" In other words, who can say, "Why did this happen to me?" Paul continues to challenge our reasoning mind in Romans 9:21. "Does not the potter have power over the clay?" It is the Potter's choice to fashion this lump of clay in whatever way He desires. And if the clay is marred in His hand, He takes it off the potter's wheel and reshapes it again, as it seems good to Him. Praise the Lord, our lives are altogether under His sovereignty.

Who can add one cubit to his stature? (Matt. 6:27). Who can control tomorrow? Who can predict what will happen next week? (James 4:13-15). We are under God's sovereign, unconditional love. In Deuteronomy 33:27, He assures us that He is carrying us in His arms: "The eternal God is your refuge, and underneath are the everlasting arms." His arms are underneath us. Thus, if we are torn, if we are stricken, that is part of the process of death and resurrection, so that the life of Christ might be exhibited through us and in us.

Take the bypass   November 14th

"I say then: Walk in the Spirit, and you shall not fulfill the lust of the flesh." GALATIANS 5:16

B efore we are regenerated, our whole being is left to itself. But at regeneration, the life of Jesus comes into our spirit. Now there is a new source for our being. At the same time, our weak flesh is still present. We feel its rumblings. We feel its weakness. We feel its tendencies, its inclinations, its downward moves. In the past, when we felt it, we went to repair it. We went to cope with it. We went to do other things to make up for the void and the lack within that flesh. But those things did not work. We just went from one thing to another, from one misery to another, until one day we discovered our spirit. We still have the same weaknesses in our flesh. The flesh has not changed. But the difference is that now there is another source for our being. That source is as close as saying "Jesus." Calling on the name of Jesus instantly ushers us into a participation in the life that is in our spirit, our new source.

To say "Jesus" is to instantly drink of the supply of His very life and nature that has overcome the flesh, that has dealt with it already. Now there is a new realm in which we live, and that is the realm of our spirit. So when we feel our flesh, when we feel our weaknesses, we know what to do. James says, "Draw near to God, and He will draw near to you." This means that our life is a life of interacting with the Lord in our spirit — the source that was established from the first day of our new birth. We know that we have received Christ and that our destiny has changed. We will not perish but have eternal life. Nevertheless, for years we may still depend upon the source of the flesh to live this life, rather than discovering that we have another source in us. Learn to pray. Learn to call "Jesus." Learn to sing to Him. Learn to fellowship. Learn to bypass all the activity in your flesh and go straight to Jesus. Go directly to your spirit. Do not do anything else. Do not solve. Do not handle. Learn to do one thing — Draw near to God. He will draw near to you.

Organic, life oneness   November 15th

"I in them, and You in Me; that they may be made perfect into one, and that the world may know that You have sent Me, and have loved them as You have loved Me." JOHN 17:23

The organic oneness between believers is revealed in the Lord's prayer in John 17. In verse 21 He prayed, "That they all may be one, as You, Father, are in Me, and I in You; that they also may be one in Us, that the world may believe that You sent Me." Here the Lord is praying for the oneness of all who would believe on Him through the apostles' word (John 17:20). In His prayer to the Father He specifies the nature of the believers' oneness — "That they also may be *one in Us*" or "That they also may be *in Us*." (The latter translation is according to some of the oldest Greek manuscripts.)

In verse 22 the Lord continues praying, "And the glory which You gave Me I have given them, *that they may be one just as We are one.*" This part of the prayer again specifies the nature of the believers' oneness — it is a oneness that is directly related to the oneness between the Father and the Son. Furthermore, in verse 23 He utters exactly *how* we are one. In other words, to be "one just as We are one" means in reality "I in them, and You in Me." This is how we are one — one in the oneness of the Father and the Son! This oneness is the Son Himself indwelling us ("I in them"), and thereby

329

bringing in His oneness with the Father ("You in Me"). This is an organic, life-oneness. It is this oneness entering into us as the gift of eternal life (John 17:2-3) that causes us to be made perfect into one.

According to the Greek text, the word "perfect" in John 17:23 is a perfect passive participle and may be translated more literally, "that they may be in a state of perfection." This means that when eternal life enters into us in the Person of the Son of God, a perfect state of oneness enters into us. It is simply the "I in them, and You in Me" that creates and establishes the oneness of believers with Christ, the Head, and all the members of His Body. It is being grafted into an organic oneness (John 15:4-5). In this way the church is Christ — by an organic, life union with the Head, who is supplying every part of Himself with His life (Eph. 5:28-30).

Understanding God's will   November 16th

"Therefore do not be unwise, but understand what the will of the Lord is." EPHESIANS 5:17

The word "understand" in this verse simply means to compre-hend. In other words, the will of the Lord is not something we cannot comprehend or something we cannot know. Rather, the will of the Lord is something we can grasp and understand with our mind. In Ephesians 5:15 Paul says, "See then that you walk carefully, not as fools but as wise." In the original Greek, the word *carefully* means *accurately* (*akribos* / ἀκριβῶς). Thus Paul is telling us to have a walk that is accurate in its aim and goal. Do not be unwise. Do not be a person without an accurate understanding of the will of the Lord. As believers our walk should be accurate according to God's one unique will.

Then Ephesians 5:16 says, "redeeming the time, because the days are evil." The context of this verse shows us that "redeeming the time" is not just having the right priorities and learning how to order and schedule our lives properly. People can do that without God. Here, redeeming the time is directly related to our having an understanding of what the will of the Lord is. The result of this understanding is that we relate to our daily life as one opportunity after another to live out the will of the Lord. Even the word "time," according to the Greek meaning, emphasizes time in the sense of opportunity. Redeem the opportunities — every kind of situation — because the days are evil. The tide of this age is evil, away from God, indifferent toward God's revealed will. Do not be unwise, but be wise. By walking accurately, or carefully, with an understanding of what the will of the Lord is, we can be wise and redeem all the time and opportunities in our life.

Live   November 17th

"And when I passed by you and saw you struggling in your own blood, I said to you in your blood, Live! Yes, I said to you in your blood, Live!" EZEKIEL 16:6

Some of us need a radical change in our relationship with the Lord, because we base God's love toward us absolutely on how we feel and on our record of failures or successes. We imagine that God either loves us or does not love us according to whether we have had "a good day" or "a bad day." But God's love is unmistakably unconditional. In Jeremiah 31:3 the Lord says to Israel, "I have loved you with an everlasting love." And in Ezekiel 16:6 the Lord says to His people, "Live!" And He made them alive and caused them to thrive and mature, and He shepherded them. They were in their own blood — this was their condition. They were wallowing in their misery, in their death. And He said, "I saw you." He found them in their blood. Has He ever caught you in that condition? One day you were in your blood, wallowing in your misery and your failure. When you deserved a spanking, God said, "I love you. I demonstrated it. Your sins are on My Son. He bore them once and for all. Now just come to Me. Come and be loved." This is relationship-changing love.

The Spirit is territorial   November 18th

"Or do you think that the Scripture says in vain, The Spirit who dwells in us yearns jealously?" JAMES 4:5

This verse reveals that the Spirit is territorial. The Spirit knows its territory. We are redeemed property, and the Spirit is yearning jealously over every part of our being. The way we know God is in us is because He is jealous over even the most infinitesimal speck of rebellion in us, or anything spotted by the world. That is why you can never get away with it. The nature of the Spirit is jealousy. We all have had personal experiences of being jealous. We know how jealousy works. It is possessive. It watches over everything that would alienate someone we love from us.

But one day the kingdom life gets into us! And now that life is jealous over every part of us. That is why you cannot even think a thought and get away with it. You lose your peace. You do not even speak out your thought. You used to say it. But now you do not say it, and you think you should be okay. Yet you are not okay. Just a little reasoning in your mind, and you cannot get away with it. He is jealously yearning over your thought life. So you say, "But what can I do? My thoughts are thinking." Years ago, when we asked our oldest son why he did not stop running when we had told him to, he replied, "I tried to stop but my feet just kept coming." That is like us with our flesh — "I tried to stop my reactions, but my emotions just kept reacting." So what do you do with this unchangeable source? You learn to bypass it and call "Jesus! Here it is again. Jesus, it's here!" Do not handle it yourself. Do not dare to touch your worst reaction. You are only qualified to do one thing. Go straight to Christ. He is your Savior. You are not the savior. He is the Savior. Go directly to Jesus and call and receive the supply from this Person.

A greater grace   November 19th

"But He gives more grace. Therefore He says: God resists the proud, but gives grace to the humble." JAMES 4:6

The phrase "He gives more grace" can also be translated "He gives a greater grace." James is saying, "Saints, in the midst of your problems, regardless of what is rumbling, God's life is in you and He is going to give you a greater grace." And right in this context James says, "Humble yourself." That means let your problem do one thing. Let it humble you. Just let your weakness humble you to come to the Lord, to draw from Him. God resists the proud. The pride in us is self-sufficient. It can make it. It can do better next time. It will not make the same mistake again. These are all forms of pride in us. Actually, we will make that same mistake again until the day we die. What we need is to be humbled, which means to be dependent upon God. Humility is not a "pious virtue." Humility is recognizing that in me dwells no good thing, and that I need the Lord every hour. Just tell Him, "Lord, I need You this morning. I need You this afternoon. I need You in the middle of the afternoon. I need You in my relationship with my associates, in my relationship with my spouse. Lord, I need You. Apart from You, Lord, I can do nothing." This is humility. Humility is dependence upon God.

God gives a greater grace. That means supply. And that supply causes me to sense that God Himself is sufficient. My God is my sufficiency. The self-life is propped up with all its supports. It lives off of others. It lives off of convenience. It lives off of what can be done for it. When its supports are taken away, it whines, it cries, it complains, it blames, because it is so centered on itself. But in grace, God Himself becomes the sufficiency for the four walls of this body, from the top of my head to the soles of my feet. Throughout my mind, emotion, and will, God becomes sufficient for me.

"I still love You" November 20th

"Blessed are those who hunger and thirst for righteousness, for they shall be filled." MATTHEW 5:6

To love Jesus does not mean that you are without problems or without the feeling of your weaknesses. Many times your love for the Lord is manifested at your lowest moments, when you are the most discouraged with yourself. I once said to a servant of the Lord, "Romans 8:28 says that all things work together for good to those who love God, but what if we do not love Him?" He said, "The fact that you say you do not love Him indicates that you love Him all the more." In other words, we are disgusted with ourself. We are disgusted with our way of life. We realize that within ourself we do not have love for the Lord. The very fact that we are aware of a lack of love for the Lord and wish we had more love for Him, *that* is desire for God. That is called "Blessed are those who hunger and thirst for righteousness," because they will be filled.

We often have deep desires for God when we are feeling weak and full of self. Even when we have failed, the Lord is there and we can say, "Right now, Lord, my mind is being badgered by some thoughts. Lord, my emotions are flat." Despite your mind and despite your emotions, you have a deeper part — your spirit where Jesus lives 24 hours a day. So you can say from within, "I still love You, Jesus. I still love You, Lord." This helps us to see that Christ is in us as everything, despite what we are passing through.

Take problem to Jesus

"And behold, they brought to Him a paralytic lying on a bed. And Jesus, seeing their faith, said to the paralytic, Son, be of good cheer; your sins are forgiven you." MATTHEW 9:2

In the Gospels we read many accounts of people being brought to Jesus. There was a blind man. They took the blind man to Jesus. Jesus touched Him. There was a woman with an issue of blood. She knew that she just had to get to Jesus. She touched Him and she was healed. Then there was a lame man. They took the lame man to Jesus. In the Gospels every problem you see is something to take to Jesus. Just take the problem to Jesus. It is the same way now. Are you disturbed over something in your life? in your plans? in a relationship? Take the disturbance to Jesus. And the way you take it to Him is by calling His name. Just say "Jesus." Today we do not have the physical Jesus walking on the earth for us to touch. But His name, which is His person, is as real as His physical presence. When you call my name, I respond. When you call "Jesus," He responds. He responds in you. Do not take responsibility for your problems. Give your problems to Jesus. And when Satan comes to harass you in your mind, in your thought life, you can pray, "Jesus, he is here again!" When the devil comes, instead of trying to overcome him in yourself, just say, "Jesus, they are here again, these visitors in my mind." By taking your problem to Jesus, what you are saying is what the Lord said — "Without Me, you can do nothing." So just keep bringing yourself to the Lord. This is the way to go on in the Christian life.

"Love has been perfected among us in this: that we may have boldness in the day of judgment; because as He is, so are we in this world. There is no fear in love; but perfect love casts out fear, because fear involves torment. But he who fears has not been made perfect in love." 1 JOHN 4:17-18

John is describing the nature of perfect love. This kind of love not only casts out fear, but it also gives us boldness in the day of judgment. There is a reason for our having this boldness: "because as He is, so are we in this world." It does not say "as He was" but "as He is." How is He? The Lord Jesus has once and for all passed through Calvary, the tomb, and the grave. His relationship with the Father can never again be characterized by judgment as the One "smitten by God" on the cross (Isa. 53:4). His present relationship with the Father in resurrection is characterized by the eternal flow of love between them. Just *as He is* enjoying this realm of love with the Father, *so are we* in this world. Thus, what characterizes my relationship with God is not judgment, condemnation, or fear, but a sweet rest in the security of that love over me *in this world* — in my condition — because God loves me just as I am. We are enjoying Him and we are with Him, just as the Son is.

Our relationship with the Lord is characterized by love-dealings. All our dealings with the Lord are actually love-dealings. Everything is love. The Lord's discipline in our lives is a love-dealing; it is altogether characterized by love. And now we love Him because He first loved us and rid the atmosphere between us of any torment and fear.

Not waiting for a better day   November 23rd

"I thank You, Father, Lord of heaven and earth, because You have hidden these things from the wise and prudent and have revealed them to babes. Even so, Father, for so it seemed good in Your sight." MATTHEW 11:25-26

Our environment demands an answer, a response. So if you have to answer your environment, how do you answer it? How do you respond to it? When everything was against the Lord Jesus, He addressed the Father as "Lord of heaven and earth." This means the Lord categorically accepted all the defaming, all the rejection — all the events taking place around Him — as being one hundred percent from the sovereignty of the Father's hand. By calling the Father "Lord of heaven and earth," Jesus is acknowledging that nothing has gone wrong on the earth, but everything is as it should be. He is not hoping for a better day, not escaping the environment; but He is giving an absolute response to the Father about that environment that is against Him. He is thanking Him for it, praising Him for it. Then the Lord Jesus further acknowledges and submits to the Father's sovereignty and His will: "because You have hidden these things from the wise and prudent and have revealed them to babes" (Matt. 11:25). He is saying, "Father, You have not made any mistakes. You allowed all these things — the rejecting, the defaming. This is from You. This is under Your control."

Brothers and sisters, the hidden self will never be exposed and dealt with until we take our environment absolutely — until we take our husband or wife absolutely, and until we take the brothers and sisters absolutely. There cannot be even one inch of reservation in us, of thinking that others are wrong, that we are not being treated fairly. As long as there is one little bit of blame toward someone and self-vindication, Satan is still there lurking in our being in this hidden self.

337

The objective and subjective cross   November 24th

"When Christ who is our life appears, then you also will appear with Him in glory. Therefore put to death your members which are on the earth." COLOSSIANS 3:4-5

Our minds must be renewed with the revelation of the objective cross in order that we could experience the subjective working of the cross. These two aspects are connected in Colossians 3:3 and 5. In verse 3 the objective aspect is given: "For you died, and your life is hidden with Christ in God." That is the fact, and nothing can change it. Our feeling cannot change it. The atmosphere cannot change it. Whether we believe it or not, it still remains a fact. Disbelief cannot eradicate it. The fact is the fact. We died. This is the objective cross.

Then in verse 5 we see the subjective side: "Therefore put to death your members which are on the earth." This is the subjective working out of the cross. So the two sides of the cross are revealed in Colossians 3: "You died" in verse 3, and "put to death" in verse 5. We put to death our members which are on the earth *because we died.* The objective truth is that we were crucified with Christ. But now subjectively we need to apply this and experience it.

By knowing the truth, you know exactly how to relate to yourself. You know how to relate to your reaction. You know how to relate to that ugly thing rising up in you. You are not looking at it, being anxious about it, or hoping that it will somehow disappear. You are not in that false kind of realm, wishing for a change. Once you have seen the fact that your old man was crucified, that you died, then when that reaction rises up in you — when you feel it, when you sense it — you know your position with it. You know exactly how to relate to it. You say, "That is not me anymore. That thing died, and right now I am going to put it to death." This is faith. This is the exercise of our spirit of faith. This is being clear and knowing what the truth is. So we can see how crucial it is for us to know the facts

338

of this revelation from the Word — that our old man was crucified. It is good to declare it. It is good to announce it and then to apply the subjective working of the cross by the Spirit.

No way November 25th

"We are hard pressed on every side, yet not crushed; we are perplexed, but not in despair." 2 CORINTHIANS 4:8

The word "perplexed" comes from the Greek word *aporeo* (ἀπορέω). The prefix means "no," and the root means "way." Thus, it is rendered "no way" or "at a loss for a way." You have no way. You have no answers. Many times God's sovereign love designs that you have no answer. You are in front of a wall. You cannot go over it, around it, or under it. There is no way that you can penetrate it. There is no answer. You just kneel in front of the wall and say, "O Lord Jesus. Hallelujah, I am in Your hands." In this kind of death situation — whatever it is — He will revive you. And on the third day, He will raise you up in resurrection. This means that God needs a little time to prove that it is not you delivering yourself. After a few days there in death, you begin to stink. You begin to realize that there is no ability in you. But then, seemingly out of nowhere, there is an inner surge, an inner welling up of life. Then your mind begins to see things differently. God is sovereign over all. He has torn and He is going to heal. He is healing you now. He has stricken you and He will bandage you up (Hosea 6:1).

God's sovereign love comes to us in a pattern — death and resurrection. This cycle is repeated over and over again in our experience. Just as the Lord Jesus passed through death and resurrection, we follow in His pattern.

"In this you greatly rejoice, though now for a little while, if need be, you have been grieved by various trials, that the genuineness of your faith, being much more precious than gold that perishes, though it is tested by fire, may be found to praise, honor, and glory at the revelation of Jesus Christ." 1 PETER 1:6-7

In a trial your mind is heavy. Pressure is on your soul. You just want to shake your head in disbelief. What has happened is almost oppressing. Something has affected you. It has affected your emotion, so that your soul feels as though it is collapsing. You feel ambivalent. Two things are going on in you at one time. You love the Lord, at least you thought you loved the Lord. And at the same time, you have these trials that have crushed your soul, and you feel heavy. Do not forget that the Lord Jesus also had a soul. In the hour of trial He said, "Now My soul is troubled" (John 12:27). And in Gethsemane, His soul was awestruck and in distress (Mark 14:33-34). The soul of the Lord Jesus went through severe testing, and it was exceedingly sorrowful.

"The testing of your faith produces patience" (James 1:3). In the testing, your mind, your emotions, and even your will feel very weak. You feel limp. Yet you will discover that after a few moments, or a few hours, or maybe a few days, something in you — despite your wanting to give up, despite overwhelming feelings of discouragement, despite it all — something in you rebounds and you say, "Lord, I still love You. Lord, I want You." This was the testing of your faith. Something happened to shatter your feelings. And in your thought life, you could not pull everything together. But there is something deeper. You start to pray. "Amen, Lord. God, I love You." You discover that this is genuine. You do love Him. Why? Because your faith will not quit. You keep coming back, you keep responding to Jesus.

The survival of faith

"And the Lord said, Simon, Simon! Indeed, Satan has asked for you, that he may sift you as wheat. But I have prayed for you, that your faith should not fail; and when you have returned to Me, strengthen your brethren." LUKE 22:31-32

Peter is the most notable example of the survival of faith. When the Lord told him that Satan desired to sift him as wheat, that meant "The devil is going to come to you, Peter. He is going to shake you up one side and down the other. You think you love Me? You think you are so much for Me? I am going to show you, Peter, that there is nothing in you for Me." And Peter denied the Lord. But before that the Lord said to him, "I have prayed for you, that your faith should not fail." This means Peter's response, his living faith, should not fail. Then the Lord added, "And when you have returned to Me, strengthen your brethren." The word "returned" can also be rendered "converted" or "turned again." So when Peter turned again, He was to strengthen the brothers. Though Peter denied the Lord, his faith did not fail. It came back. On the day of Pentecost, there was power with Peter, because his faith had survived the test. It had proved to be genuine.

Sometimes we pass through trials, environments that shake us down to the bone, and we feel, "God, there is nothing in me for You." But we just need to give ourselves a little time. We will discover that deeper than our mind, deeper than our emotions, there is a response in us. And that is what surfaces in us. It is called faith. And it sounds like, "Jesus, I love You. I love You even more." This shows that we experienced Christ in a genuine way.

James tells us that the testing of our faith produces patience (1:3). The word "patience" comes from a compound Greek word. The first part of the word means "under," and the second part of the word means "remain." So patience means to remain under. When there are pressures, difficult environments, we experience patience by remaining under the environments. When we do not get what we want, we remain under that situation. When we feel deprived, or things are delayed, we remain under. When things do not happen the way we think they should, we know how to remain under. And that remaining under, that patience, is Jesus Christ. He is patience. When you are there under a certain environment and you are saying "Jesus," you are experiencing Another life that is able to remain under with joy. With joy! Not with grumbling, not with complaining, not with "I cannot wait to get out of this situation." But you can remain under. This is patience. This is the faith that does not fail. It survives despite the intensity of the testing.

Grace as power   November 28th

"But by the grace of God I am what I am, and His grace toward me was not in vain; but I labored more abundantly than they all, yet not I, but the grace of God which was with me." 1 CORINTHIANS 15:10

Grace is not just God's attitude toward us. It is also God's power toward us. Grace is Christ Himself as resurrection power coming into us to change us and to do in us what we could never do in ourselves. We may have thought that grace is merely God looking favorably at us from the heavens while remaining detached from us. But grace is Christ actually coming into us, operating in our heart, taking away the stony heart, and inclining us to love Him. Grace is an inner, divine operation in our will to produce a willingness that we do not have in ourself. It is Christ doing everything in us by His own resurrection energy. It is a ceaseless working, whether we feel it or not. Our life is hidden with Christ in God, and day by day this Person is operating in us to effect a change in our being. It is all grace. Indeed, He is "the God of all grace" (1 Pet. 5:10).

Grace is a word that describes the sum and substance of our Christian life. On God's side, grace is both His attitude and His power. On our side, grace is enjoyment. Just as Mephibosheth sat at King David's table in the Old Testament (2 Sam. 9:13), we sit at the table with our deformed feet out of sight, and feed on the word of God's grace. Grace means that we learn to feed on Christ and enjoy Him by coming to Him just the way we are. We learn how to lay our self aside. We learn how to bypass solving our own problems by going directly to the source of our supply — to eat of Him and to drink of Him. So on our side, grace is enjoying and partaking of God. On God's side, it is His favorable attitude toward us while at the same time He is working inwardly to transform us.

Handling love November 29th

"I drew them with gentle cords, with bands of love, and I was to them as those who take the yoke from their neck. I stooped and fed them." HOSEA 11:4

This love is "handling love." It is the way God handles us in our rebellion. In Hosea 11:2 there is rebellion. God sent His servants to His people, and the people turned away from them. They went back to their Baals and they sacrificed. Do you know what God's unconditional love does in that state? He says, "I taught Ephraim to walk, taking them by their arms; but they did not know that I healed them" (11:3). This describes the tenderness with which the Lord handled His people. Then He amplifies on how He handled them: "I drew them with gentle cords, with bands of love." Gentle cords and bands of love are in apposition to one another. The gentle cords are the bands of love.

In these verses Ephraim is pictured as a stubborn, rebellious heifer. Usually, stubborn heifers would be handled with thick ropes to control their rebellion. But God does not do that with us. He does not throw those heavy ropes over our rebellion and try, so to speak, to force us to the ground, and then draw us like a beast. He does not handle us in that way. Even when we are rebellious, He is so delicate and so gentle. He draws us with gentle cords — cords of a man, not cords of a beast. Using thin, gentle cords, He tugs slightly and draws until our rebellion begins to be subdued.

How to transfer   November 30th

"For the weapons of our warfare are not carnal but mighty in God for pulling down strongholds." 2 CORINTHIANS 10:4

Stop yourself and open wholly to the Lord. You cannot do anything to change yourself, but you are connected to the source of power, to the Triune God, to the name of Jesus, to the Spirit of God who casts out demons. You are one with that Spirit. Stay one with Christ, hold Him as the Head, stay with your spirit, believe the truth, and stand with the Body. This is how to have a transfer. It is to stop ourself and open to the Lord and contact Him.

We have been interpreting our own life. We have been doing the living. We have lived to ourselves, and we are a subjective mess — deceived and filled with demonic activity. Now we need to disassociate ourself from the enemy. And this enemy is not merely an objective enemy. It is a subjective enemy enmeshed with our soul, possessing us with our own state of mind and our own moods. You have to disassociate yourself from your mood, from your own feeling. The enemy hates this word. Acting on this word will deliver us all.

The best kind of prayer to deliver us from this subjective state is to exercise our spirit and draw a line. On this side of the line, speak boldly to the enemy, "You fallen angel, you devil, you demons, I have been enmeshed with you. I have thought your thoughts, I have believed your feelings. You have caused me to be shut up to myself. But this day, I am drawing a separating line between you and me. I declare war with the weapons of my warfare that are mighty through

344

God. My real person is Christ. It is no longer I. I have been crucified with Christ. Now *Christ* lives in me. I am regenerated in my *spirit*. The *truth* is mine and I stand one with the members of the *Body*." Take these four pillars and you will overthrow the stronghold of self. You will drive out every subjective state that keeps you in bondage to self. The transfer will be there.

December

"Thy words were found, and I did eat them; and thy word was unto me the joy and rejoicing of mine heart." JEREMIAH 15:16 (KJV)

Many years ago I began to learn the secret revealed in this verse. After being a Christian for about nine years, I came to a point where I felt dry, discouraged, and defeated. I tried to overcome my failing self in many areas, but found I lacked the necessary strength. This went on for several weeks, and then somehow it occurred to me that I should begin reading my Bible three times a day in a regular way. So I began reading the Old Testament in the morning, Psalms and Proverbs at noon, and the New Testament in the evening. It was amazing to see what happened to me within one week. I discovered that the Word of God was food! At that time the Lord impressed me with Jeremiah 15:16.

Formerly, my time with the Lord in the Word was mainly an exercise of my eyes and my mind. But when I discovered that the nature of God's Word was food, I began to read the Word with a praying spirit. The Bible became a new book in my hands. It became a book of enjoyment, a book from which I could feed upon the living God. I found myself reading and praying simultaneously and then taking up a verse or a phrase and beginning to fellowship with the Lord with the very words of Scripture. I found I did not have to strive to find what to pray. The Word of God itself became the content of my prayer. While doing this I found a mysterious yet real supply spontaneously infusing my inner man. No longer was I merely looking at black and white letters on a page or trying to mentally understand things, which had often left me spiritually deadened. For the first time in my Christian life, I began to enjoy God Himself in the pages of the Bible.

Eating three square meals a day by feeding upon the Word taught me experientially that my inner man requires food just as my physical body does. The reason for my defeated Christian life, I discovered, was simply lack of nourishment. In studying the Bible for seven years, it had become to me a book of theology, sermons, and outlines, rather than a book of enjoyment and supply. I realized that the mere knowledge of the Bible could not change me. It was only when the Bible was translated into food by my praying with and over the verses that it turned into enjoyment rather than mere thought. I realized then, as I do today, that one of the secrets of spending time with the Lord is to feed upon the Word.

How to be filled   December 2nd

"And do not get drunk with wine, for that is dissipation, but be filled in spirit." EPHESIANS 5:18 (NASV)

Since Christ Himself dwells in our spirit, the secret of experiencing Him is to use our spirit. So the apostle Paul exhorts the saints to be filled in spirit in order to experience the shining of Christ on them. In Ephesians 5:14 he says, "Awake, sleeper, and arise from the dead, and Christ will shine on you" (NASV). Then in verse 18 he reveals *how* Christ will shine on them: "And do not get drunk with wine, for that is dissipation, but be filled in spirit." The verb "be filled" is in the present tense in Greek, stressing a continuous kind of experience. It is also in the passive voice, indicating that something is causing the filling. And finally, it is in the imperative mood, which means it is a command. However, the command Paul gives here seems to be outside the reach of our experience. According to our thought, to be "filled in spirit" requires inspiration, a special feeling, or excited emotions. But Paul does not mention these things as the means to be filled in spirit. What then is the means or cause of the filling?

To find the cause of being filled in spirit, we do not need to look far. There are at least five participles in the succeeding verses that are grammatically connected to the verb "be filled." The word "participle" itself reveals its function in a sentence — it *participates* in the action of the verb. Thus, when Paul says, "Be filled in spirit," his thought is linked to the five participles that follow in verses 19 to 21: *speaking, singing, psalming* or *making melody, giving thanks,* and *submitting* to one another. These five participles express simultaneous action with the verb "be filled." They are the means for being a person continuously filled in spirit and shining with Christ. To experience Christ shining upon us so that He is everything to us, we need to be filled in spirit *by* speaking, singing, psalming, giving thanks, and submitting to one another.

Calvary-imputed righteousness   December 3rd

"For I through the law died to the law that I might live to God."
GALATIANS 2:19

In Galatians 2:20 Paul says, "I have been crucified with Christ; it is no longer I who live." This "no longer I" is the old "I." It is the "I" of the flesh. It is the "flesh-I" that tries to please God. It is the "I" that tries to keep the law. Verse 19 tells us how Paul arrived at "no longer I": "I through law have died to law that I might live to God." Paul took up the law, and through the law he eventually died to it in order that he might be transferred to live to God. So Paul could say, "I am crucified with Christ; and it is no longer I who live." The "I" trying to attain, trying to keep the law, is the "I" that has been crucified.

There may be religious striving in us. This kind of striving can be found in any set of religious activities. We may be reading the Bible. We may be praying. We may be doing good deeds. Yet we are doing these things with the motive *to do something* that will please God. Hebrews 9:14 calls these religious works of the flesh "dead works." Dead works are works in us that have no regard for the cross. They are works that seek to establish a righteousness based upon personal attainment, rather than righteousness that is imputed to us as a gift based upon what Christ did on the cross (Gal. 2:21). If this is the case in our experience, we will never feel accepted by the Lord. We consciously and unconsciously examine our conduct to find a reason to feel better and to feel closer to the Lord. We strive to attain acceptance by some means of our own.

This is why it is crucial to know Romans 8:10: "The spirit is life because of righteousness." Righteousness in this verse is Calvary-imputed righteousness. This means that my spirit is released *before* I do anything. My spirit is released, not because *I* released it, but because *His righteousness* released it! My spirit *is* life because of righteousness. It is not going to be life after I have prayed, called on the Lord, read my Bible, or adjusted my conduct. No! My spirit is in a constant state of life because of a blood-bought righteousness won for me at Calvary!

Reckon   December 4th

"Likewise you also, reckon yourselves to be dead indeed to sin, but alive to God in Christ Jesus our Lord." ROMANS 6:11

The Greek word for "reckon" is *logizomai,* a mathematical term. Paul used this word to convey that Christ as our relationship with sin is just as reliable as a mathematical equation. He meant that we could rely upon Christ as our relationship with sin just as we rely upon the fact that $2 + 2 = 4$. When you wake up in the morning and it is stormy weather outside and the electrical power has gone out, it does not change the fact that $2 + 2 = 4$. Whether it is good weather or bad weather — any kind of weather — this equation will always hold true.

In the realm of the Spirit, to reckon means to trust and rely upon what exists in that realm. What exists there? Victory over sin in Christ Jesus! No wonder Paul broke forth in Romans 7:25 and declared, "Thanks be to God *through* Jesus Christ our Lord!" (NASV). At that moment he saw Christ as his relationship with sin. Sin could no longer intimidate him. He was freed from the torment of sin because he saw his new relationship with sin in the Person of Christ. Instead of living in the mode of being miserable and wretched, he started living in the mode of thanksgiving. When we experience Christ in this way — as our relationship to sin — the church increasingly becomes a life-giving expression of Him.

Subjective condemnation   December 5th

"Thanks be to God through Jesus Christ our Lord! So then, on the one hand I myself with my mind am serving the law of God, but on the other, with my flesh the law of sin." ROMANS 7:25 (NASV)

Being subjective will always manifest itself in one's life by a stream of condemning thoughts. The real source of condemnation with many people is simply subjectivity. This is the kind of condemnation referred to in Romans 7 and 8 — subjective condemnation. A person lives with condemnation because he believes his own feelings and his own state of mind. Thus, he is set up for the accuser of the brethren. If we do not stand with four objective facts — Christ, our spirit, the truth, and the Body — we are left to the onslaught of condemnation from the enemy. This is because we are identifying with the sin in our flesh. It reacts, it moves, it has its tendencies, and it seeks to act itself out (Rom. 6:12). Paul's description of his subjective state in Romans 7 reveals that there was a fierce struggle going on within his being because he had no objective base to lay hold of. There was no truth, no spirit, no Christ, and no Body. So he ends up with a desperate cry, "O wretched man that I am!" (v. 24). His wretchedness was due to being confined to his own thoughts and emotions. His subjectivity in handling himself resulted in subjective condemnation.

Then Paul bursts forth in Romans 7:25, "Thanks be to God through Jesus Christ our Lord" (NASV). And again in Romans 8:1-2 he declares, [1] "There is therefore now no condemnation to them that are in Christ Jesus. [2] For the law of the Spirit of life in Christ Jesus made me free from the law of sin and of death" (ASV). These two facts uttered by Paul reveal the way he was delivered from subjective condemnation. When he said, "*Through* Jesus Christ," coupled with "the law of the Spirit of life . . . made me free," he disclosed *how* he was delivered. His deliverance did not come from any experience that he passed through. His deliverance came as a result of moving out of his subjective state into the objective reality of Christ, the spirit, and the truth. Not only did he know himself *in Christ,* but he also saw that everything now was to be processed *through Jesus Christ.*

Man's day versus the Lord's day December 6th

"But with me it is a very small thing that I should be judged of you, or of man's day: yea, I judge not mine own self."
1 Corinthians 4:3 (KJV)

Man's day is a term used in contrast to *the Lord's day*. Man's day means that man's opinion and man's judgment hold sway. Man's day means that it is man's turn to judge, view, and analyze. The Lord's day means that the Lord comes in, as in Revelation 1:10: "I was in spirit on the Lord's Day." On the Lord's day the Lord came in to walk among the churches to judge them (Rev. 2—3). The Lord's day means that now it is the Lord's turn to judge. With this realization Paul says, "Yea, I judge not mine own self." He is saying that he is not trustworthy to analyze himself.

Then in verse 4 Paul continues, "For *I know nothing against myself,* yet I am not justified by this; but He who judges me is the Lord." To deal with our fallen state of subjectivity, we just need to stop ourself. Do not interpret anything concerning yourself or others. Do not argue or debate with yourself. Do not analyze yourself. Do not trust your view, opinion, and reasoning. Call a halt to this self that has controlled and lived out its life for so many years. The way to be transferred out of your self and into the spirit is to stop your self. Say, "Lord, I open to You with Jeremiah 17:9, 'The heart is deceitful above all things, and desperately wicked; who can know it?' " Who can know the heart? Who can know our real state? Verse 10 says, "I, the Lord, search the heart, I test the mind." The Lord is the One who is qualified to know you and change you. In the New Testament, there is a compound Greek word translated "heart-knower." The Lord is the Heart-knower. He is the One who really knows your heart accurately.

The bulging of grace   December 7th

"And God is able to make all grace abound toward you, that you, always having all sufficiency in all things, have an abundance for every good work." 2 CORINTHIANS 9:8

We need to appreciate the relationship between grace and good works. It is very simple. Good works are just grace abounding (2 Cor. 9:8). And grace abounding is grace bulging. Do you know what it is to bulge? To bulge is to expand. When grace bulges, it becomes good works. Good works are the bulging, the expansion, of grace. They are not something different from grace. They are the coming out of grace. Good works are the issue, the fruit, the result of grace. They prove that the grace in us is genuine. They are an extension of our enjoyment of grace. So when we are enjoying God's life and following that life, what comes out are good works.

353

Our experience of grace in a genuine and practical way is a testimony of the kingdom on this earth. For example, Matthew 5:16 says, "Let your light so shine before men, that they may see your good works and glorify your Father in heaven." Let your good works be seen. But do not forget that our good works are just the outshining of this life that we are enjoying. So when we are enjoying Christ as our light, the issue will be good works. John 1:4 says, "In Him was life, and the life was the light of men." To *let* our light so shine before men is to let the inner life of Christ as our light come out of us. It is not to hold a little candle out for men to see. It is to let the shining from our inner enjoyment of Christ beam out of us in the form of good works. Thus, good works are another form of grace. Ephesians 5:8 tells us that we are now "light in the Lord." When I enjoy the light and stay in the light, I *let* it shine. Then there is an outflowing. That outflowing is called good works. These are practical deeds and actions particularly in relation to others. Good works are Christ applied in a specific way to meet the needs of others.

Initial faith and tested faith   December 8th

"My brethren, do not hold the faith of our Lord Jesus Christ, the Lord of glory, with partiality." JAMES 2:1

When James talks about faith in his Epistle, it is not in the same sense that Paul speaks of faith in Romans and Galatians. In those Epistles, Paul is speaking of initial faith for initial justification. Initial faith comes by hearing the gospel. Through this faith we are saved and justified in a split second. This initial experience of salvation is by grace and not of works (Eph. 2:8-9). It is in this sense that faith is used in many of the passages in Romans and Galatians. But the faith James is talking about is an already existing faith, an indwelling faith. This faith dwells inside of us and needs to be stirred up (2 Tim. 1:5-6). It is faith that can also be tested and tried to such an extent that it proves to you that your salvation experience was not just something emotional. You can pass through trials and tribulations, counting it all joy. This genuine faith passes through the trials and continues all the way to the judgment seat of Christ.

When genuine faith is tested, it always has works with it. For example, James 2:1 tells us not to hold faith with partiality in our hearts. How do you hold faith? How does it dwell in you? In which way do you possess faith? Is it hypocritical? or is it genuine? James is talking about an existing faith that lives in us. He is telling us not to hold the faith of our Lord Jesus with something incompatible with it. So James is not talking about *receiving* faith but of *holding* faith in a way that is compatible with the Lord. In this Epistle good works are very precious because they are the expansion, the outflowing, of faith and grace.

Oneness   December 9th

"Being diligent to keep the oneness of the Spirit in the bond of peace." EPHESIANS 4:3

B rothers and sisters, our oneness is the oneness of the Spirit. It is not a made-up oneness. We do not need a movement for oneness. We are not attempting to create oneness through conferences and revivals. Oneness is not the cooperation of denominations; nor is it interdenominationalism. That is not the oneness in the New Testament. Oneness is God Himself entering into us. We are one because *He* dwells in us! We have the oneness of the Father and the Son installed into our spirit, and the best we can do is to *see* it and say, "I am one with all the saints." We *see* the oneness. We cannot create it, produce it, or arrange it. We can only *keep it* and *arrive at it* in a progressive and deeper way in our experience.

Nevertheless, this oneness has an outward expression. Its expression is revealed in 1 Thessalonians 1:1: "Paul, Silvanus, and

355

Timothy, to the church of the Thessalonians in God the Father and the Lord Jesus Christ: Grace to you and peace." The church identified as being in God the Father and the Lord Jesus Christ has a practical expression. It meets in Thessalonica. It is the church of the Thessalonians *outwardly*, but *inwardly* it is in God the Father and the Lord Jesus Christ. Thus, there is a practical expression of the oneness that we have in the Triune God. To have the practical church life is *how* I can keep the oneness created by the Spirit. This oneness is the very oneness of the Godhead flowing into me, making me a member of the Body of Christ in the city where I live, with all the saints there expressing the oneness of the Triune God.

Interrupt the flesh   December 10th

"I say then: Walk in the Spirit, and you shall not fulfill the lust of the flesh." GALATIANS 5:16

When you say "Lord Jesus" from your spirit, at that point you are walking in the Spirit and not carrying out the lust of the flesh. The flesh has many facets to it. It can be angry one minute, lustful the next, and then turn into a deep depression with morbid introspection. Although we may have these feelings of the flesh, we can interrupt them by walking in the Spirit and not carrying them out.

In my early Christian life, I did not know how to interrupt the flesh and walk in the Spirit. I just did not know how to apply Christ at the times I needed Him the most. For example, I used to have problems knowing what to do with my mind. Certain thoughts were so forceful that they would plague and torment me. The only thing I knew to do to handle those thoughts was to drive down the freeway for miles. I would just drive my car, hoping to shake the thoughts out of my head. I did not realize at the time that the secret to handling those thoughts was to exercise myself in the realm of the Spirit, that is, to walk in the Spirit. To call upon the Lord in the midst of the thoughts is the way to walk in the Spirit and not fulfill them. The name of Jesus is the name that interrupts the flesh to let Christ be our relationship with our thoughts.

Empty out December 11th

"But emptied Himself, taking the form of a servant, and coming in the likeness of men. And being found in appearance as a man, He humbled Himself and became obedient unto death, even the death of the cross." PHILIPPIANS 2:7-8

We need to allow the cross to operate to completely terminate this self and to germinate resurrection life. In this way, the life that is manifested in us is life out of death (2 Cor. 4:10-11). Life out of death! For this we need to let the cross operate. And how do we let the cross operate? Philippians 2 gives us the way: we empty ourselves, not grasping anything, just as the Lord Jesus emptied Himself. And then He humbled Himself and became obedient unto death. In that emptying and humbling, God was operating. These verses are in the context of Philippians 2:13, "It is God who operates in you." Let God operate. You cannot do anything. You simply empty. Empty out your energy, your striving, your self in its religious workings. This is the meaning of Paul's word, "I have been crucified with Christ; it is no longer I" (Gal. 2:20). Terminate and end that self. Just empty it out. And then humble yourself. The humbling is uniquely related to obedience. Though you cannot change yourself and you cannot reproduce resurrection life, you can let God operate by emptying out your own energy and self and then obeying. Just go along with whatever He is saying, whatever He is doing.

In our emptying and in our obeying, God is operating. The cross is operating. Death is operating to change us, to transfer us out of our self into the Spirit, and to reproduce Christ in our being until we are completely conformed to His image. This is God's New Testament economy (Rom. 8:29).

Willingness is a barometer December 12th

"And not only as we had hoped, but they first gave themselves to the Lord, and then to us by the will of God." 2 CORINTHIANS 8:5

Willingness is a barometer of our real state with the Lord and with the Body. In 2 Corinthians 8:3-5 Paul refers to the willingness of the churches of Macedonia: [3] "For I bear witness that according to their ability, yes, and beyond their ability, they were freely willing, [4] imploring us with much urgency that we would receive the gift and the fellowship of the ministering to the saints. [5] And not only as we had hoped, but they first gave themselves to the Lord, and then to us by the will of God." Paul says that the believers freely, willingly, gave. Their willingness was an indication that their relationship with the Lord was fresh and their relationship to the Body was real and genuine.

This shows us that a lack of willingness, a closed life, a self-centered life, a tight-fisted life, indicates a deficiency in our relationship with the Lord and with the Body. Many times when there has been an urgent need, I have known in my spirit immediately who I could call. Some saints are available at a moment's notice. They are ready for anything, without hesitating, without calculating. I do not mean that there are not legitimate circumstances that may prevent us from being able to meet a need. But the point is, are we willing? Do we have relationships with one another in this kind of way? Such willingness indicates the health of our relationship with the Lord and with the Body.

When you see your lack of willingness, what do you do? You say, "Wretched man that I am. But Lord, grow in me. Thank You for Your life in me. I lay my hand on You as the burnt offering. You are the willing One. So Lord, transmit Your kind of life into me."

"Under it" or "over it" December 13th

"That the righteous requirement of the law might be fulfilled in us who do not walk according to the flesh but according to the Spirit." ROMANS 8:4

Whenever negative thoughts are rising up in us or bothering us or trying to leech on us, we know that it is just a sign to us saying, "You need to get into the law of the Spirit, and you will find another set of feelings. You will find another mind, another evaluation." But some of us would rather talk about our problems. We would rather talk than call upon the Lord and get to God. We are in such a syndrome that it seems we really do not want God. We would rather just talk. But it is wonderful to know that there is another law in us. It is the law of the Spirit that freed us from the law of sin and death. It is a realm where we are freed, literally freed, from that whole scenario that leaves us depressed, discouraged, and anxious. Follow those symptoms back to their source, and you will discover that they come from the good flesh trying to outdo the bad flesh.

God sent His Son. His Son came into us. Now we are in union with Him in order that the righteous requirement of the law might be fulfilled *in* us. Notice that it does not say "fulfilled by us," but "fulfilled in us." This means that something is happening in us. Who is the "us"? It is those who "do not walk according to the flesh but according to the Spirit." This shows that when we walk according to the Spirit, we are walking in the transcendency of Christ's life that is freed from the law of sin and of death. To experience this life is to experience a transcendent life. You can know what realm you are in by whether you are "under it" or "over it." In the Spirit, there are feelings of "over it." But when you are in the other realm, you feel "under it." When you touch the Spirit, you discover that there is a ready-made life that has already won the victory.

The Christian life is entering into Christ. It is merging with Him. It is being transferred out of your self into Him. It is not morbid introspection. It is not religious effort. It is not struggling and straining or using our own energy to try to get to God. That is not it. This life from the start is transcendent. It comes to us that way. You receive transcendency when you receive Him. You do not receive a process. You receive the finished product. You and I receive the One who passed through every kind of experience. Now we call on Him. We call "Jesus." This is participation. This is entering into the Person who is transcendent, who is "over it."

The liberty of the saints

December 14th

"For the kingdom of God is not eating and drinking, but righteousness and peace and joy in the Holy Spirit." ROMANS 14:17

By observing Paul's interaction with the saints in the New Testament letters, we can see that he was always careful to speak in a way that preserved the liberty of the saints (Philem. 12-14; Rom. 1:11-12; 2 Cor. 8:7-8). Study the fine points in Paul's dealing with the churches, and you will see a relationship between an apostle and the saints in which freedom was maintained.

Brothers and sisters, for freedom Christ set us free! We are all here willingly. There is no forcing or compelling. There are no unspoken or hidden agendas. There is not an expected way to meet or practice the church. Whether we meet this way or that way, as long as Christ is not nullified, we are all happy. This is to be in the reality of the kingdom of God, which is righteousness, peace, and joy in the Holy Spirit. We are not here with formed ideas and concepts, or even the scriptural way to practice the church. Of course, nothing is wrong with the scriptural way of gathering believers. But what is more important is *the way* these kinds of things are handled, because it determines whether the atmosphere of freedom is preserved or lost. If freedom is lost, then Christ is nullified, and the Spirit cannot operate. Spiritually speaking, everything comes to a halt, even though outwardly the meetings and activity of the church life continue.

This is why it is so serious for the law to come into the church in any form. It kills the ability of the Spirit to be released and the ability of the divine love to flow. This happened among the Galatians. When the saints were put under a yoke of slavery, they discovered that they not only lost the love between themselves, but they were also biting and devouring one another. They were consuming one another because the freedom was lost (Gal. 5:14-15). When freedom returns, Christ returns, and love toward all the saints returns.

Intrinsic love   December 15th

"How can I give you up, Ephraim? How can I hand you over, Israel? How can I make you like Admah? How can I set you like Zeboiim? My heart churns within Me; My sympathy is stirred."
HOSEA 11:8

Hosea 11:7-9 shows us God's heart of love toward us. Verse 7 says, "My people are bent on backsliding from Me. Though they call to the Most High, none at all exalt Him." In other words, they mouth the words, but they do not mean what they say. They do not really exalt Him. They are bent on backsliding. Then the Lord says in verse 8, "How can I give you up, Ephraim? How can I hand you over, Israel? How can I make you like Admah? How can I set you like Zeboiim?" These two cities are associated negatively with Sodom and Gomorrah in Deuteronomy 29:23. When God destroyed Sodom and Gomorrah, He included Admah and Zeboiim. So here He is saying to Israel, "How can I do that?"

In a sense, judicially, we deserve that kind of judgment because of our rebellion. But listen to God's intrinsic love, the love that is part of His very being. He is talking in a way that tells us He cannot help Himself. He loves us. But you ask, Why? There is no reason.

361

It is electing love. It is because God chose to love you. God decided to make you an object of His love. So regardless of where you are — in blood, in death, in rebellion, in sin, in the world — you are an object of the love of God, you are a victim of that love. And one day you will come face to face with the fact that God loves you. Indeed, God's love and God's heart churns within Him. His sympathy is stirred over us. This is the kind of love God has toward rebellious people.

Do not shut Christ down   December 16th

"You have become discharged from Christ, you who attempt to be justified by law; you have fallen from grace." GALATIANS 5:4

Paul's word is very strong concerning how we can shut Christ down in our lives. To be discharged from Christ means to be brought to nought from Christ, to be separated from Christ, or to become idle in relation to Christ. This does not mean that we lose our salvation. But it does mean, according to the Greek word, *katargeo*, that we nullify Christ and put Him out of operation.

In my computer there is what is known as "the system folder." This folder is the key to the operation of all the other programs. If the system folder is up and running, then everything else runs smoothly. But if something goes wrong with the system folder, everything on the computer shuts down. Even though there are many good programs that can do many things, if the system folder is damaged in any way, then nothing works. In the same way, if you and I come under the law in any form and are brought again under a yoke of slavery, we are discharged from Christ and He is nullified in our practical experience.

This word from Paul in Galatians is helpful to all of us. It may explain our own experiences when we have felt like the Lord was virtually absent from us. The atmosphere of freedom was lost. Christ was nullified. This word will also preserve us as we go on together in the church life. May we always cherish the blood-bought atmosphere of freedom, which brings in the full enjoyment of Christ. Then the church will be maintained in the reality of Christ.

The two great mysteries   **December 17th**

"That their hearts may be comforted, they being knit together in love, and unto all riches of the full assurance of understanding, that they may know the mystery of God, Christ." COLOSSIANS 2:2 (ASV)

Of the mysteries mentioned in the Bible, two are basic. The first is the mystery of God. The phrase "the mystery of God, Christ" is an appositional statement. That is, the mystery of God *is* Christ. Christ is the unveiling of God! If we want to *know* God, if we want to *see* God, if we want to *touch* God, if we want to *understand* the mystery of God in this universe, then we must see that this mystery is embodied in Christ. To look at Christ is to look at God! To know Christ is to know God!

The second basic mystery in the Bible is the mystery of Christ. After Paul speaks concerning some of the details of this mystery in Ephesians 3:3-5, he then unveils what the mystery is in verse 6: "That the Gentiles should be fellow heirs, of the same body, and partakers of His promise in Christ Jesus through the gospel." Thus, the mystery is the one Body of Christ, made up of both Jews and Gentiles. Paul continues to refer to the mystery of Christ in Ephesians 3:9 by saying, "And to bring to light what is the administration of the mystery . . ." (NASV). Then he specifies in verse 10 that the administration, or the economy, of the mystery is being worked out through the church. Thus, the mystery of Christ is the church! If we want to know Christ, touch Christ, hear Christ, and see Christ, we must realize that Christ is revealed in the church. The mystery of Christ is His Body, the church, the fullness of the One who fills all in all (Eph. 1:22-23). The church is the expression of

363

Christ. It is Christ Himself lived out in a corporate way through His members. The revelation that the mystery of Christ is the corporate Christ was the unique revelation of Paul's ministry. It was given to him in order that all believers might enter into his understanding. In other words, there is not going to be another revelation of the church for us to enter into. No! All believers are required to enter into Paul's revelation and understanding.

His enlargement   December 18th

"But I saw no temple in it, for the Lord God Almighty and the Lamb are its temple." REVELATION 21:22

When this verse reveals that God Himself is the temple, it does not mean that God is the temple by Himself. Rather, it means that God is so thoroughly and completely embodied in His people that *they* have become *an enlargement of Him* as a temple (1 Cor. 3:16; 2 Cor. 6:16). They are His dwelling place to such an extent that they perfectly express Him and have His glory (Rev. 21:9-11). God's building at the end of the Bible is composed of God Himself built into every saint transformed and conformed to the image of His Son (Rom. 8:29).

When you look at the holy city depicted in Revelation 21 and 22, you are impressed with the fact that the whole city is God! God is the temple! The Lamb is the lamp! He is the light that illumines the entire city! The river of the water of life is flowing to every part of the city, supplying it with God Himself (Rev. 22:1-2, 17). What we behold in the holy city is God the Father, God the Son, and God the Holy Spirit. This triune God is the inner content and reality of His finished work, His dwelling place for eternity! The city has the glory of God! It is not existing for itself or making a name for itself, like Babylon (Rev. 17:1-5). It is just God Himself enlarged in the Body of His Son (Col. 1:18-19), supplying everything directly as the Spirit

364

(Rev. 22:1), flowing as a river for all to freely drink (Rev. 22:17)! What oneness and solidarity between God, the Lamb, and the city!

The holy city is not only the consummation of all God's work throughout the ages, but it is also the present goal toward which we should pursue (Heb. 13:14). Thus, the proper church life today should be a miniature of the holy city. The church should simply express Christ, having God's glory shining through it (2 Cor. 4:6-7). When people touch the church, they should be able to touch Christ in all the members. What people should be impressed with is simply Christ living and flowing from all the saints. May it be so with us.

Their oneness between us   December 19th

"And let the peace of Christ rule in your hearts, to the which also ye were called in one body; and be ye thankful." COLOSSIANS 3:15 (ASV)

Christ as the inner reality of the church is just the oneness of the Father and the Son flowing into us and shared between us. Thus, *our oneness* is not a oneness that is distinct or separate from *Their oneness*. *Our* oneness is *Their* oneness. The oneness of the Triune God has entered into us and is now settled in us. Our part is simply to recognize this oneness between us and keep it. We are sharing and participating in Their oneness! That is why Paul can say to the believers in Ephesians 4:3, "Being diligent to *keep* the oneness of the Spirit in the bond of peace." Just keep it! To keep it means that we already have it resident within us.

Brothers and sisters, have you recognized the oneness of the Spirit in your relationships? Have you seen that *Their* (the Father and Son's) oneness is *your* oneness in your marriage life? Are your children being raised in an atmosphere where the oneness of the Spirit is recognized in day-to-day living? What about our relationships as brothers and sisters in the church life? Do we see that our relationships are not in the natural realm, but in a transcendent realm? When we see that the church is Christ embodying the oneness of the Spirit, then between us the governing principle in all our interactions and dealings is "the peace of Christ" ruling and arbitrating in our hearts (Col. 3:15). For example, when I am tempted to remain in my disagreeable disposition with my wife, I now have a new kind of realization: I am not merely having a disagreement with her; I am interacting with God Himself between us. Are you going to be mad at your spouse for a few hours? Do you realize that you are touching a member of Christ? Apparently the disagreement is over some problem that has arisen, but actually the real issue is the oneness of the Spirit between us.

The two spirits   December 20th

"For ye received not the spirit of bondage again unto fear; but ye received the spirit of sonship, whereby we cry, Abba, Father." ROMANS 8:15 (ASV)

There are two sister verses in the New Testament that show us the two spirits. In Romans 8:15 we see "*a spirit* of sonship," and in Galatians 4:6 we see "*the Spirit* of His Son." To understand these two spirits, we need to carefully consider both verses. Romans 8:15 says, "For ye received not the spirit of bondage again unto fear; but ye received the spirit of sonship, whereby *we cry*, Abba, Father." And Galatians 4:6 says, "And because you are sons, God has sent forth the Spirit of *His Son* into your hearts, *crying out,* Abba, Father!" When we compare these two verses we have to ask, who is doing the crying? In the Galatians verse *the Son* is crying, but in the Romans verse *we* are doing the crying. The reason for the apparent contradiction is simply that the two spirits are mingled into one. From one angle it is the Son crying; from another angle it is our crying. These are not two separate cryings. It is only one crying due to the mingling and oneness of the two spirits. The Son's crying is mingled with our crying, and His crying does not happen apart from our crying.

When we ask how the church becomes the reality of Christ, the answer is — the mingled spirit! Christ lives in us and moves through us as we give Him the track of our spirit. For example, our praying is His praying (Rom. 8:26-27, 34), our preaching is His preaching (2 Cor. 5:20), our witnessing is His witnessing (Matt. 10:19-20), our love is His love (1 John 4:12), our experiences are His experiences (2 Cor. 4:10-11). Christ is all and in all! This is the church. It is Christ!

The dynamic of the two spirits   December 21st

"The Spirit Himself bears witness with our spirit that we are children of God." ROMANS 8:16

In this verse we see the dynamic that takes place in the mingled spirit. In verse 15 when we cry with *our* spirit of sonship, "Abba, Father," then in verse 16, "The Spirit Himself bears witness with our spirit that we are children of God." What did our spirit do that causes the Spirit Himself to witness with our spirit? In other words, what is the factor that causes the Spirit of God to respond? The answer is in verse 15 — it is our crying "Abba, Father" that causes the Spirit of God to respond and testify in us. In our religious mentality, we usually read these verses the opposite way. Our thought is that the Holy Spirit takes the initiative and does the crying, and then our spirit bears witness with His Spirit. But it is just the reverse — the Spirit Himself witnesses with our spirit. To cry "Abba, Father" is to take the initiative to exercise Christ in our spirit.

Based upon this principle of the mingling of the two spirits, the church becomes the fullness of Christ. For example, when we come to the meetings of the church, we come exercising our spirit with Christ. When we do this, the meetings are brought into the realm of the reality of Christ. We do not wait for an inspiration or for someone to make the meeting happen. The meeting is not a spectator event like entertainment or sports. Nor is the meeting an impersonal program being carried out. No. The meeting is the mingling of the two spirits crying "Abba, Father." This mingling, through the exercise of our spirit, causes the meeting to release Christ. When we pray, fellowship, speak, sing, and open up to each other as members of the Body of Christ, the dynamic of the two spirits is felt — His Spirit witnesses with our cooperating spirit.

Our spirit and our mouth   December 22nd

"But since we have the same spirit of faith, according to what is written, I believed and therefore I spoke, we also believe and therefore speak." 2 CORINTHIANS 4:13

The apostle Paul shows us the importance of our spirit and mouth in experiencing Christ in the midst of our environments. In this verse Paul quotes David from Psalm 116:10. There David describes his afflictions and trials, and then speaks of how he called upon the name of the Lord in the midst of them. When Paul says, "We have *the same* spirit of faith," he is identifying himself with David — both with David's trials, as well as with how he handled his trials. David's way and Paul's way of passing through trials was to release their spirit of faith by speaking.

To understand the spiritual law of opening our mouth to draw from our spirit of faith is the key to experiencing Christ in a practical way. This is how Christ can become our relationship to everything. It is also how the church is Christ in its expression. For example, in the middle of your feelings of hurt and bitterness — when you can feel them wanting to take you over, when the feelings are turning into anger, when your reasonings begin to fuel your feelings and you are about to give vent to them in words and deeds — at that moment you can exercise your spirit by opening your mouth and saying, "Lord

Jesus!" When we call His name, He operates within our spirit to change us. Thus, He becomes our relationship with others. This is how the content of the church is Christ.

Eternal life   December 23rd

"And this is eternal life, that they may know You, the only true God, and Jesus Christ whom You have sent." JOHN 17:3

Eternal life is not some substance or commodity. Eternal life is the Person of God Himself. It is not a ticket we are holding. Eternal life is our relationship with the Father and the Son. It is that current of life between the Father and the Son in the flow of the Spirit. Eternal life is that current which has been flowing for eternity between the Three in the Godhead. And God has given Their relationship to us. He has given us Their flow. He has put within us Their reciprocal relationship one with another. He has included us in that flow because we are the Body of the Second in the Godhead. We are the Body of Christ. He is the Head, and we are the members. He is the Anointed, and we are the anointed ones. He is the Christ, and we are the Christians. We are one with Him in our union with Him.

We can know we have eternal life. How? Because the Father's testimony concerning His Son was not just a historical event 2,000 years ago (Matt. 3:13-17). What He spoke then out of the heavens is now in the Spirit. So when we say — "Lord, You are the Christ. You are the One living for me now. Live in me. I refuse to handle this, Lord. I refuse to live apart from You. Without You I can do nothing. I am just a branch drawing and absorbing from You" — His Spirit will be constantly bearing witness within us and testifying, "Yes, yes, that is right." This is because the Father handles everything with His Son. And now we too can live handling everything the way the Father does — in Christ, through Christ, and unto Christ.

369

"You are"   **December 24th**

"All things have been delivered to Me by My Father, and no one knows the Son except the Father. Nor does anyone know the Father except the Son, and he to whom the Son wills to reveal Him." MATTHEW 11:27

W e cannot know the Son apart from the revelation of the Father. And we cannot know the Father apart from the Son revealing Him. In other words, Theirs is an exclusive relationship. It is the only relationship in the universe. It is this relationship that has become the gift of eternal life to all of us. So when I receive Christ, the Spirit of God's Son comes into my heart crying, "Abba, Father." I begin to know the Father the way Jesus knows the Father. I begin to know how to be an object of love and grace and mercy. I begin to know how to receive the love of God again and again. I am in the beloved One. I have been graced in Him. I am getting showered with the love of God because I am in the Son of God.

Do you have any personal problems? Do you have any inferiority complexes? Come and let us talk about you in Christ and Christ in you. Just keep saying, "Lord, You are." In every problem and every situation, say "You are." The Lord Jesus told the Jews that He is the "I AM" (John 8:58). Whatever we need, He is. So we can say to Him in our daily life, "Lord, You are. You are peace. You are patience. You are endurance. You are power. You are faith." We just keep saying, "You are."

An all-inclusive utterance   **December 25th**

"When Jesus came into the region of Caesarea Philippi, He asked His disciples, saying, Who do men say that I, the Son of Man, am?" MATTHEW 16:13

The centrality of Christ is the "rock" upon which the Lord builds the church. Where there is the centrality of Christ, there is the building of the church. The Lord opens up the significance of building upon this rock in Matthew 16:13-18: [13] "When Jesus came into the region of Caesarea Philippi, He asked His disciples, saying, Who do men say that I, the Son of Man, am? [14] So they said, Some say John the Baptist, some Elijah, and others Jeremiah or one of the prophets. [15] He said to them, But who do you say that I am? [16] And Simon Peter answered and said, You are the Christ, the Son of the living God. [17] Jesus answered and said to him, Blessed are you, Simon Bar-Jonah, for flesh and blood has not revealed this to you, but My Father who is in heaven. [18] And I also say to you that you are Peter, and upon this rock I will build My church, and the gates of Hades shall not prevail against it."

Peter's confession, "You are the Christ, the Son of the living God," is both definite and singular: Christ is uniquely *the* Son, and He is the *only* Son, distinct and particular. The Lord responded to Peter's confession by saying that what he saw was not revealed to him by flesh and blood, but by the Father. Although these verses are familiar to us, we may have overlooked their real impact on our Christian lives. To make a confession based upon revelation that Jesus, the Son of Man, is the Christ, the Son of the living God, is to be a person who is reduced, focused, and centered upon one Person. It is a confession that Christ is the unique anointed One — He is the One appointed to live out the Father's life, do the Father's will, and accomplish everything in God's economy. To confess that Jesus Christ is the Son of the living God is to acknowledge Him as the One who has the approved relationship with the Father, as well as the proper relationship with all things, both negative and positive. This confession is an all-inclusive utterance concerning the Christian life. It is a confession that recognizes that Christ is all and in all.

"Then Jesus said to His disciples, If anyone desires to come after Me, let him deny himself, and take up his cross, and follow Me. For whoever desires to save his soul-life will lose it, and whoever loses his soul-life for My sake will find it."
MATTHEW 16:24-25

To lose our soul-life means losing our soul-life as the initiator! In these verses the Lord is saying, "Lose setting your mind on the things of men. Lose it! Take Me! You will find your soul when you take Me as your relationship with all things. Your relationship to your self is Me! Lose your self; do not find your self. When you lose your self to find Me, then you will find your self in a proper way."

For the church to be in the reality of Christ, we need many experiences of starting to do something out of ourself and then stopping ourself by calling on the Lord. By this we bring our being back to Christ. We sink back into our mingled spirit. We stop ourself from initiating, thinking, acting, deliberating, and bring ourself back to Christ as our source. At that point, we lose our soul-life. The more we lose our soul-life, the more Satan comes out of our system, and the more Satan cannot destroy the church through our undealt-with mind and opinion.

When Peter took the initiative to rebuke the Lord concerning His going to the cross, the Lord looked at him and said, "Get behind Me, Satan!" That means Satan was in Peter's system. He was occupying Peter's soul. This is where the problems and division in the church really come from — our undealt-with soul. Satan will be ejected out of our system if day by day and hour by hour we do not initiate anything, but lose our soul-life to find it in Christ. When the self initiates things, Satan is unrestrained in his attack on the church. We must all learn not to initiate! Do not live! Do not reason! Do not introspect yourself! Just say, "Lord, You are the Christ, the Son of the living God!" Then, like Peter, we will learn to eject Satan out of

372

our system; and our independent, undealt-with self will not be Satan's door into the church.

God's administration   December 27th

"Unto an administration of the fullness of the times, to head up all things in Christ, the things in the heavens, and the things upon the earth; in Him." EPHESIANS 1:10 (ASV)

God's economy is His administration, or the working out of His plan from eternity past through time into eternity future. This administration overarches the history of humanity according to the divine will in this universe. Within this administration there are various periods of time, commonly referred to as "dispensations." Thus, dispensation is an aspect of the word "economy." This is seen in Ephesians 1:10, where "economy," or administration, is related to "the fullness of the times, to head up all things in Christ." This shows that God's administration embraces time periods. In this qualified sense, administration or economy is understood as "dispensation" — when it refers to a time period or a stage within the overall carrying out of God's administration.

Economy, stewardship, administration, and *dispensation* are all translations of the same Greek word, *oikonomia.* This word has a compound meaning, including the word *law* and the word *house.* It may be understood as "the law of the house." These root meanings have evolved into the idea of the management of a household. Thus, God's economy is His management of the universe. This is the economy of God. He has a plan and a purpose. He is governed by His own purpose. He created this universe to administrate His purpose.

Everything that frustrates God's purpose, He is dealing with according to His own management, to bring it into line to match His purpose. Thus, it is not a small matter to experience Christ and let Him occupy our soul. This kind of experience is dispensational in nature.

373

It is related to God's over-all administration. To live with our soul-life dependent on God, and not seek to save it or love it, is to correspond with God at this time in history. By this we cooperate with His administration for the specific purpose of ushering in the kingdom age.

The Father handles the universe with Christ   December 28th

"Blessed be the God and Father of our Lord Jesus Christ, who has blessed us with every spiritual blessing in the heavenly places in Christ." EPHESIANS 1:3

The Lord builds the church with brothers and sisters who handle everything in their daily life with Christ. God's intention is that Christ would be our relationship with every item in our lives, whether inward or outward. But His intention does not extend just to us. Have you ever realized that even the *Father Himself* handles everything with Christ? He handles the entire universe with Christ. He does not touch the universe apart from Christ.

It is enlightening to see that the Father handled His eternal purpose, His plan, and the good pleasure of His will with His Son. Ephesians 1:3-4 says, [3] "Blessed be the God and Father of our Lord Jesus Christ, who has blessed us with every spiritual blessing in the heavenly places in Christ, [4] just as He chose us in Him before the foundation of the world, that we should be holy and without blemish before Him in love." In eternity past the Father chose us in His Son, His Beloved. This is how the Father began to handle the universe. Before the universe was created, the Father was at the "drawing board" considering all those who would be in His family and who would be part of His habitation for eternity. And what came out was an eternal plan that had everything to do with His Son. God did not come forth with a plan that was apart from His Son. The Father's plan was in Christ. And the Father chose us in Christ.

Verse 5 continues, "having predestined us to sonship through

Jesus Christ to Himself, according to the good pleasure of His will." It was the Father's good pleasure to handle His eternal plan with Christ. God's good pleasure is to have many sons. He has predestined us for this. But He has done it through Jesus Christ and through His redemption. It is by His one unique Son that God gets His many sons.

Double vision   December 29th

"But if your eye is evil, your whole body will be full of darkness. If therefore the light that is in you is darkness, how great is that darkness!" MATTHEW 6:23

The vision of God's eternal purpose gives us a single eye, with the result that our whole body is full of light. This means vision brings in light that shines through our entire attitude, causing us to view life in a renewed way. It brings in an attitude of seeing God in all the affairs of our life — "Blessed are the pure in heart, for they shall see God" (Matt. 5:8). This is why the Lord said that if your eye is single, your whole body will be full of light. Vision causes us to reinterpret our problems in the light of God's economy. It changes our values from the vanity of the material realm to the reality of the spiritual realm. This is the effect vision has on our attitude.

In Matthew 6:22-23 the Lord contrasts a *single* eye with an *evil* eye. This means that if I have my eye on God and on something else at the same time, my eye is evil. In the Lord's estimation, to have double vision is to have evil vision. Having a hidden reservation about fully following the Lord can cause us to have an evil eye, or double vision. Double vision expresses itself in an attitude that says, "I will follow the Lord as long as it does not interfere with the other goal in my heart." That goal may be a self-motivated ambition. It may be a relationship. It may be money. It may be a job, clothes, or a car. It may be anything. Whatever usurps the place of God in my life and does not give Him the preeminence is another goal that causes me to have an evil eye.

When our spiritual eyesight is double, it is considered by the Lord to be dark: "If therefore the light that is in you is darkness, how great is that darkness!" Double vision influences your whole mentality. It has an effect upon your attitude and entire way of thinking. It clouds everything. Our need, then, is for a single, governing vision. We need God's light to shine through our whole being so that we will evaluate everything according to the divine view and feeling. When the light that is in you is the light of God's eternal purpose, your eye is single, and your whole body will be full of light. Your attitude will not only change, but it will be governed by a heavenly vision. The heavenly vision needs to be continually refreshed in our being.

The wrong person living   December 30th

"For whoever desires to save his soul-life will lose it, and whoever loses his soul-life for My sake will find it." MATTHEW 16:25

The soul is not the leading part of our being. The soul does not have the first place in our being. Christ in our spirit has the first place. Christ is your source. To lose your soul-life means that you do not take your soul-life as your person. Christ is your person. You do not take your soul as your source. Fellowship with Him. Take Him as your point of reference. Cast everything upon Him. He is the One. We lose *our* soul-life, with its religious or spiritual endeavors. It is Christ who has first place. He takes the lead. He is the One we handle. We touch Him. To touch Him first is the way to lose the soul-life. By touching Him we find our person. We truly find our soul-life in Him.

Our soul is not our person. Our soul should only be the expression of our spirit — our real person. My mind is a faculty that is wearing a person. My emotions are another part of me that wears my person.

Soul, you are wearing a person! When I am enjoying Christ from my spirit, my soul expresses His image, and His image is drawn upon my soul (Luke 1:46-47). We need to know the order of our being and not live the wrong person. We need to keep Christ, our real person, as our person.

The sense of need   December 31st

"Blessed are the poor in spirit, for theirs is the kingdom of heaven." MATTHEW 5:3

A sense of need is always at the base of our making progress in the Christian life. This is a spiritual principle. To be poor in spirit means that we sense our need for God, realizing that we have absolutely nothing in ourselves. What often motivates us to spend more time with the Lord is an ever deepening realization of our need of Him. So our sense of need becomes the factor of our spiritual progress because it causes us to seek Him and spend time with Him.

To be without a sense of need in our Christian life is a sure sign of spiritual decay. The Lord's diagnosis of the church in Laodicea in Revelation 3:14-20 reveals that lukewarmness, pride, and self-sufficiency are all directly related to a lack of spending time with the Lord. He says to the Laodiceans, "Behold, I stand at the door and knock. If anyone hears My voice and opens the door, I will come in to him and dine with him, and he with Me" (v. 20). The Lord was virtually saying to them that they had not opened the door of their hearts to spend time with Him in fellowship. Yet He is also patiently standing at the door and knocking, seeking to get His believers to find time to dine with Him. The Greek verb *deipneo* (δειπνέω), translated "dine" or "sup" in Revelation 3:20, refers to the daily time that was set apart to eat the main meal. In Luke 14:17 it is called "the dinner hour" (NASV). In other words, the Lord's supreme desire for us is that we would sense the need to have a daily dinner hour, spending time with Him.

377

Title Index

381

386

Subject Index

only one, 101
poured-out, 131-32
keeping in the love of God, 153
victims of, 83-84
Loving God, 272-73
Lord's voice, the, 5-6, 37
a life-voice, 233
an inner drawing, 256-57
an inner knowing, 279
an inner persuasion, 287-88
an inner supply, 259-60
and comprehension, 262-63
compatible with, 216
disciplined to hear, 102-3
inner inclinations, 165-66
in our consciousness, 121-22
obeying, 97-98
remembrance, 140
still small, 108-9
the Shepherd's, 280
your teachers, 102
Lust of the flesh, 26-27

Mysteries
the two great, 363-64
Mystery of His will, 127
Murmurings, 173-75

New covenant, 157

Obedience, 96-97
Oneness
in life, 329-30
in the blood of Christ, 210-11
keeping and arriving at, 355-56
of the Spirit, 15, 248-49
of the Triune God, 365-66
Opinion, 80-81
Organic union, 162-63, 187, 204-5
the organic "I," 163-64, 189-90

Participation in Christ, 226
Participation in God, 166-67
Peace
compatible with, 270-71
Perfection, 34-35, 38, 39-40
our state of, 268-69
perfect love of God, 302-3
Personalized cross, 27-28
Personhood, our, 317-18
Prayer life, the
and our environment, 195
drawing a line, 344-45
God passing through us, 142-43
God's desires, 151-52
God's flowing, 282
God's intentions, 150-51
the benefit of, 149
the Lord's, 58-59
the prayer of God, 281
withdrawing to pray, 238-39
Praying in the Holy Spirit, 153,
209-10
Problems, 100-101
solving, 104
Purpose
according to, 24-25

Reading the Bible, 28-29
Reasoning, 53-55, 173-75
Receiving
Christ, 1-2
one another, 71-72
Reckon, 106, 350
Redemption
its meaning, 132-33
Regeneration, 51-52
Repentance, 186
Revelation
living by, 31
governing vision, 197-98

Scripture Index*

---

* The page numbers in bold type indicate the leading verse for each day.

New Testament

398

400

401

Book Index Key

* unpublished

Book Index*

Date	Book	Pages		Date	Book	Pages
January				**February**		
1	ATC	6-8		1	STWTL	43-44
2	STWTL	2-3		2	WOL1	98-99
3	STWTL	23-24		3	CAS	6-7
4	GUL	1-2, 4-5		4	CAS	10-11
5	HTLV	8-9		5	HTLV	30-31
6	HTLV	9-10		6	GUL	193-94
7	VCL	6-7		7	GUL	135-36
8	VCL	9-10		8	GUL	188-89
9	OCO	163-64		9	CAS	22
10	GUL	215-17		10	HTLV	45-46
11	CIC	35-36		11	CIC	71-72
12	CIC	37-38		12	CIC	72-73
13	CIC	39-40		13	CAS	32, 28-29
14	OCO	207-8		14	CAS	33-34
15	OCO	208-9		15	GUL	217-19
16	WOL1	95-97		16	GUL	218
17	WOL1	97-98		17	CIC	88-89
18	WOL1	156-57		18	CIC	87-88
19	CIC	74-75		19	STWTL	28-30
20	GUL	65-67		20	HTLV	44-45
21	WOL1	145-46		21	HTLV	50-51
22	STWTL	4-5		22	CAS	58-60
23	STWTL	57-58		23	CAS	66-67
24	WOL1	12-13		24	STWTL	54-55
25	WOL1	13-14		25	CAS	200-201
26	CFS	2-3		26	STWTL	25-27
27	CAS	191-93		27	STWTL	27-28
28	DOS	7-9		28	CAS	27-28
29	OCO	32-34		29	FK	120-22
30	WOL1	148-49				
31	WOL1	146-48		**March**		
				1	STWTL	8-9
				2	HTLV	39-40
				3	CIC	61-62
				4	CIC	62-63
				5	STWTL	37-39

* The book index identifies the book and page number from which each selection was taken.

Date	Book	Pages	Date	Book	Pages
6	CIC	81	12	HTLV	18-19
7	CIC	82-83	13	KH	89-90
8	CIC	83-84	14	KL	145-46
9	CIC	94	15	OCO	166-68
10	OCO	164-65	16	CAS	12-13
11	CIC	66-67	17	HTLV	13-14
12	CIC	67-69	18	BOL	28-31
13	CIC	75-76	19	BOL	37-38
14	GOS	31-33	20	STWTL	21-23
15	GUL	220	21	BOL	43-44
16	CAS	29-30	22	BOL	49-53
17	GOS	35-36	23	BOL	55-57
18	GOS	36-37	24	CIC	79-80
19	CAS	13-14	25	GOS	43-45
20	CAS	56-57	26	GOS	45-46
21	CIC	76-77	27	GOS	46-48
22	GUL	5-7	28	GOS	48-49
23	GUL	10-11	29	GOS	50-51
24	GOS	37-39	30	HTLV	15
25	STWTL	5-6			
26	GUL	8-9	**May**		
27	GOS	39-40	1	STWTL	13-14
28	STWTL	33-35	2	GOS	33-34
29	CAS	286-87	3	BOL	79-80
30	GOS	3-5	4	CMC	37-39
31	OCO	168-69	5	CMC	41-42
			6	CIC	95-96
April			7	CIC	98-99
1	CIC	36-37	8	CIC	113-14
2	CAS	15-16	9	STWTL	46-47
3	GOS	40-41	10	GUL	223-24
4	GOS	41-42	11	BOL	116-19
5	HTLV	10-11	12	STWTL	49-50
6	HTLV	11-12	13	KL	159-60
7	KH	83-84	14	KL	161-63
8	KH	87-88	15	CIC	51-52
9	KH	91, 93	16	CIC	52
10	GUL	221	17	CAS	30-31
11	HTLV	17-18	18	HTLV	16
			19	BOL	57-59

Date	Book	Pages	Date	Book	Pages
20	STWTL	72-73	27	CMC	44-45
21	CIC	201-2	28	CAS	268-69
22	HTLV	74-75	29	CAS	270-72
23	CMC	33-34	30	STWTL	61-62
24	CMC	48-49			
25	CIC	100-101	**July**		
26	CIC	104-5	1	STWTL	24
27	STWTL	73-74	2	CIC	77-78
28	STWTL	76-77	3	WOL2	42-43
29	STWTL	79-80	4	WOL2	43-44
30	STWTL	62-63	5	WOL2	46-47
31	GUL	226-27	6	OCO	118-19
			7	VCL	46-48
June			8	VCL	55-56
1	STWTL	15-16	9	CAS	52-54
2	STWTL	17-18	10	GUL	228-29
3	BOL	87-88	11	STWTL	81-82
4	CAS	261, 264-65	12	VCL	3-5
5	CAS	278-80	13	VCL	17-18
6	WOL2	17-19	14	VCL	20-22
7	WOL2	6-7	15	HTLV	36-37
8	WOL2	36-38	16	CAS	275-76
9	WOL2	39-40	17	VCL	66-67
10	HTLV	31-32	18	CIC	78-79
11	HTLV	32-34	19	WOL2	44-46
12	BOL	69-71	20	WOL2	51-53
13	CIC	202-3, 205	21	WOL2	59-60
14	CAS	292-93	22	GUL	121-22
15	CAS	293-95	23	GUL	128-30
16	BOL	94-95	24	GUL	141-42
17	CMC	35, 37	25	OCO	102-4
18	CAS	284-85	26	VCL	61-63
19	CAS	287-88	27	CIC	136, 138
20	CAS	288-89	28	CIC	136-37
21	CAS	1-2	29	HTLV	51-53
22	CAS	2-3	30	HTLV	53-54
23	CAS	4-6	31	WOL1	32-33
24	GUL	213-14			
25	GUL	214-15	**August**		
26	CMC	42-43	1	STWTL	44-46

Date	Book	Pages
2	CIC	53-54
3	CIC	56-57
4	CIC	96-97
5	GUL	176-77
6	CIC	117, 118
7	CIC	119-20
8	CIC	140-42
9	GUL	114-15
10	CIC	191-92
11	CIC	193-94
12	CIC	206-7
13	CIC	208-10
14	CIC	210-11
15	HTLV	40-41
16	CIC	114-15
17	CIC	121-22
18	CIC	163-64
19	CIC	164-67
20	STWTL	64-65
21	BOL	71-72
22	CIC	130-32
23	CIC	150-52
24	CIC	176-77
25	STWTL	30-32
26	STWTL	32-33
27	CIC	143-45
28	GUL	142-44
29	GUL	144-45
30	CIC	135-36
31	STWTL	63-67

September

Date	Book	Pages
1	STWTL	65-66
2	WOL2	48-51
3	VCL	22-23
4	CIC	54-56
5	CIC	211-12
6	HTLV	21-22
7	CIC	85-86
8	CIC	91-93

Date	Book	Pages
9	HTLV	27-28
10	HTLV	28-30
11	HTLV	80-82
12	HTLV	84-85
13	GUL	67-68
14	CMC	46-47
15	CIC	223-24
16	HTLV	88-90
17	CAS	290-92
18	CIC	184-86
19	HTLV	91-92
20	HTLV	41-42
21	HTLV	42-43
22	HTLV	97-98
23	BOL	72-74
24	CIC	213-15
25	CMC	230-31
26	CIC	222-23
27	WOL1	60-61
28	WOL1	73
29	HTLV	25, 27
30	HTLV	26-27

October

Date	Book	Pages
1	STWTL	69-71
2	STWTL	71-72
3	CAS	276-78
4	VCL	34-36
5	VCL	36-38
6	CIC	58-59
7	HTLV	23-24
8	WOL1	45-46
9	WOL1	46-47
10	WOL1	48-49
11	CAS	77-78
12	CAS	78-80
13	CAS	99-101
14	SFC	46-48
15	HTLV	47-48
16	HTLV	48-50

Date	Book	Pages	Date	Book	Pages
17	WOL2	1-3	24	CAS	184-86
18	WOL2	3-4	25	GUL	90-91
19	BOL	75-77	26	KL	58-60
20	BOL	77-79	27	KL	60-62
21	CIC	147-48	28	KL	91-92
22	CAS	97-98	29	GUL	92-93
23	WOL1	62-63	30	CAS	101-2
24	WOL1	83-84			
25	WOL1	99-101	**December**		
26	WOL1	118-19	1	STWTL	55-57
27	WOL1	127-28	2	CIC	43-45
28	WOL1	159-60	3	WOL2	56-58
29	WOL1	161-62	4	CIC	59-60
30	KL	151-53	5	CAS	84-86
31	GUL	207-8	6	CAS	95-97
			7	KL	94-96
November			8	KL	97-98
1	BOL	80-82	9	WOL2	177-78
2	CAS	280-81	10	CIC	47-48
3	WOL2	55-56	11	CAS	221-22
4	GUL	199-201	12	WOL2	25-26
5	HTLV	110-11	13	WOL1	39-41
6	HTLV	107-8	14	CIC	194-95
7	CAS	118-19	15	GUL	97-98
8	CAS	136-37	16	CIC	199-200
9	CAS	137-39	17	CIC	21-22
10	CAS	151-52	18	CIC	25-26
11	CAS	246-47	19	CIC	31-32
12	GUL	125-27	20	CIC	41-42
13	GUL	88-90	21	CIC	42-43
14	KL	21-23	22	CIC	46-47
15	CIC	27-29	23	CIC	181-83
16	HTLV	87-88	24	CIC	178-79
17	GUL	86	25	CIC	159-60
18	KL	31-33	26	CIC	168-70
19	KL	35-36	27	WOL2	72-74
20	KL	51-53	28	CIC	173-74
21	KL	56-57	29	VCL	57-59
22	GUL	204-5	30	WOL2	54-55
23	CAS	133-34	31	STWTL	1-2

Other Ministry Publications

Writings by Bill Freeman

The Supplied Life (Daily Selections)
The Triune God in Experience
Our Common Oneness
The Cross and the Self
The Church Is Christ
God's Unconditional Love
Spending Time with the Lord
– A Lesson Workbook for STWTL
Hearing the Lord's Voice
Seeing and Feeling the Church
Vision in the Christian Life
– A Lesson Workbook for VITCL
The Basic Truths of Our Common Faith
How They Found Christ
– in their own words –
The personal testimonies of Bunyan, Wesley, Whitefield,
Finney, Müller, H. Taylor, Spurgeon, and W. Nee

Booklets

One Will — One Purpose — One Economy
Christ — Our Relationship with Everything
Where Do Your Struggles Come From?
Christ Formed in Us
Concerning the Bible
Concerning the Triune God
Concerning the Person of Christ
Inward and Outward Christians
The Assurance That Christ Is in You

God's Eternal Purpose
The Father's Good Pleasure
Gaining Christ in Daily Life
The Dividing of Soul and Spirit
The Conflict between Flesh and Spirit

Writings by Kirk Eland

Christ: the Christian Life

Booklets

What Does It Mean to Be Born Again?
Being Right with God
Baptism
Our New Identity in Christ
Discovering Your Human Spirit
Knowing the All-Sufficiency of Christ

ORDER FROM:

Ministry Publications
P. O. Box 12222
Scottsdale, AZ 85267 • USA
(800) 573-4105 / (602) 948-4050
Fax – (602) 922-1338